THE ART OF TURNED-WOOD BOWLS

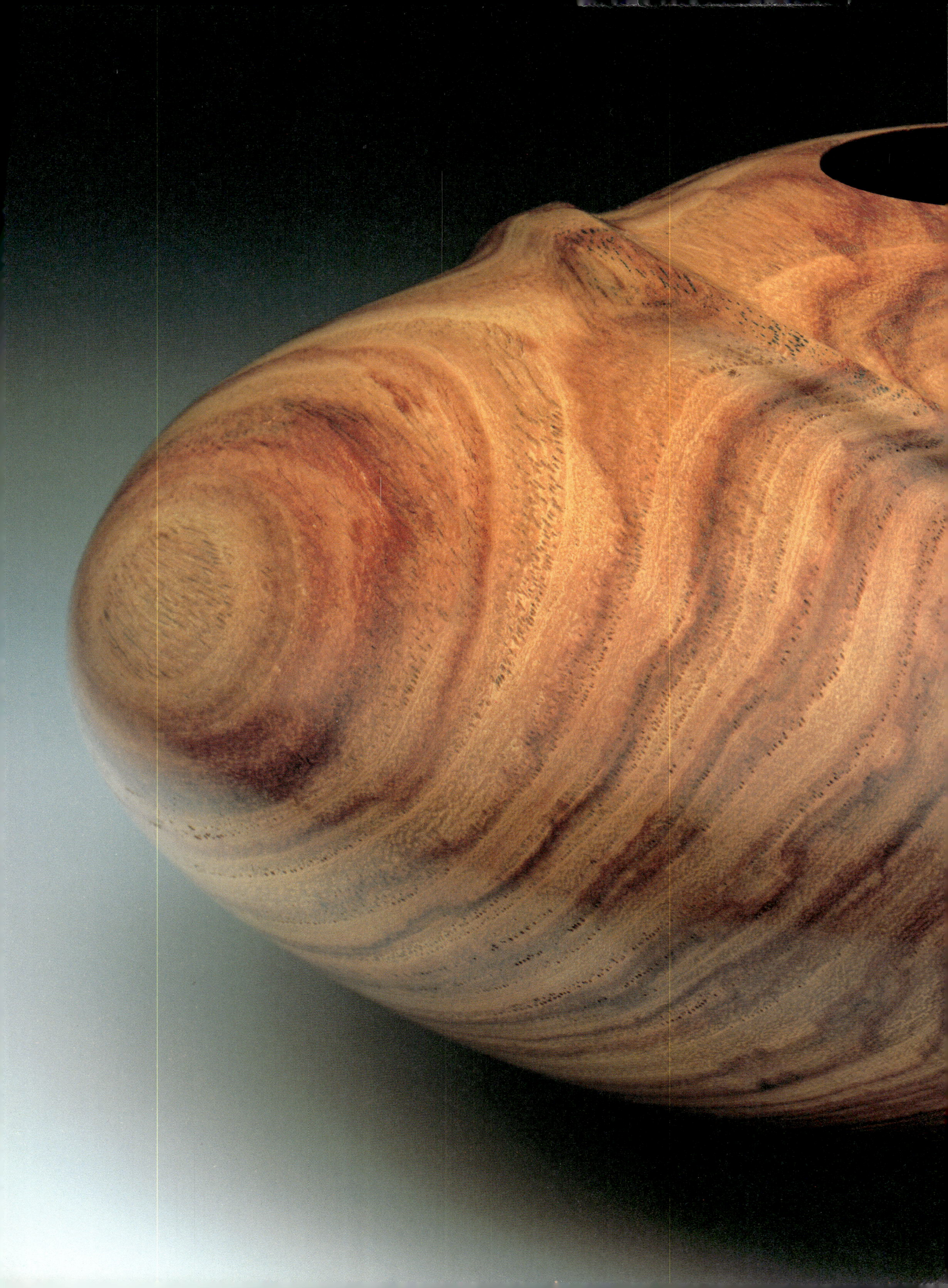

THE ART OF TURNED-WOOD BOWLS

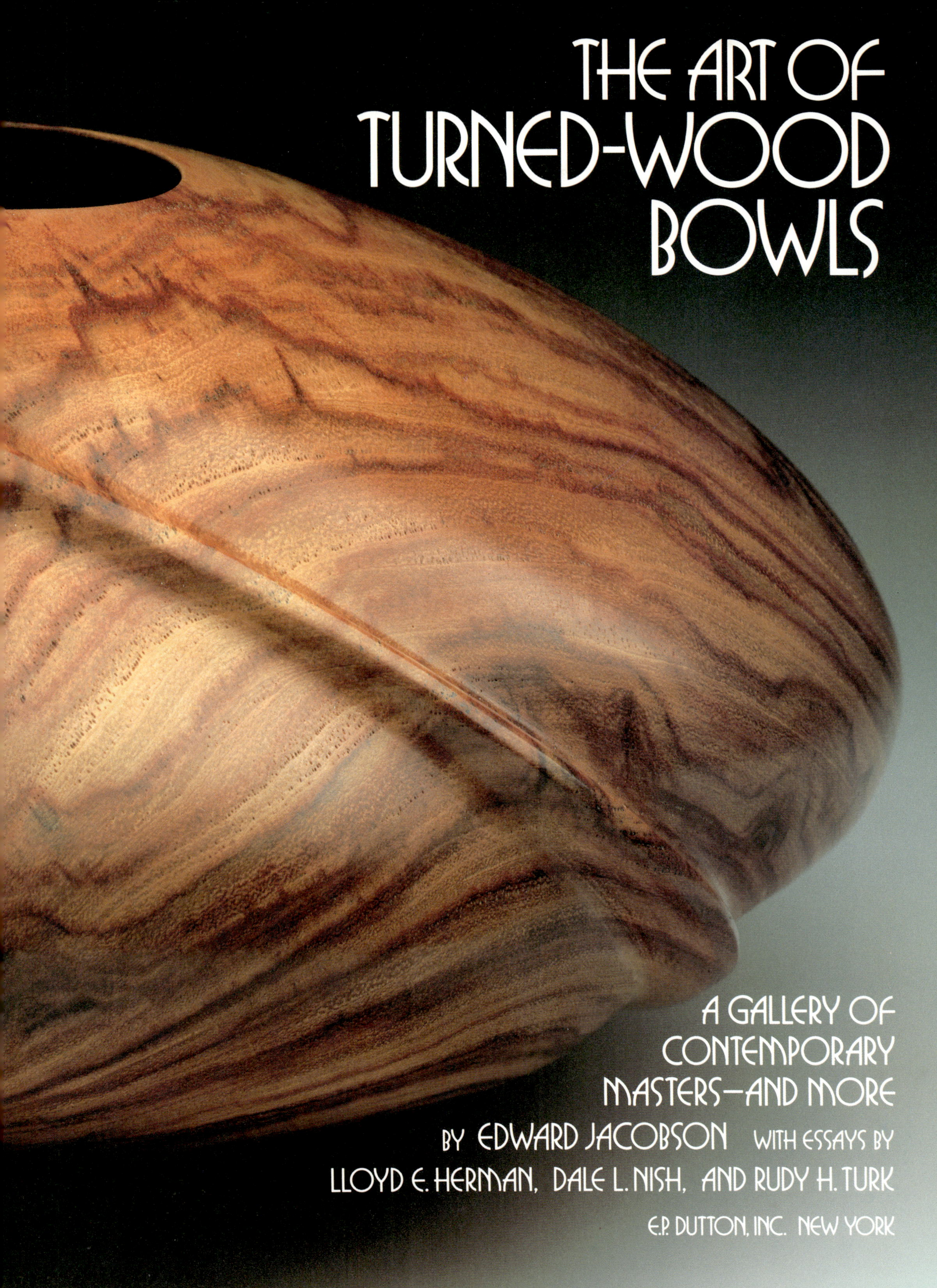

A GALLERY OF CONTEMPORARY MASTERS—AND MORE

BY EDWARD JACOBSON WITH ESSAYS BY
LLOYD E. HERMAN, DALE L. NISH, AND RUDY H. TURK

E.P. DUTTON, INC. NEW YORK

(Overleaf) Enlargement of *Tulipwood Orb* by Bill Hunter. See page 37.

First published, 1985,
in the United States by E.P. Dutton, Inc.

For information contact:
E.P. Dutton, Inc.,
2 Park Avenue, New York, N.Y. 10016

Library of Congress Catalog Card Number: 85-70224

Printed and bound by
Dai Nippon Printing Co., Ltd., Tokyo, Japan.

ISBN: 0-525-24328-3 (cloth) 0-525-48165-6 (DP)

Published simultaneously in Canada by
Fitzhenry & Whiteside Limited,
Toronto

Book design by Marilyn Rey

W

10 9 8 7 6 5 4 3 2 1

First Edition

CONTENTS

THE ART OF TURNED-WOOD BOWLS

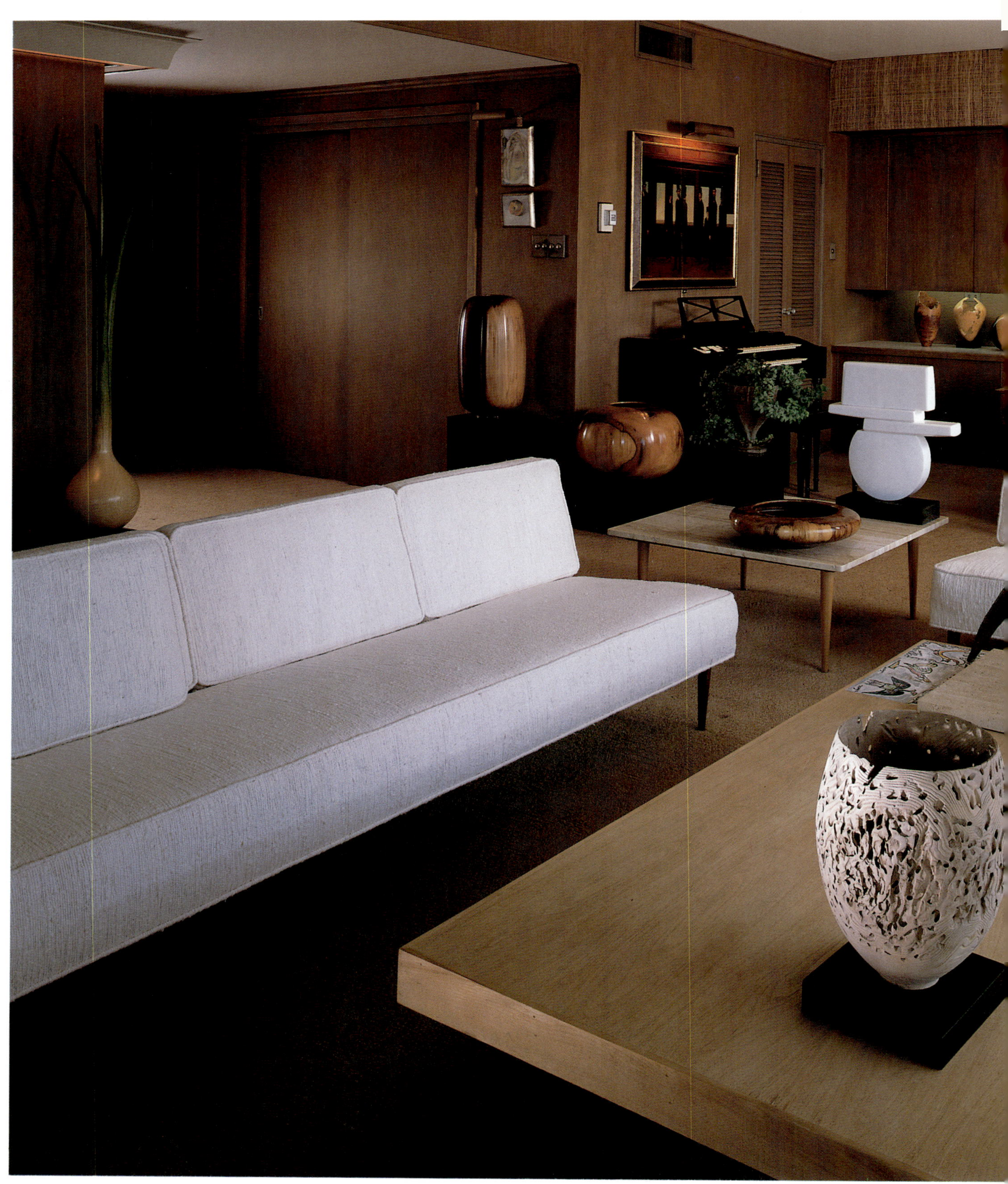

The north end of the author's living room showing some of the handsome bowls illustrated in this book displayed with fascinating examples of modern painting and sculpture.

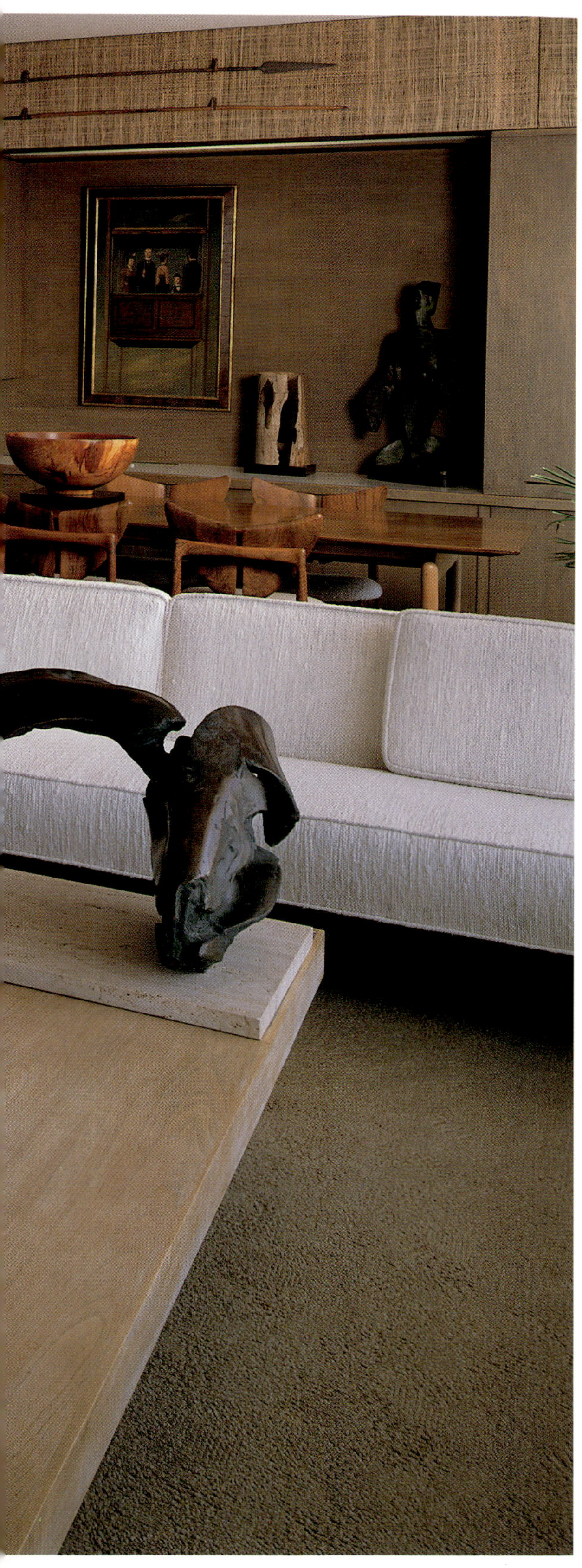

PREFACE

Why would a moderately sane professional who is not a hobbyist woodworker and who had never before collected or been particularly interested in craft objects put together a collection of over ninety turned-wood bowls in the past seven years? More than once I have asked myself that question.

One answer is the human response to beauty. The special dignity of great trees, the varied patterns of sapwood, heartwood, burl, and bark, different for each species, the visual and tactile elegance of beautiful finishes, and the subtle grace of the many bowl shapes captured my eye and my heart. I made my first purchase on November 1, 1977, at The Hand and The Spirit, a distinguished craft gallery in Scottsdale, Arizona. It was an Ed Moulthrop bowl of tiger-striped Georgia pine (see p. 54, top). My response to its beauty continues undiminished to this day.

Another answer to the question of why a collection of turned-wood bowls, is the conviction that the works of the contemporary master turners deserve to be seen by the art—in addition to the craft—audience.

A few master craftsmen, in fields other than wood turning, were beginning to achieve that goal. They and their works were becoming subjects for serious review in the art press. Art galleries began to show and sell their works. Even art museums, which traditionally neither collected nor displayed craft objects (with the exception of historical pieces in the decorative arts collections), began selectively to do so. In clay, these craftsmen/artists included Peter Voulkos and Richard DeVore; in glass, Harvey Littleton and Dale Chihuly; in furniture, Wendell Castle. Others followed. For a few, the market was beginning to broaden; the circle of appreciation was enlarging; a new audience was being reached. But contemporary woodturners were not among this group.

In January 1981, however, a gathering in Phoenix, Arizona, seemed to demonstrate that the time had come for contemporary master turners to enter this new and larger arena. The Phoenix Art Museum was host to the annual meeting of the American Association of Art Museum Directors, an organization composed of the directors of approximately one hundred and fifty of the largest art museums in the nation. As many as possible of our local museum's trustees, including myself, were called upon to help entertain our guests.

It was then that I had the opportunity to watch a number of these directors closely examine nine turned-wood bowls displayed in my small apartment. So concentrated was their interest that it was as if the furniture and furnishings in the room (including the art) had been removed. What was happening? Some of the best art-trained eyes in the nation were seeing great turned-wood bowls for the first time, and it was evident that they genuinely and deeply admired what they saw. Here were some of the ultimate arbiters for the art audience quietly giving their serious approval to objects traditionally viewed as craft.

Those who subscribe to craft publications and visit craft galleries and museums are, by and large, not the same people as those who subscribe to art magazines and frequent art museums and art galleries. Craft and art seem to draw different audiences, even though other distinctions between craft and art have all but disappeared. Attempts to validate other than audience distinctions tend to raise more questions than they answer. For example: (1) What is the difference between art and craft? (2) What objective evidence can be marshaled to support any answer to that question? (3) Have answers previously given stood the test of time? (4) Might this question be of little use other than as a topic for panel discussions? My answers to these questions would be: (1) I do not know, nor, do I believe, does anyone else. (2) Very little. (3) No. (4) Probably yes.

It is generally agreed that the traditional tests formerly used to distinguish between art and craft are no longer applicable. The "household use" test suffers from the fact that, but for handmade furniture, few of the items for sale in today's fine craft galleries are designed for such use.

The "manual skills versus aesthetic value" test is flawed because high aesthetic values are precisely what is being sold in today's fine craft galleries.

Craft galleries are no longer the only galleries dealing with objects made of fiber, clay, glass, and wood. Objects made of all these materials (and others) are also commonly found in art galleries.

Language scholars tell us that the comparative use of the two words *art* and *craft* began at about the time of the Norman conquest (1066). The Norman-derived word *art* was reserved for the higher-priced items made for the conquerors. The Anglo-Saxon–derived word *craft* was reserved for the lower-priced items made for the conquered. But these days even price is no longer a reliable distinction.

Walter Gropius, speaking through the Weimar Bauhaus manifesto, probably said it best:

> No essential difference exists between the artist and the craftsman of heightened awareness. . . . But the basis of craftsmanship is indispensable to all artists. It is the prime source of all creative work.

If only the audiences remain to separate the arts from the crafts, and if even this differential is being slowly erased, where do contemporary turned-wood bowls fit into this changing landscape?

There are a few (but only a few) hopeful signs of art-audience attention. Several art museums have begun to collect the bowls of the master contemporary turners. The credits listed after the turners' names in this book will indicate which ones. The list includes some of the most important art museums in the nation, although, except for The Metropolitan Museum of Art's early acquisition of James Prestini's work, most of these collections are of recent vintage and, unfortunately, display in art museums has been infrequent.

However, in April 1985, as a part of the University's Centennial Celebration, the Arizona State University Art Museum will mount a show of the collection pictured in this volume, and it is hoped that this show will travel. In addition, arrangements have been made to ensure that the collection will be donated to the public.

The art press is also beginning to stir. Art critics in at least two of the nation's leading daily newspapers, *The New York Times* and *The Wall Street Journal*, have recently written articles on contemporary master turners.

However, the art-book field remains barren. Although there have been many fine how-to craft books devoted to turning, this may well be the first volume devoted to the art of the turned-wood bowl. Next best to seeing (and touching) the bowls themselves is seeing photographs of them and reading about them in a book. It is my hope that both readerships, craft and art, will encounter and enjoy this volume.

The work of the master contemporary turners deserves a significantly wider circle of appreciation. That is what this collection—and this book—are all about.

Most books are the results of the efforts of a good many people. This is especially true of art books, where the photography, catalogue information, and much of the text are frequently not the work of the author but of others. Such is the case here.

All photographs for the book were taken by Chuck Garner of Vermillion Photographic. The collection was catalogued by Karen C. Hodges, Curatorial Assistant for the Phoenix Art Museum. Packaging the collection, both for museum shipment and storage, was accomplished (both design and construction) by David Restad, Preparator for the Phoenix Art Museum. The typing (and retyping), the scheduling, and the record keeping were done by my secretary, Linda Winter. Learning which turners to collect was based on suggestions that came principally from the turners themselves.

Finally, I was encouraged and supported by four close friends: Jean Lipman, noted art author and neighbor; James Ballinger, Director of the Phoenix Art Museum; Rudy Turk, Director of Art Collections, Arizona State University in Tempe; and Michael Fox, Director of the Heard Museum in Phoenix. All of them admire these bowls and, I believe, agree with the major premise of this book.

EDWARD JACOBSON

Phoenix, Arizona

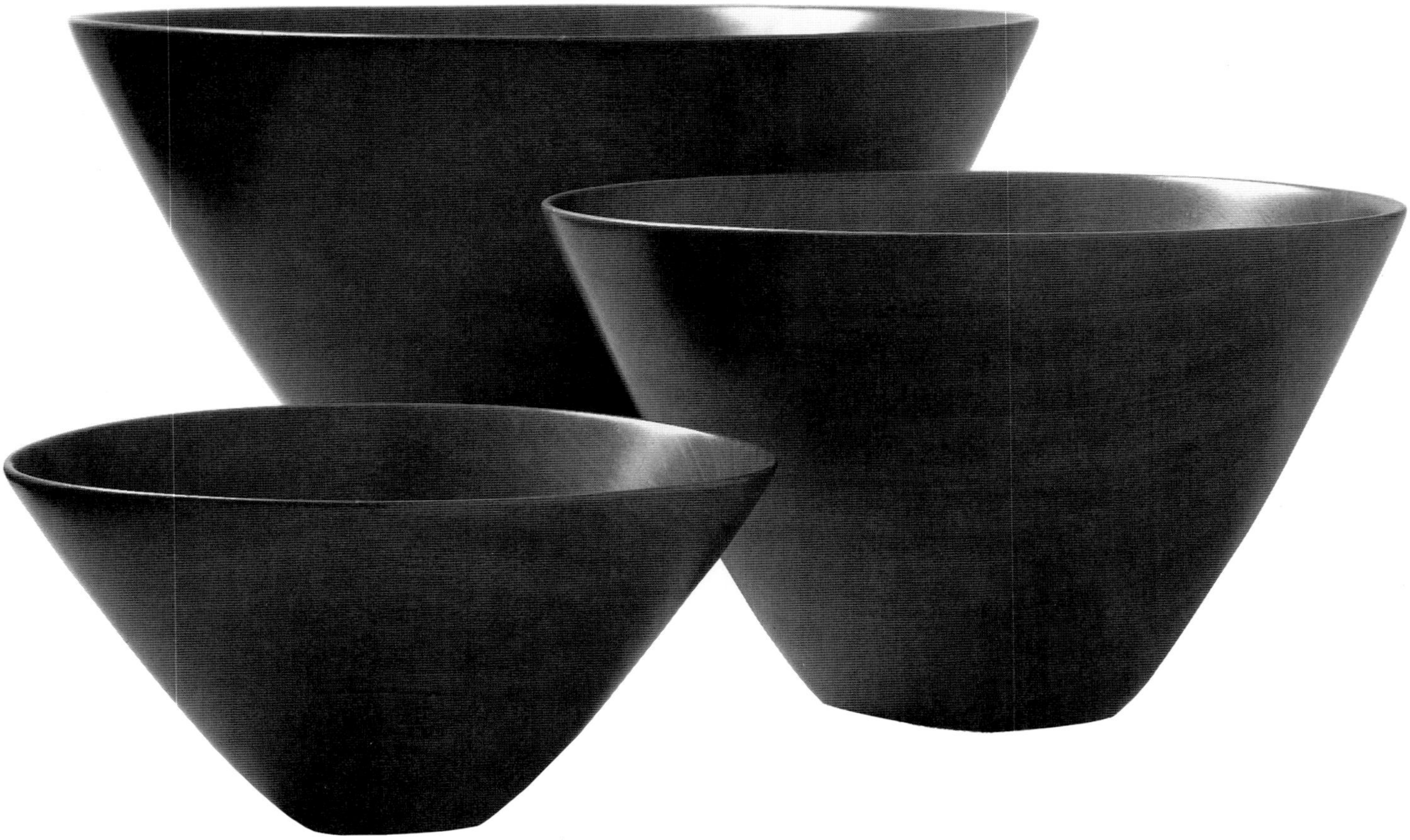

In 1933 James Prestini began his twenty-year exploration of the turning process to create elegantly formed, thin-walled vessels. These examples, in various woods, are among twenty in the collection of the National Museum of American Art, Smithsonian Institution. H. 4″–13″. (Gift of the artist)

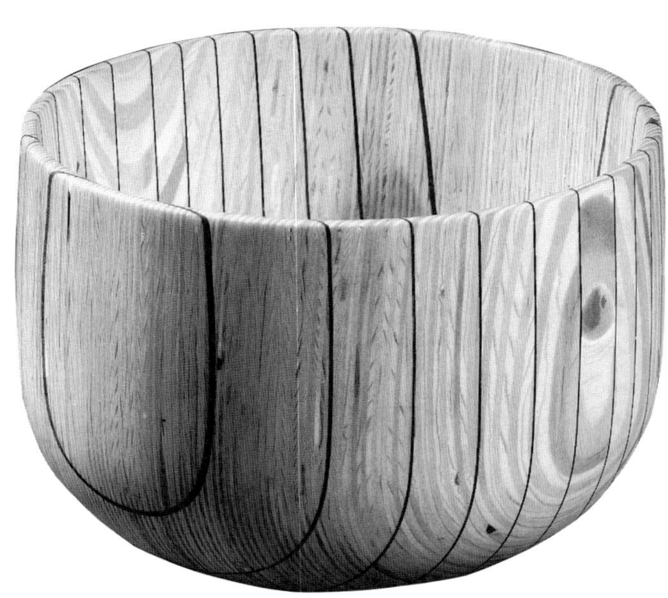

Rude Osolnik is well known for his bowls turned from solid wood. This example, however, is made of birchwood laminated with walnut, and it was selected in a national competition for handcrafted multiples held in 1975 at the Renwick Gallery, National Museum of American Art. H. 7″; Diam. (rim) 11″. (Museum Purchase)

THE ART OF TURNED-WOOD BOWLS

Human beings today have acknowledged human creativity—almost from the beginnings of human life as we know it—as art. Writing, painting, carving, composing music, and designing shelter have qualified for the designation as art, though not always within the lifetimes of those responsible for the creative product. Art, it seems, goes through almost constant reevaluation. The concepts of beauty and harmony have generally governed the recognition of art, whether it emerged as an object to contemplate and appreciate or as a song or story in performance. Utility and practicality in furniture, architecture, clothing, or tableware have rarely been considered important in the discussion of art objects made by hand or with the aid of manufacturing techniques. Instead, aesthetics alone governs our identification of art in everyday things.

What, then, of the turned-wood bowl as art? The origin of the bowl probably dates from early man's need to cup his hands to hold water for a cooling drink. Surely he discovered soon after that indentations in rocks could be enlarged to hold liquids or food and that leaves when folded or intertwined could provide containment for solids, too. It was only a step or two more to learn how to form vessels from clay or wood. But when did such containers ever strive for—or achieve—recognition as art? Archaeological collections in museums worldwide display early earthenware bowls, or pounding and grinding vessels made of stone. Wood, however, is subject to rot and destruction by vermin. Early examples of wood containers made by any process are not found very often; the earliest turned bowl, dating from 600 B.C., was found in a burial mound in Bavaria, West Germany. Yet it is not necessary to look for the earliest wood bowls to evaluate their legitimacy as art.

It is the bowl form itself that deserves first consideration. The very presence in art museum collections of ceramic and glass bowls made by other peoples in other times is evidence enough that they have been kept and treasured as art objects. They are not exhibited only as cultural artifacts that speak to us of the daily rituals of those people who made or used them. They are there because they are visually pleasing. Men and women have prized them since they were made and have preserved them, passing them on to others so that they might be seen and admired by future generations. Their forms and their surface embellishments have been found to be beautiful. It matters not to us today whether they were made for ritual purposes, to hold grain, or for the pure delight of seeing and touching. These bowls may be of bronze, iron, ceramic, glass, stone, or wood. We respond intuitively to their shapes and sizes, as well as to their colors, textures, and surface patterning. The bowl is a familiar shape to all, held by human hands since childhood. We all have some idea of how a bowl should be shaped and how it should feel when held. We evaluate its weight, its surface, the edge of its lip, and the sureness of its base as it sits on a flat surface.

Can one deny the beauty of classical bowls from Greece, formed of clay and decorated with human figures in their daily pursuits? Is a simple porcelain bowl from China, unadorned but for its colored, glassy sheen, less beautiful? Why not, then, consider that a bowl made of wood can also be beautifully formed, its lustrous surface revealing the years of life it experienced as a tree?

Wood has been one of the earth's most abundant natural materials for human manipulation. Although this book deals with it as a material suited for artistry on a

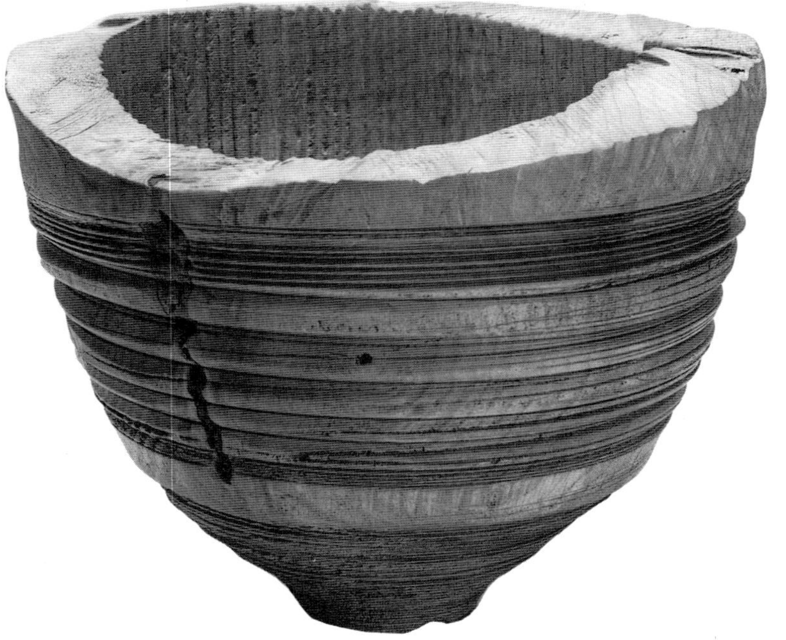

Mark Lindquist, with his father, Mel, first gained serious recognition for the vessels he turned from spalted wood. *Ascending Bowl #3,* 1981, in the collection of Renwick Gallery, National Museum of American Art, marked his departure from smoothly finished, richly figured bowls, and the beginnings of his sculptural treatment of the turned bowl's surface. Walnut. H. 8½"; Diam. (rim) 11½". (Museum Purchase)

turner's lathe, it has been used in other ways to make containers. The process of scorching wood, then cutting away the charred wood to create a cavity in a solid wooden block, has been used by primitive peoples to make canoes as well as storage and serving bowls. The native tribes in the northwestern United States and Canada used bending techniques to make containers for food that were often carved and painted as gifts for the potlatch. The tree's bark alone has also been used to form containers, folded and lashed together at the corners. Although more frequently seen in the exhibits in anthropology museums than they are in the context of art, this variety of bowl form visually rewards and reminds us of the world's plurality in creative expression.

The turning of bowls on a lathe is hardly a new phenomenon; for some three thousand years craftsmen have used sharp tools to cut whirling blocks of wood into vessels and other functional and decorative objects. Scholars speculate that the lathe may have developed simultaneously among the Etruscans in Italy, the Celts in Great Britain, and the residents of the Crimea around 1000 B.C. The simple vertical bow lathe that turned the object being carved forward and back, but allowed cutting only in the forward direction, was gradually improved with the addition of a crank. Although that fifteenth-century development permitted steady turning in one direction, a helper was still needed. It was not until the advent of motorized equipment that a turner could operate his lathe alone. Adjustable speeds and improved blades were further improvements.

However, industrialization brought faster methods of forming functional objects of clay, glass, and metal, and by 1850 the need for turned-wood bowls for the kitchen hardly existed. Wood turning by the late nineteenth century seems to have been directed more to the manufacture of turned architectural ornaments for Victorian houses, parts for furniture, or models for metal castings. But even though the industrial revolution seriously threatened the future of handcrafts except in rural areas where changes took place more slowly, the late nineteenth century witnessed a renewed interest in the quality of handmade goods. The English Arts and Crafts Movement gave birth to an American manifestation of its effort to bring dignity and honesty to handcrafted domestic furnishings that continued roughly until World War I. Like its English counterpart, the American movement rejected the excesses of inappropriate ornamentation of manufactured items. Instead, the movement's followers championed simplified shapes for wood furniture, and ornamentation—where still needed or desired—was reduced to simplified naturalistic decoration. Furniture relied principally on the beauty of the wood itself, with its honest joinery visible as a prominent decorative element. It is unlikely that bowls produced for use during this period changed very much; the turning process did not encourage the elaboration of decoration popular in the late nineteenth century. Leaders of the Arts and Crafts Movement would have had no stylistic axes to grind in their zeal to bring honest craftsmanship to the turning of bowls; it had never been forsaken.

It can probably be safely said that the market for turned-wood products neither grew nor faltered seriously during two world wars and the period between. Turning simply became a method for the factory, not the independent professional craftsman. In the 1950s, however, postwar prosperity and optimism began to give Americans new ideas for their newfound leisure time. The home workshop was born. Hobbyist craftsmen turned to the power saws and lathes that they had installed in garages and basements and began to experiment with building birdhouses, lawn chairs, and other simple furniture. Turned bowls could not be far behind.

Parallel to the burgeoning interest in hobby crafts in the postwar years was the growth of craft classes in the curricula of art schools and university art departments. Returning war veterans sought new opportunities for education and creative fulfillment; the GI bill provided the means to earn a college education. Opportunities to study woodworking came later than courses in ceramics, textiles, jewelry, and metalworking, and it was not until the 1960s that national recognition came to established American furniture craftsmen like Wharton Esherick, Sam Maloof, George Nakashima, and Wendell Castle. Not one of them turned bowls. Art museums began to exhibit their work; contemporary woodworking was finding acceptance. Curators and critics were beginning to see that modern craftsmen had the ability to take a familiar material and give it creative form while revealing its natural beauty.

The rise of such a group of professional furniture craftsmen indicated an increasing interest that home craftsmen also shared: their love of wood. It is probably coincidental that the exhibition that opened the Smithsonian's Renwick Gallery in 1972, "Woodenworks: Furniture Objects by Five Contemporary Craftsmen," took place only a couple of years before Taunton Press launched *Fine Woodworking*, the first crafts magazine devoted to wood. This periodical brought the readership of home woodcraftsmen together with professionals creating unique furniture. Its mixture of technical articles and picture spreads of current professional work of significant quality helped to focus on the creative possibilities for the medium. Turners had found their forum.

In the past decade the number of woodworkers has grown tremendously. Furniture makers have been joined by turners in the pages of art journals and exhibition catalogues. A master turner like James Prestini, whose elegant, thin-walled bowls and platters had won many admirers since he began making them from scrap wood in 1933, is revered anew for the grace and serenity of his creative output of twenty years. (His career subsequently turned to steel sculpture of a larger scale when he had explored to his satisfaction the possibilities of turning wood.)

Master craftsman Bob Stocksdale, who had been turning decorative bowls professionally since the late 1940s, found that younger turners were inspired by his sureness of form and technique. His willingness to teach others in an increasing number of turning workshops around the country has further strengthened the regard in which he is held personally and professionally by his followers. His technical perfection, use of exotic woods, and the vocabulary of forms he calls on to enhance the beauty of the wood grain have made him an exemplar of the modern wood-turning movement.

Since the advent of a modern wood-turning movement, the outpouring of turned bowls, large and small, flat and tall, of domestic and exotic woods, has enabled those of us who are interested in American art made in the "craft" media to begin making comparisons within the context of turning as well as the other methods and materials used to produce bowls.

Unlike throwing ceramic vessels on the potter's wheel, the craftsman working at his lathe turning wood does not have an infinite variety of forms his material can take. A potter begins with a lump of pliable clay, centering it on the wheel and stretching it up into the form of a vessel. The walls may be pushed out or pinched in. It may have a wide, flared opening or be pulled in again to permit little more than a pinhole for an opening.

A block of wood fixed to a woodworker's lathe is solid. Although various woods have different working qualities, it is safe to say that the unsure hand (and the unsharp tool) can splinter or gouge its surface, perhaps ruining it completely. Clay can be pushed together again and re-formed. A mistake when turning a bowl may render it suitable only for firewood. Unless a smaller bowl can be salvaged from the turned block the effort (and the material) may be lost forever. The turner's error will not be forgiven by the unyielding material.

Yet, although the processes of forming a bowl of wood, metal, clay, or glass are different, we bring much of the same aesthetic viewpoint to the consideration of each. What pleasure does the bowl hold for us? Is the form graceful; that is, balanced between the base and the top opening? Is its real or apparent thinness appropriate for its shape, size, texture, and pattern of the wood? Has the turner chosen to finish it with a polished surface, heightening the wood's natural beauty? Or has the quality of the wood dictated another surface treatment? How does the finished bowl compare with other examples of its maker's work? Is its form, finish of outer surface, size, or inner volume unique to the style of the turner who made it?

We have been told so often that art is in the eye of the beholder, and to a large extent that is true. Each person relies on accumulated visual experience in choosing work that he or she qualifies as art. Beyond the most basic visual pleasure in seeing an object for the first time, it is often important to discern whether it will become boring after a day or two or a week or two. Is there always something new to enjoy in it? Will it continue to fascinate the eye when seen under artificial light as it does in the glow of sunrise? Does the wood's grain provide changing pleasures as one examines a bowl in the round?

Mark Lindquist's *Ascending Bowl #3*, in the collection of the Renwick Gallery of the Smithsonian's National Museum of American Art, provides an interesting contrast to Ed Moulthrop's (see p. 55) and to Bob Stocksdale's (see p. 75, bottom). Lindquist, after years of turning smoothly polished bowls of beautifully figured and spalted woods, here chose to reveal the marks of his tools and the turning process in his work. The bowl is heavy-walled, lifting gracefully from a small base and almost appearing to whirl toward its top edge. The interior of the unpolished, dry-looking vessel has been gouged out with his tools from the top downward, and the primitive carved effect of the inside contrasts with the apparent spinning movement of the outside. Light cast on the bowl's sculptured surface produces deep shadows in its grooves; it is interesting to see from any side and under all lighting conditions.

Moulthrop typically turns figured tulipwood, choosing the grain and color variations carefully so they will be enhanced as the bowl takes shape. The large ovoid forms are highly polished, forming a perfect foil for the rich patterning in the wood. The apparent thinness of his turning where one perceives it at the vessel's opening might make one think of these large turned forms as gigantic wooden bubbles, so thin that they might break as easily as an eggshell.

Bob Stocksdale works on a more intimate scale, choosing exotic figured woods and determining which form will best reveal that wood's color and texture. His bowls usually have a small base, flaring out and up. He is masterful in bringing to our attention a wood's color variation by turning it so that only the bowl's edge color contrasts with that of its body. Rude Osolnik not only turns solid wood—often that native to Kentucky, where he lives—but laminates contrasting woods and turns them into practical, artful bowls.

Each turner has a distinct style, as do the other turners in this survey. They have succeeded in elevating the craft of turning, directing their materials and techniques toward the service of their unique visual ideas. Although there is no hard line between *craft* and *art*—a continuum that at one end depends on technical skill and at the other end on the ideas served by that skill—these turners have taken their rightful place in the elusive stratosphere of art. Others will follow, finding their own individual ways of imbuing their turned bowls with creativity and originality. It is wonderful to be a part of their generation and to see it happen.

LLOYD E. HERMAN,
Director, Renwick Gallery of the
National Museum of American Art,
Smithsonian Institution,
Washington, D.C.

AN OVERVIEW OF THE HISTORY OF FINE TURNED-WOOD BOWLS

In the early history of America, three groups of colonists settled in different localities, separated at that time by great distances. The Virginia colonists settled at Jamestown in 1607, New England colonists landed and settled Plymouth in 1620, and William Penn and the Quakers established Philadelphia in 1683.

Although these early settlers brought with them from Europe the language and culture of their ancestors, they were forced to adapt to the different environments they encountered in the New World. The mild climate of Virginia produced a style of living quite different from the spartan life-style forced on the New Englanders by the rigorous weather and short growing seasons, while the Quakers took advantage of the densely forested area and built with wood and stone, furnishing their homes in much the same style as in the old country.

Necessity required each homeowner in the Colonies to be a jack-of-all-trades and a master of some. Exceptional skill allowed one to barter and trade for necessities and luxuries, raising one's standard of living as well as giving personal satisfaction and security.

Woodenware, or treenware, was an important part of the day-to-day housewares used by the early colonists. The woodenware used in New England and Virginia was sturdy, crude, and simple, performing various functions as required. That used in Pennsylvania was a little more refined and was frequently decorated with carvings or paintings.

Woodenware was either imported or produced locally by craftsmen experienced in the work. The type of work produced in the Colonies varied little from the work being done in England, as the pieces produced were usually copies of turnings currently in hand. Also, if a turner had previous training, he likely would have received it in England or from a fellow colonist who had been trained in England.

Eating bowls and plates were called *turner's ware*, as they were made on the lathe. The men who did this type of work, called *dish turners*, were respected craftsmen, working alongside the coopers, chairmakers, carpenters, cabinetmakers, carvers, wheelwrights, and the spindle turners, who also used the lathe to fashion parts for chairs, beds, and other furniture.

The first lathe used in the Colonies was the *pole lathe*, which was powered by a slender sapling fixed horizontally overhead. The cord from the pole was wrapped once or twice around the work, with the end fastened to a treadle. The work was supported between centers; and as the treadle was pressed down, the work rotated through several revolutions, permitting the turner to form the surface of the stock with a turning chisel. Releasing the treadle caused the pole to spring back, rotating the stock backward and raising the treadle in preparation for another cut. The work was tedious and tiring, but the process was far superior to burning the interior of a bowl or laboriously using bone, shell, or stone scrapers to form a wooden vessel.

A lathe used in the late seventeenth and eighteenth centuries was the *mandrel lathe*. This lathe had a continuous rotating action and was turned by a treadle, water-, man-, or animal power. A handheld chisel formed the piece while it was rotating in the lathe. The pieces produced were said to be *hand-turned*, as distinguished from the machine-made pieces produced by factories later.

The mandrel lathe, with refinements in engineering, is still with us today. However, the power source now is usually electricity, with ball bearings, cast-iron parts, and precision machining contributing to convenience, accuracy, and speed. Although the modern lathe used by the hand woodturner may be superior to the wooden machinery of yesteryear, the pieces produced on modern lathes are not always better.

From the early nineteenth century onward, the need for skilled craftsmen decreased as the use of mechanical technology increased. Individuals worked to the pace and rhythm of the machines. The worker no longer worked on a piece from start to finish; instead, he generally performed a single task over and over again.

During colonial times, the term *craftsman* was used to refer to many different kinds of people who worked with their hands. Other terms used to refer to such workers were *artisan* or *tradesman*. At the top of the colonial hierarchy was the *master craftsman*. Highly skilled and respected in the community, the master usually owned his own shop, supervised his own workers, often designed his own pieces, and set the standards for craftsmanship in his shop. The wealthy were frequently his customers, and while the master craftsman generally worked within the limits established by European fashions and gave the customer satisfaction, he interpreted fashion and design from his own experience or by the limitations placed on him by his tools and materials.

The colonial journeyman was the result of the apprenticeship system, usually serving about seven years under the watchful and demanding eye of the master. Skill was developed by constant repetition, and patience for doing the dirty work required. The early years of apprenticeship allowed little opportunity for personal interest or creative work. In fact, the apprentice was the last in the shop to receive the better duties, accommodations, food, or leisure.

The apprenticeship system produced skilled craftsmen, but the industrial revolution brought with it an insatiable appetite for common workers. The advent of mechanization required new directions in apprenticeships, and new skills had to be developed to feed the mechanical appetites. In most cases, the craftsman did not fare well.

Much that previously had been produced by hand could now be produced abundantly in the factories. Manufactured glass, clay, and metal containers rapidly took the place of woodenware. Mass production reduced costs to the point that most Americans could afford at least the rudimentary necessities produced by the factories. Technology and industry combined to change the life-style and aspirations of most Americans. The attitude commonly prevailed that factory-made was superior to handmade; in fact, many felt that handmade was only for those without the means to purchase factory goods.

The craft of wood turning declined drastically during those years, with the dish turner disappearing and being absorbed into the industrial machine. The hand-turner also largely disappeared, and those who survived were primarily spindle turners who worked in a semi-mass-production shop producing porch posts, bedposts, newel-posts and spindles for staircases or legs, and spindles for small chair plants. Others were employed as pattern or prototype makers in furniture manufacturing plants.

Manual arts programs in public schools and post-secondary institutions provided instruction in the rudiments of wood turning, but seldom did the students develop a high level of skill. The elementary skills survived in the educational programs and with a few isolated turners in various parts of the country. However, a general decline in interest and skill continued until the 1970s.

Occasionally, a star appears during a declining period, sometimes intentionally, other times with other purposes in mind. One such person is James Prestini. From 1933 to 1953 Prestini was a serious woodturner. He turned and sold hundreds of bowls, although professionally he was involved in engineering, design, mathematics, and teaching. Although wood turning was a hobby for him, he was the first seriously to turn the wooden vessel with other than utility in mind. His approach to wood turning was to subject function to form. The concept of turned bowls and plates has been with us for hundreds of years, but Prestini has added a new dimension. The lathe had been used to shape and produce forms in wood; but Prestini used the lathe to produce forms *he* wanted, selecting the wood for grain, color, and texture to suit his purpose. These forms became a statement in wood, design, and art. For the first time, Prestini originated forms in wood that became recognized as art forms. The shapes were new for wooden forms, but history can find them in glass or clay.

The astounding thinness of Prestini's bowls is a first. No one before him had pushed the material toward its limit. He was the first to establish the artistic viability of wooden vessels, and his work established a firm dimension of credibility for the wooden bowl as an art form. He has had shows in museums and galleries across the country, with a major show being held in New York at The Museum of Modern Art in 1949. His pieces were photographed and displayed in magazines, adding even greater credibility to the concept of the decorative bowl. His bowls were collected by private individuals and purchased by museums. He is, indeed, the pioneer of the bowl as an art form.

A quotation from the introductory essay by Edgar Kaufmann, Jr., in *James Prestini: Art in Wood* (New York: Pocahontas Press, 1950) summarizes his work:

> It is hard to make a place for Prestini among conventional craftsmen, and his place among artists would be exceptional and marginal. Yet his place is secure as a maker of beautiful, pure shapes.... Perhaps we must be ready to grant Prestini a unique position.... He has made grand things that are not overwhelming, beautiful things that are not personal unveilings, and simple things that do not urge usefulness to excuse their simplicity. They are not precisely works of science or art, craft or convenience. Yet in their restraint and in their superb, direct assurance they touch our scope and potentialities, our limits and desires. It is this wide frame of reference that gives Prestini's bowls and platters their audience; art or not, craft or not, bowls or plain shapes, they speak directly and amply of our day to our day. Some other day will find a category for them; for the present, they remain Prestini's pure forms.

Following Prestini, master woodturner Bob Stocksdale developed a new level of craftsmanship and form that established a benchmark for shops, galleries, and aspiring bowl turners. Stocksdale works with exotic woods from around the world, using technical expertise and an intuitive sense of form to develop bowls unexcelled in beauty. During a workshop he conducted at Brigham Young University in Provo, Utah, a participant queried Stocksdale about the source of forms for his bowls—whether inspiration, training, or otherwise. Stocksdale replied that at one time he had checked out some books on Oriental porcelains and pottery and found that Chinese and Japanese potters had been "copying my designs for two thousand years." Although a tongue-in-cheek comment, his forms were undoubtedly influenced by porcelain and pottery. But Stocksdale has developed a style of turning unique to himself. His bowls have long served as the technical standards against which other turners measured their work. The Stocksdale bowl has few shortcomings. There are no abrupt changes in thickness or form, wall thickness ranges from one-eighth to three-sixteenths of an inch, and the smooth surfaces are free from tear-out or sanding scratches. He is the Shoji Hamada of wood turning, using traditional tools and techniques adapted to his forms and method of work. He was foremost in establishing national bases for marketing at upper-level shops, eventually evolving into galleries and one-man shows. Since the late 1940s, Stocksdale has been a professional turner of bowls, and because of his expertise, he has become an inspiration for many young American turners.

Another American craftsman, not so well known nationally as Stocksdale, but certainly a dominant force in the Southern Highlands region of Kentucky, North and South Carolina, West Virginia, and Tennessee, is Rude Osolnik from Berea, Kentucky. Osolnik was a faculty member of the Industrial Arts Department at Berea College for forty years; at the same time his output of bowls and other turned objects was prodigious. Early in the 1940s, Osolnik realized that a bowl or platter did not require a smooth rim. Working largely from offcuts from veneer and lumber mills, Osolnik utilized the natural surface of the stock from which the bowl was turned. While selecting stock with a form in mind, Osolnik did not turn the surface of the outer rim, but utilized the beauty of the natural surface to complement or contrast with the turned surfaces of the piece. Another characteristic of an Osolnik bowl is the informal rim, which he hand-shapes after turning. Intentionally trying to break up the symmetry of the bowl, he follows the grain of the wood, shaping the edge parallel to the growth rings, creating a turned piece like an optical illusion. His work was sold nationally in gift catalogues, shops, and galleries during the 1950s and 1960s. One of Osolnik's bowls was purchased from America House in New York City by Eleanor Roosevelt as a wedding gift to the then Princess Elizabeth of England.

As the result of working with waste slabs from the wood industry, Osolnik was given a national award in 1955 by the Museum of Science and Industry in Chicago for the best utilization of waste wood. In 1950 he received a National Award for Contemporary Design for his candlesticks.

Osolnik is a complete woodturner, equally at home with bowls, spindle work, rolling pins, twig pots, or large laminated bowls made from stacked veneers or layers of plywood. Always the innovator, he has led the woodturners in his area and set a high standard of excellence.

In 1948, early in his career, Osolnik became actively involved and assumed a leadership position in the Southern Highlands Handicraft Guild, serving as president three different times. Currently, the guild has five sales galleries, featuring all areas of craftwork and producing over one million dollars in yearly sales. He founded the Kentucky Handicraft Guild in 1960 and has been actively involved ever since.

Mel Lindquist, formerly of Schenectady, New York, and now living in Henniker, New Hampshire, must not be overlooked in the history of wood turning, as he was the first turner to explore seriously the possibilities of spalted wood, which is penetrated with fungus decay. Until he and his son, Mark, began exhibiting work at craft shows, spalted wood was just a useless curiosity to most woodworkers. He also realized the artistic merit of using a rim or area on a piece to show the original surface of the tree. Although hollow turnings of stone have been with us for centuries, as evidenced by pieces constructed by Roman and Greek artisans, Lindquist was an early turner of hollow, narrow-necked vases turned hollow through the neck openings. He called this process *blind boring*, as he could not see into the piece during the turning procedure. A retired engineer for General Electric, he has a natural curiosity about new ways to do things and has developed basic bent-shaft tools to use in his work.

As we move into the 1970s, several forces come into play, each having had a tremendous effect on wood turning.

In the winter of 1975, *Fine Woodworking* made its debut. This magazine was the forum woodworkers needed. Dedicated to promoting woodworking at a high level, *Fine Woodworking* set a standard of excellence not seen before by the dedicated woodworker. Wood turning has received a deserved place in nearly every issue.

The Bicentennial year of 1976 promoted all types of crafts, woodworking probably being the most popular. Marketing people and designers emphasized early American craft, and crafts were promoted nationally and given credibility by such people as Joan Mondale, wife of then Vice-President Walter Mondale.

Also in 1976, Albert LeCoff, along with his brother, Alan, and Palmer Sharpless of the George School in Newtown, Pennsylvania, conducted a wood-turning conference, which was attended by fifty turners. The first of ten such conferences, it set the stage for numerous wood-turning and woodworking workshops at craft schools, universities, woodworking tool stores, and craftsmen's guilds.

During the 1970s a number of woodworking books began to appear on the market. These books were well illustrated with photographs and drawings, and many aspiring craftsmen purchased them and applied the information and techniques to their own work. Seeking further information, they became eager participants in workshops and symposia. Never in history has so much information on materials and techniques been so readily available to the woodturner.

Beginning in the early 1970s, a number of contemporary woodturners became visible at the national level. One of these was Mark Lindquist of Henniker, New Hampshire. As a boy, Mark worked with his father, although he left wood for a few years while pursuing a degree in fine arts and then working as a potter. He is an innovator. Driven by a sense of perfection and by recognition of his work, Mark developed new techniques and perfected methods of turning spalted wood. Never satisfied with the status quo and working with energy and dedication, he established the credibility and marketability of spalted wood, burls, and distressed wood at galleries and museums. His work is in the collections of several museums, including The Metropolitan Museum of Art in New York City, and he has had major exhibitions at numerous museums and galleries. Currently producing work with toolmarks and abraded surfaces, Lindquist is constantly striving to break tradition and the limitations of wood turning.

A discussion of contemporary woodturners must include Ed Moulthrop of Atlanta, Georgia. A part-time turner for many years, Ed gave up his thriving architectural practice about eleven years ago and began turning full time. Although simple in their design, his giant globes, lotus forms, and chunky doughnuts have given him national recognition as one of America's finest turners. Moulthrop has developed a market among interior designers, collectors, galleries, and museums, including the Smithsonian's Renwick Gallery, the Vatican Museum, New York's Museum of Modern Art, and The Metropolitan Museum of Art. The sheer size of his giant bowls as well as the five-figure prices commonly paid for his work established Moulthrop in a class by himself.

Another woodturner who has established himself in the elite group of woodturners is David Ellsworth of Quakertown, Pennsylvania. While there may be a question about who created the first hollow wooden turnings in America, there is no argument about who is currently doing the finest work. His work is incredible. In fact, I would venture to say that as few as ten years ago, most knowledgeable woodturners would have said it was impossible to turn the hollow vessels and cylinders Ellsworth is now producing. Never content with his present pieces though, Ellsworth has developed tools and techniques unique to his method of work. At the same time, he is actively teaching and encouraging woodturners across the country. His work is the rule by which others' work is measured.

When woodturners gather to discuss technique and craftsmen, Stephen Hogbin from Ontario, Canada, is another who is always mentioned. A sculptor who uses the lathe as a tool, Hogbin has shown how to break out of the restrictions commonly imposed by circular motion. Working from the principle that a cross section of a turning may be more interesting than the whole, Hogbin has reassembled sections and created new forms. He has added a new dimension to wood turning, if one has the foresight and courage to plan and experiment.

In conclusion, one must ask where wood turning is going. If the past ten years are any indication, we are in for continual advancement in work and technique that most of us cannot envision. Today in America, there are more interested, competent, and dedicated woodturners than at any time in our history. Progress in the last ten years has been incredible, and I see no reason why the future will not bring more of the same.

DALE L. NISH,
Professor of Industrial Education,
Brigham Young University,
Provo, Utah

AN APPRECIATION

Edward Jacobson has created the only comprehensive collection of wood bowls by contemporary American turners. This is a monumental achievement, all the more so as it becomes apparent that his is a collection of masterpieces. The collection testifies to a rare uniformity of standards and taste that can be achieved only when collecting is done solely and completely for the sake of beauty, and when beauty essentially is concerned with a sense of values.

The ultimate joy and reward for the conscientious collector is not in the bringing together of objects, no matter how beautiful they may be, but in making the collection available to others. This is the natural extension of the process and of self. The logical culmination of Jacobson's initial response to the beauty of a turned-wood bowl will be the exhibition without walls presented in this volume and the exhibition in 1985 of the collection at the Art Museum at Arizona State University in Tempe.

The reader of this book and the visitor to the gallery now have an opportunity to share the aesthetic experience of the collector. Like the collector, the viewer has all the necessary tools for understanding and appreciating this collection: eyes and heart. No special training, reading, or lectures are necessary. If anything, they are to be avoided. What then is the viewer advised to do? The answer is simple: look. It is amazing how quickly and how well our eyes recognize the basic truths and wonders of materials, shapes, textures, patterns, colors, contrasts, and variations. All perceptions, including tactile and kinesthetic, can emanate out of the visual experience. Look, and intuitive perception of beauty will follow or even coincide with the sensual perception of the object. A sense of beauty may be quickened or heightened by knowledge, but never is it dependent on intellectual exercise.

Look then at these wondrous bowls in a multiplicity of colors from black-dark to white-light, from soft honey to golden red to deep copper, from gentle and delicate hues to iridescent audacity. See the figured patterns, the bold striations, the humorous speckles and dots, and the lovely and seemingly infinite variety of grains. See and feel the real or apparent textures, the rough and the smooth. Smooth like glass, like satin, like silk—polished and shining. Rough like rocks, like broken earth, like the bark and burl of trees—most often matte and dull. Look again and list the shapes: tall and short, large and small, ovoid and flat, spherical and hemispherical, footed, tapered, elongated, and flattened. Take time and pleasure in naming the woods represented in this collection. How easy and familiar are cherry, apricot, butternut. How comfortable the litany of Georgia pine, hard maple, walnut burl, holly and magnolia, wild lilac and tulipwood, emery oak and tanbark oak and white oak. How exotic in oral and written form are lignum vitae, cocobolo rosewood, paloverde, and putumuzu. Domestic and exotic, the variety of choice and use seems infinite.

After seeing (conscientious, deliberate, and detailed observation) the objects, and creating a dictionary of words appropriate to the patterns and colors and textures and shapes, the multiplicity of combinations that are represented in this collection should be obvious. Equally obvious is the variegated nature of the turned-wood bowl. Infinite pluralism, it must be recognized, is basic to the nature of wood and the nature of man. And it follows that each bowl in this collection is, by its very nature, unique and totally incapable of replication.

The plethora of historic art styles may be found repeated endlessly in the work of contemporary turners. For example, the dainty elegance of the rococo is presented once again in the works of Sakwa (see pp. 68–69) and Ebner (see p. 20); Prestini's work (see pp. 65–66) proclaims the simplicity of a classic era, just as Mark Lindquist's exuberant and massive bowl (see p. 43) may be acclaimed as baroque. The values of the classic world and the romantic world alike are implicit in the works included in the Jacobson collection.

Knowledge of the secondary or nonperceptible aspects of an object may enhance one's appreciation of an object, but it is not essential to that experience. For example, it is titillating to learn that putumuzu wood comes from Brazil, thuya burl from Morocco, and paloverde from Arizona, but that type of knowledge should not affect an evaluation of the turner's art. However, if that kind of knowledge does determine one's judgment, then one is using a system of values that has very little, if anything, to do with beauty. One last recommendation and challenge: go with the eyes and the heart.

If the reader has come to the conclusion that much of the above reads like an introductory course in aesthetics or art appreciation, that conclusion is justified. That a turned-wood collection of such high quality now exists and is available to viewers throughout the nation is cause for celebration and commitment. It would be unfortunate if anyone would fail to take advantage of this superb collection because of a completely unnecessary sense of inadequacy. Follow the simple instructions for perception and judgment set forth above. Basically, you are advised to trust yourself.

Through this beautifully illustrated and informative volume, as well as through exhibitions, the Jacobson Collection will reach a wide audience. These opportunities to experience the wondrous creations of master contemporary turners constitute the culminating achievement of a consummate collector, a gentleman who knows how to use his eyes and his heart.

RUDY H. TURK,
Director of Art Collections,
Arizona State University,
Tempe

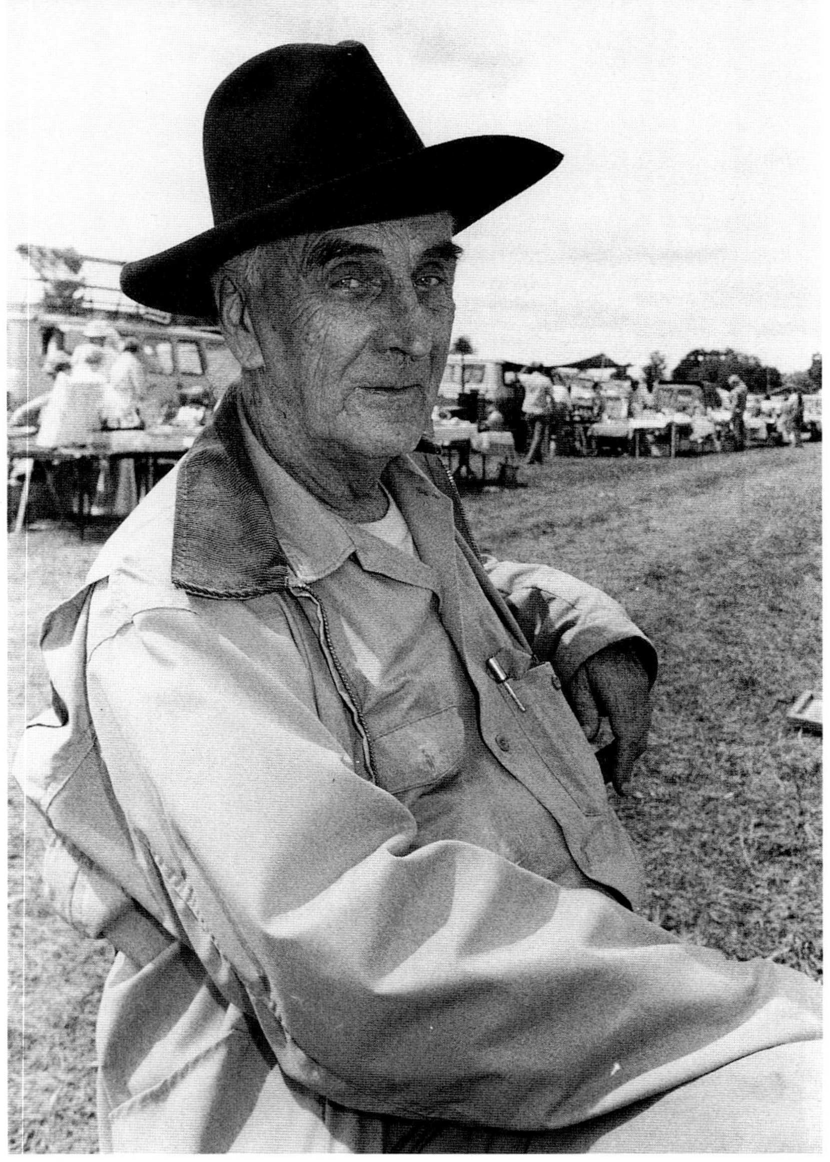

EARLY SETTLERS

The photograph is of the late Devere A. Card, renowned antiquarian of central New York State. Of his large collection of burled white ash bowls four examples are illustrated in this section.

In very early times the American Indian saw the possibilities of creating bowls from the burly growth frequently found on the huge ash trees in the forests. The natural shape of the growth suggested to the Indian that it could be made into a handsome and useful artifact.

The growth was cut from the tree and was then hollowed out by burning and scraping. The final size and shape of the piece was, of course, largely determined by the dimensions of the burl. It was not until much later that the Indian used a lathe to form the outside of the bowl. The larger bowls were used for serving food, and the smaller ones for eating.

Note: Height (H.) precedes diameter (Diam.); Thickness is always the thinnest measurement; Base may be footed (foot). Width = W.; Depth = D.; Length = L.

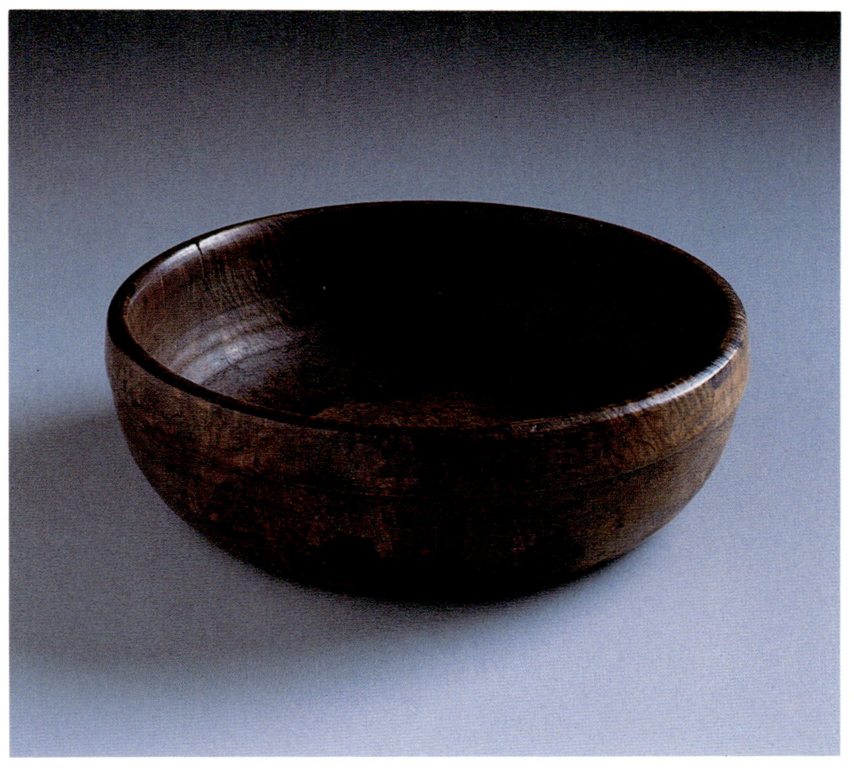

Unidentified craftsman (early American): Medium-size shallow bowl. 18th century. White ash burl. H. 2½″; Diam. (rim) 7⅞″; Thickness .36″; Base 6 1/16″.

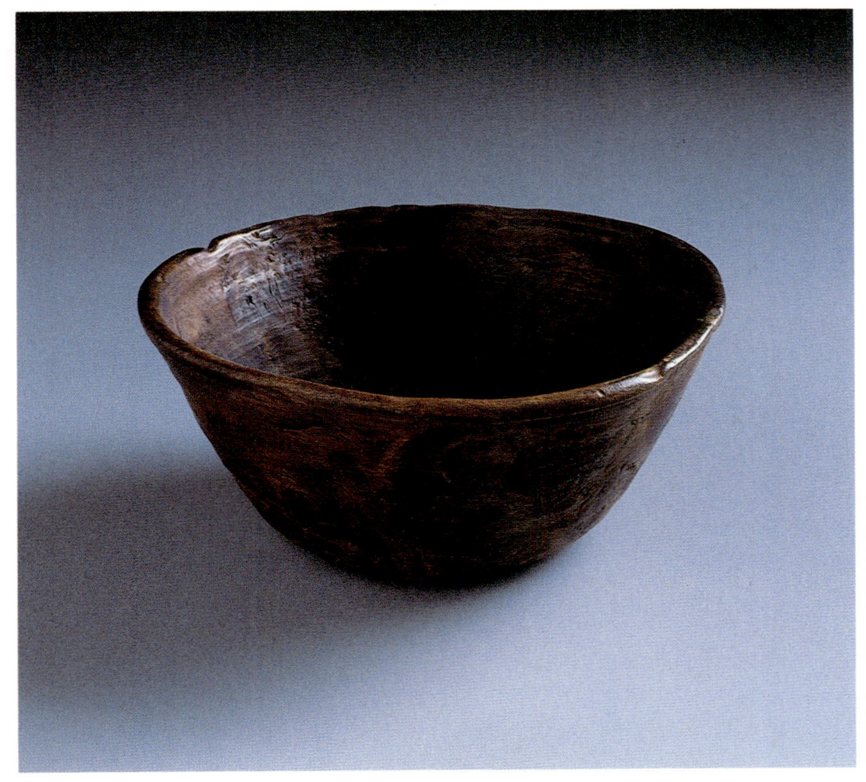

Unidentified craftsman (early American): Small bowl. 18th century. White Ash Burl. H. 2⅞″–2 15/16″; Diam. (rim) 6 11/16″–6 13/16″; Thickness .221″; Base 3 7/16″.

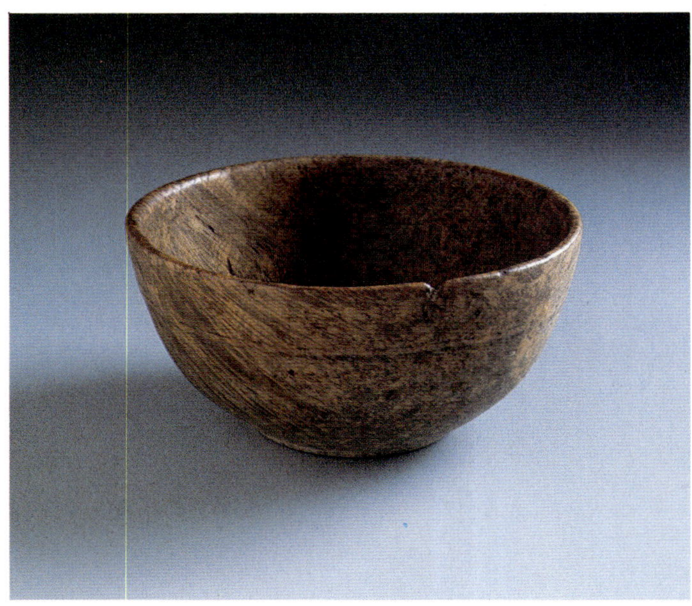

Unidentified craftsman (early American): Medium-size bowl. 18th century. White ash burl. H. 4⅜″; Diam. (rim) 9³/₁₆″; Thickness .336″; Base 4¼″.

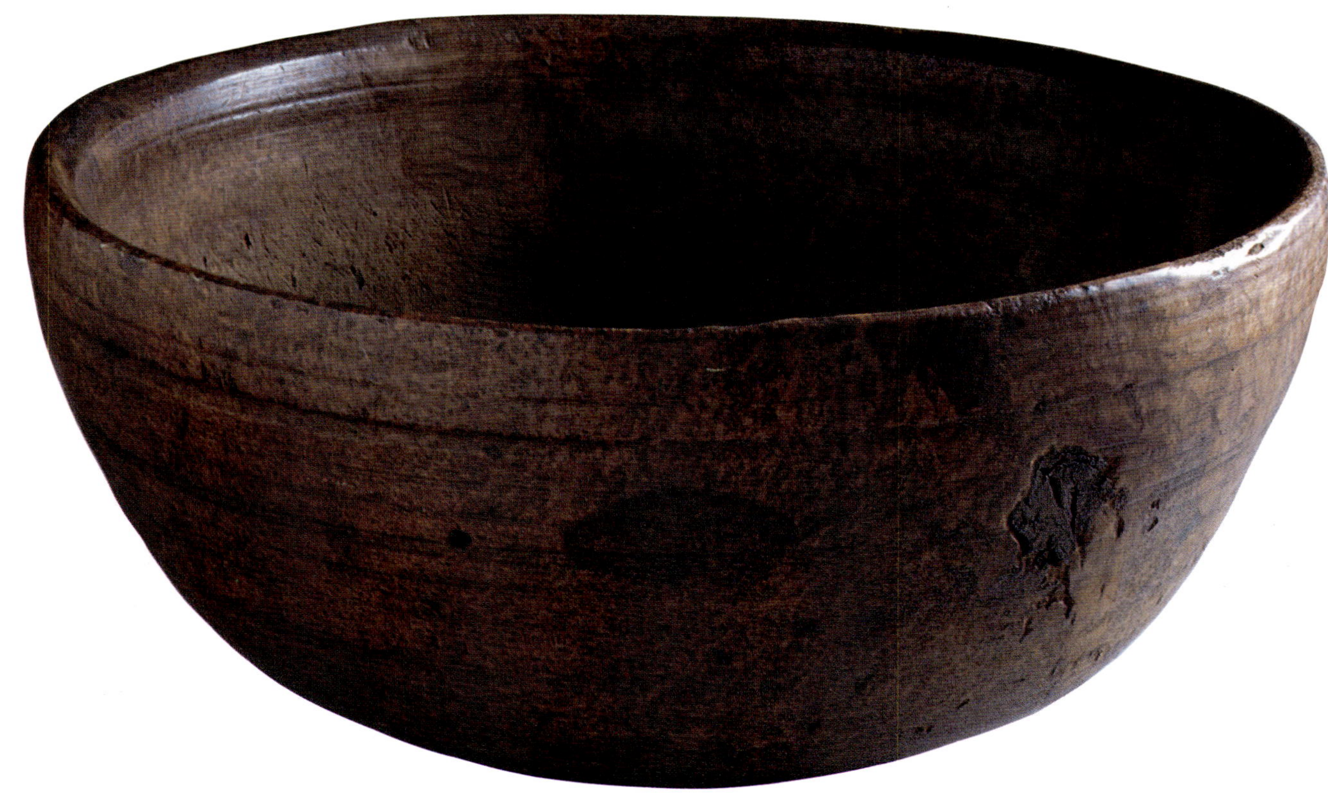

Unidentified craftsman (early American): Large bowl. 18th century. White ash burl. Diam. (rim) 15¹⁵/₁₆″; Thickness .739″; Base 6½″.

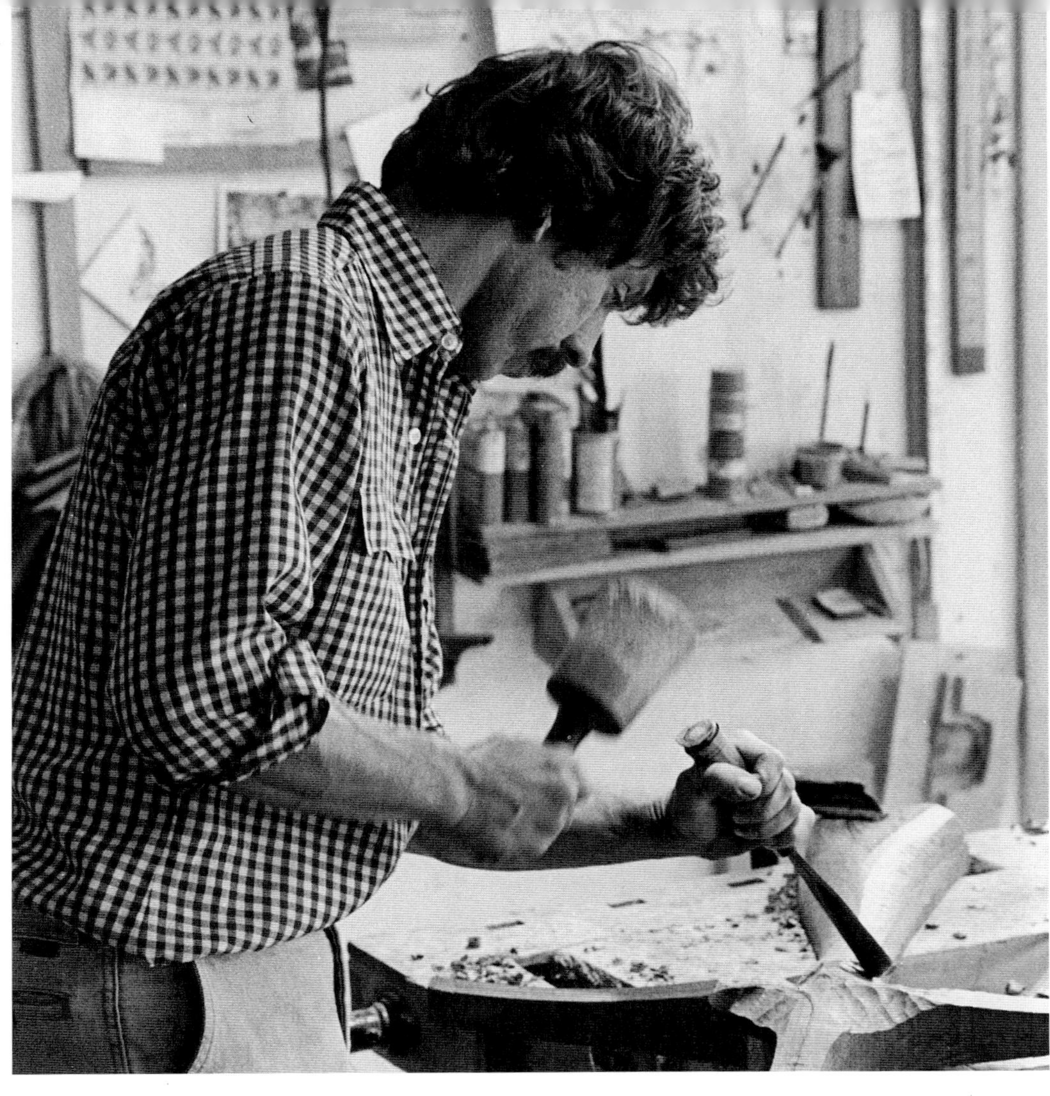

DAVID N. EBNER

31 Beaver Dam Road
Brookhaven, New York 11719

David Ebner has a BFA (1968) from the School for American Craftsmen of the Rochester Institute of Technology, New York, and took advanced studies at the London School of Furniture Design and Production, London, England, in 1969. His work is represented in the collections of the National Collection of Fine Arts, Smithsonian Institution, Washington, D.C., and the Museum of Fine Arts, Boston, Massachusetts. Mr. Ebner shows at the following galleries: Joanne Lyon Gallery, Aspen, Colorado; Pritam & Eames, East Hampton, New York; Gallery Henoch, New York City; The Swan Gallery, Philadelphia, Pennsylvania.

STATEMENT FROM THE ARTIST

The lathe is the first piece of woodworking equipment that I learned to use. I started by turning my own baseball bats at the age of eleven. Later, I started to turn bowls out of kiln-dried hardwood and to use the lathe to make parts for my furniture. As turning techniques developed and articles on the techniques on them were published, I found myself back at the lathe with many new avenues open to me. The spontaneity of turning green wood holds the most attraction for me. I apply the same design focus to my turnings as I do to my furniture—that is, I strive to have my designs reflect the inherent qualities of the material I am working in. When turning green burls, I prefer to leave the bark on the wood when possible, for I feel that by doing so the finished piece reflects the totality of the burl. The fact that I work with open shapes allows the finished piece to move as it dries, resulting in a finished piece that has a textured surface and a wandering edge.

My studio produces work in four different areas: turned bowls, sculpture, sculptural furniture, and classical impressions of furniture, by which is meant interpreting traditional furniture forms in a personal, contemporary way by using classical proportions and eliminating embellishment. In my sculptural furniture I am chiefly inspired by forms found in bones, shells, and trees.

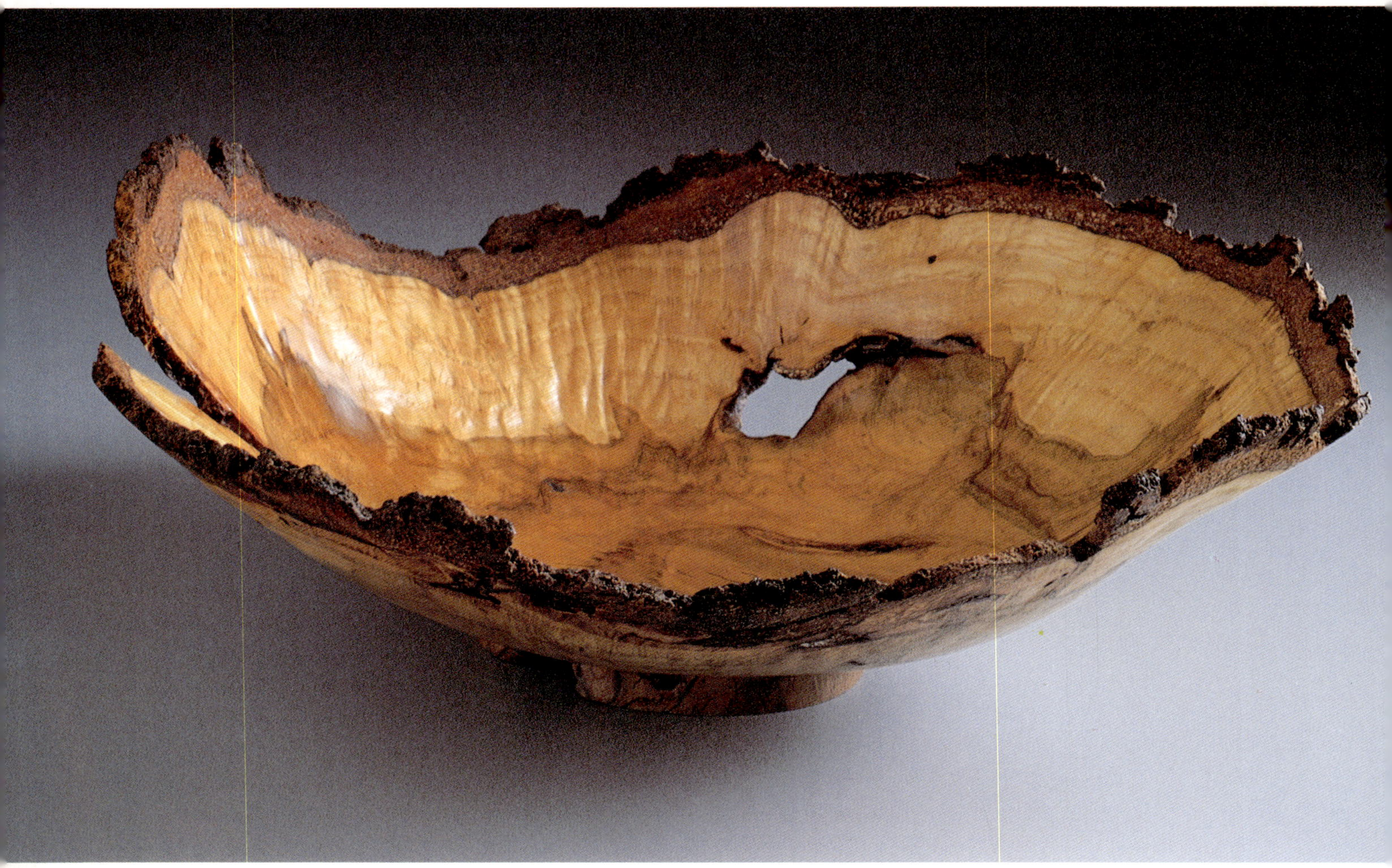

David N. Ebner: Deep footed bowl. 1981. Wild cherry. H. 3⅛″–5″; Diam. (rim) 5 9/16″–6 3/16″; Thickness .076″; Base (foot) 2¼″.

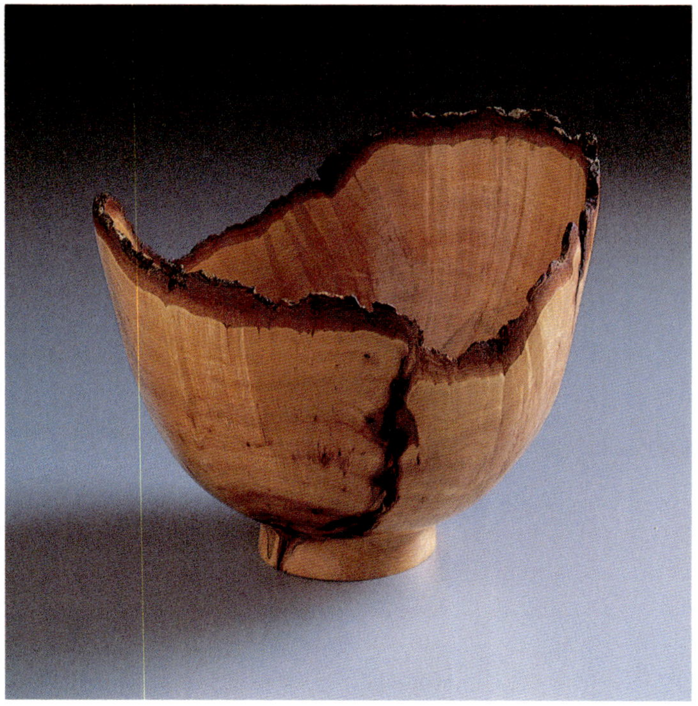

David N. Ebner: Shallow free-form footed bowl. 1981. Locust burl. H. 2 7/16″–4⅜″; Diam. (rim) 11 1/16″–12 1/16″; Thickness .205″; Base (foot) 3⅞″.

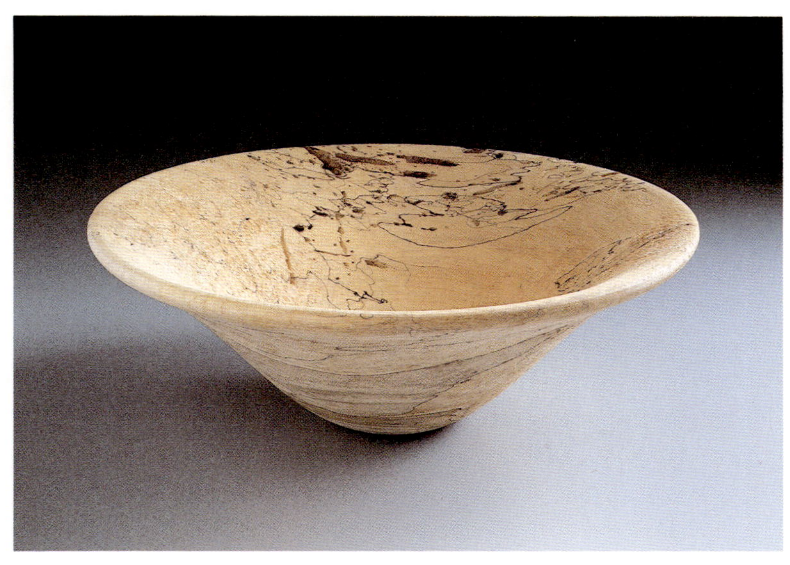

David N. Ebner: Large bowl. 1981. Spalted maple. H. 5¼″; Diam. (rim) $14\frac{13}{16}$″; Thickness .521″; Base 3″.

David N. Ebner: Wooden olla. 1981. Spalted maple. H. $7\frac{3}{16}$″; Diam. $3\frac{13}{16}$″ (mouth)–$7\frac{13}{16}$″ (belly); Thickness .625″; Base $3\frac{5}{16}$″.

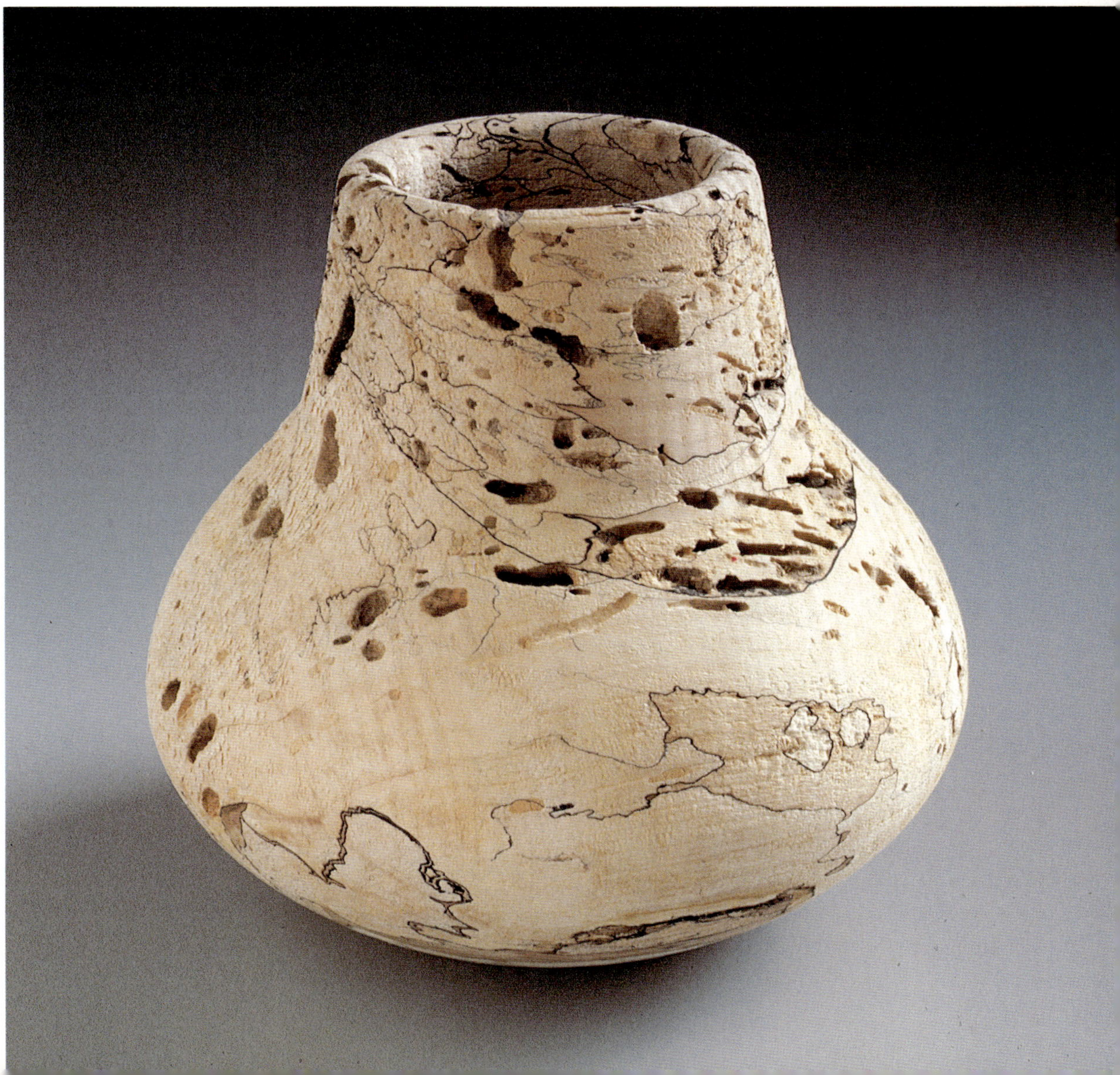

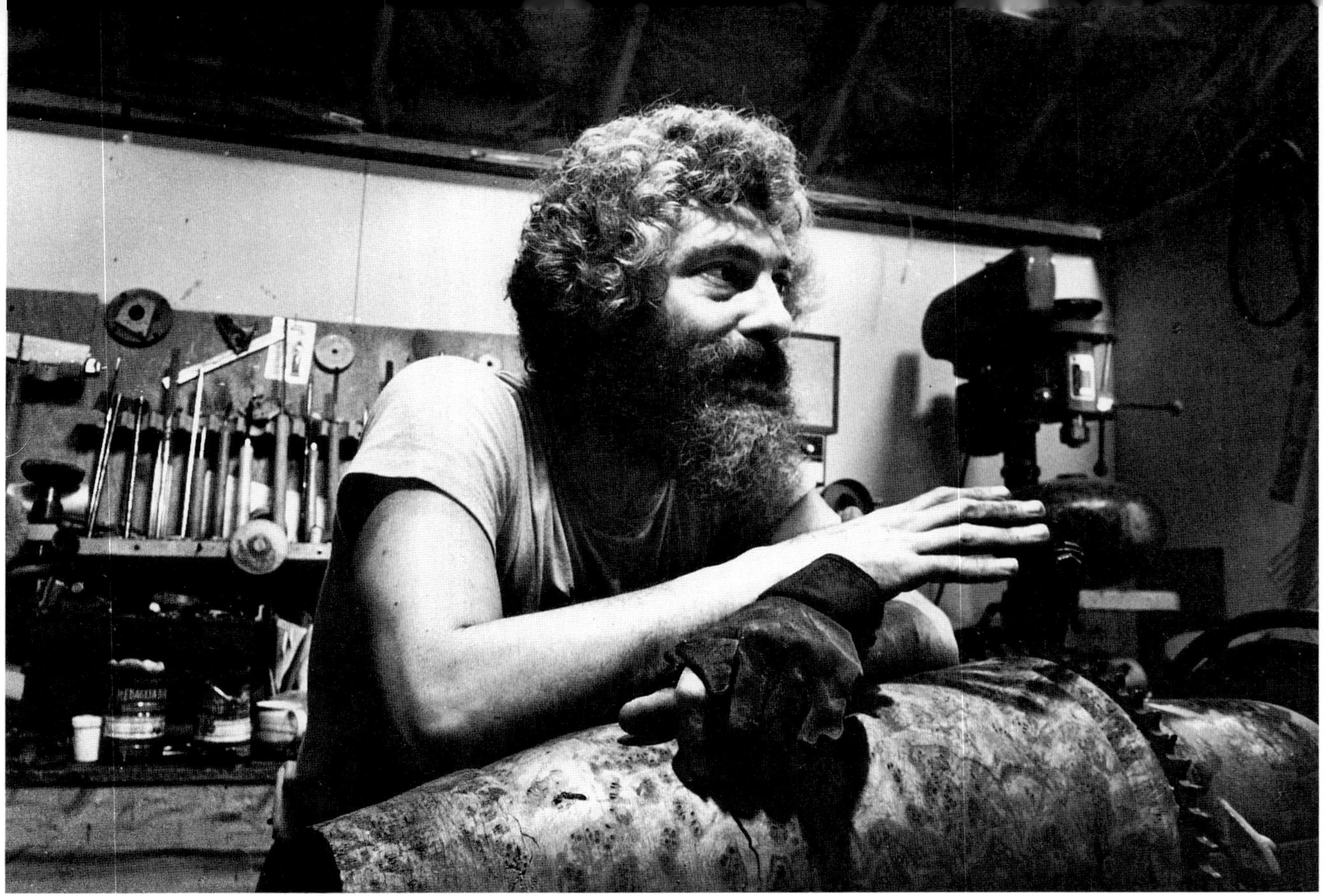

DAVID ELLSWORTH

Fox Creek R. D. 3
Quakertown, Pennsylvania 18951

David Ellsworth has a BFA (1971) and an MFA (1973) from the University of Colorado. His work is in the collections of the Denver Art Museum, Denver, Colorado, and the Sheldon Memorial Art Museum, Lincoln, Nebraska. Mr. Ellsworth has lectured in New York City; Philadelphia; Rochester, New York; Provo, Utah; Oakland, California; Marlboro, Ontario, Canada; and Shannon, Ireland. His work has been illustrated in books and included in museum exhibitions. Mr. Ellsworth is represented by the following galleries: Snyderman Gallery, Philadelphia, Pennsylvania; Pritam & Eames Gallery, East Hampton, New York; The Hand and The Spirit Crafts Gallery, Scottsdale, Arizona; Gallery Fair, Mendocino, California; Elaine Potter Gallery, San Francisco, California; and Susan McLeod Gallery, Sarasota, Florida. In September 1984 Mr. Ellsworth was awarded a $15,000 fellowship grant from the National Endowment for the Arts.

STATEMENT FROM THE ARTIST

Like most woodworkers, I began turning wood in an Industrial Arts class in the eighth grade of elementary school (1958). I maintained my interest in wood turning throughout high school and college while studying architecture and the fine arts, receiving my degrees in sculpture, drawing, and design.

My current work in hollow forms—vessels in wood—began in 1975, when I opened a studio as an independent craftsman in the mountains of Colorado. I developed a series of bent turning tools (see "Hollow Turnings," *Fine Woodworking* magazine, May/June 1979) that enabled me to hollow out a solid form through a small opening in the top—often reducing the thickness of the vessel's wall to as little as 1/16″—thus giving the object a levitative quality in its lack of mass, and a sense of mystery as to its construction. Obviously, these pieces were no longer functional bowls in the traditional sense, and in the early years I don't think that people quite knew what to call them.

As a sculptor working in a craft discipline, it has been my desire to push the technique of lathe turning beyond its traditional limits: to elevate the concept of the wooden *bowl* to that of the wooden *vessel.* What characterizes my work most is that each piece is designed to be one of a kind, and in direct response to what I see in the raw material—be it root, trunk, or burl.

Within each vessel that I produce there must exist a sense of history: Beginning with my knowledge of wood and my sense of design, each piece evolves into a form with a specific personality of its own. It is this personality, and the subtle interaction between the object and the observer, that is both the function and the future of my work.

David Ellsworth: Tall, inverted-ovoid vase. 1981. Box elder burl. H. 6¾″–$12\frac{3}{16}$″; Diam. 1⅞″ (rim)–$8\frac{9}{16}$″ (shoulder); Thickness .167″; Base $1\frac{11}{16}$″.

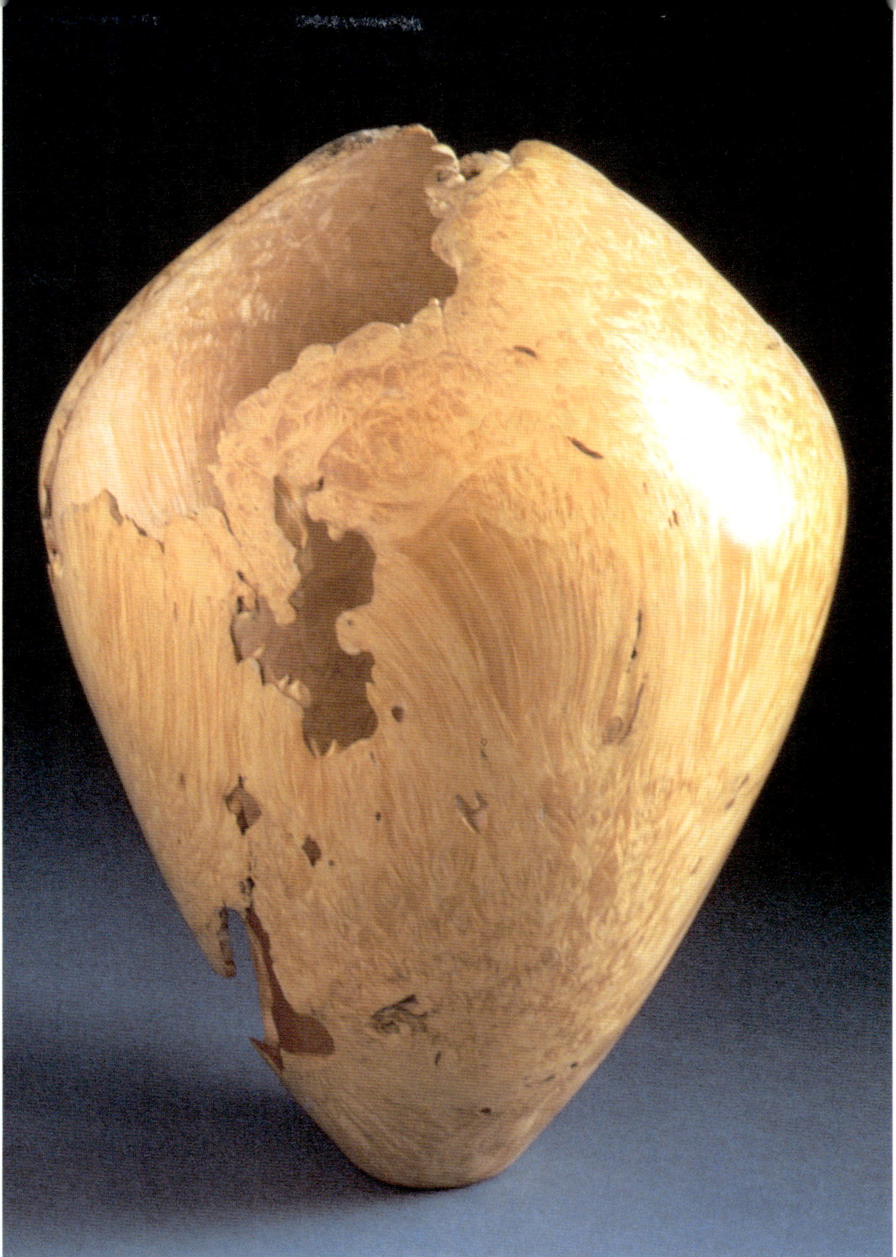

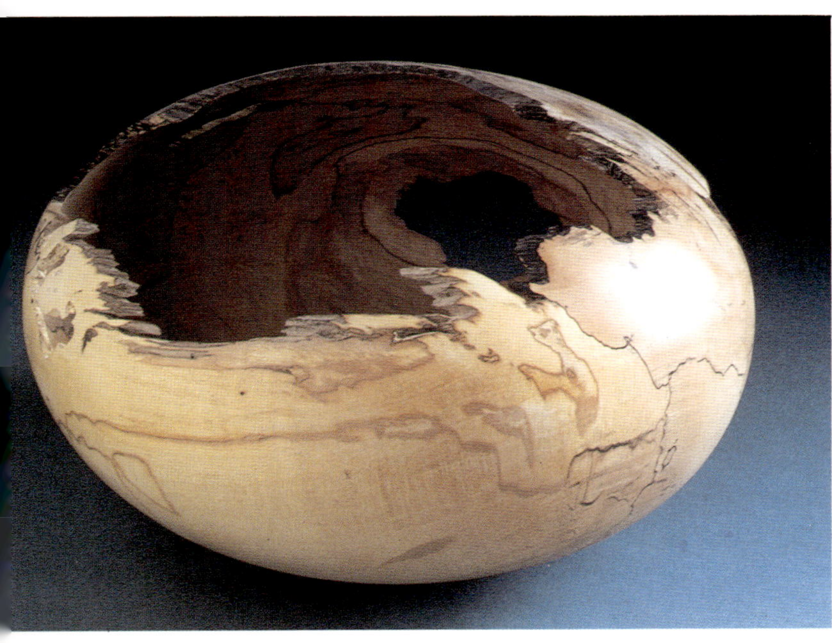

David Ellsworth: Flattened spherical bowl. 1983. Spalted sugar maple. H. 5⅞″–6⅝″; Diam. (belly) 10″; Thickness .156″; Base $2\frac{1}{16}$″.

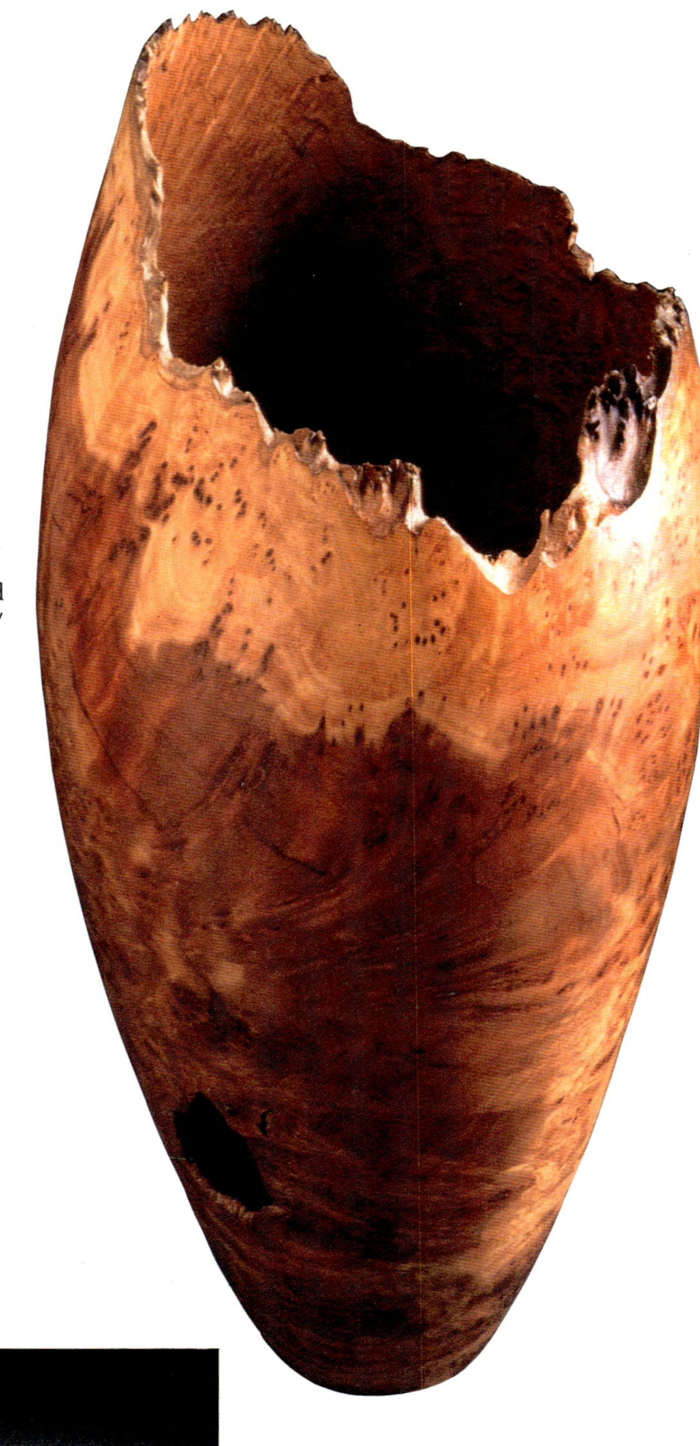

David Ellsworth: Large calyx vase. 1983. Redwood lace burl. H. 10 3/16″–14 5/8″; Diam. 5 7/8″ (rim)–7 1/16″ (shoulder); Thickness .154″; Base 1 5/16″.

David Ellsworth: Flattened hemispherical bowl. 1978. Cocobolo rosewood. H. 2 1/4″; Diam. 3 5/8″ (mouth)–10″ (shoulder); Thickness .155″.

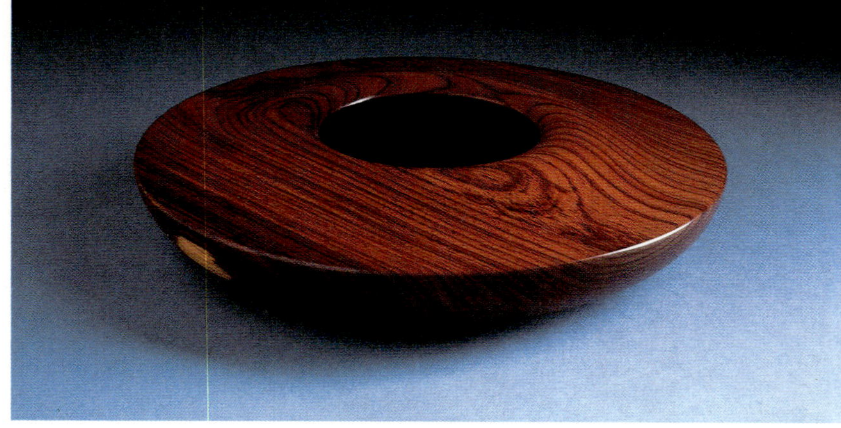

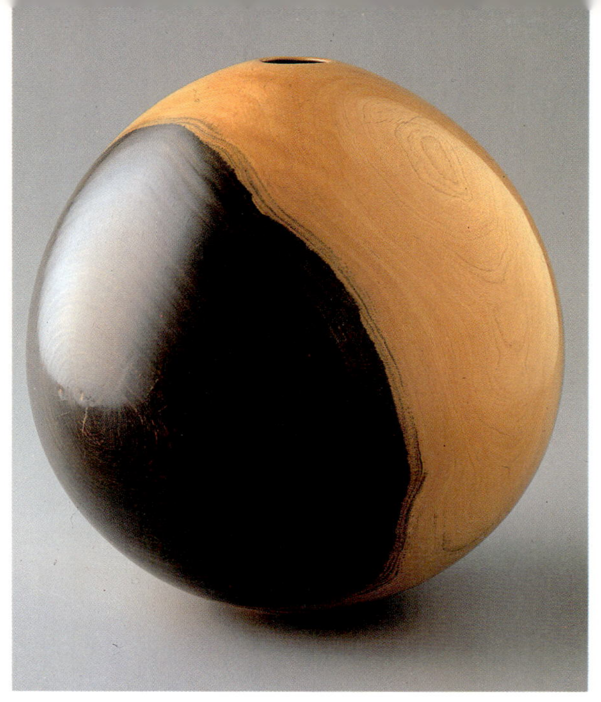

David Ellsworth: *Emerald Moon.* 1982. Lignum vitae. H. 9½″; Diam. 1 3/16″ (mouth)–7¼″ (belly); Thickness .0625″; Base 1 15/16″.

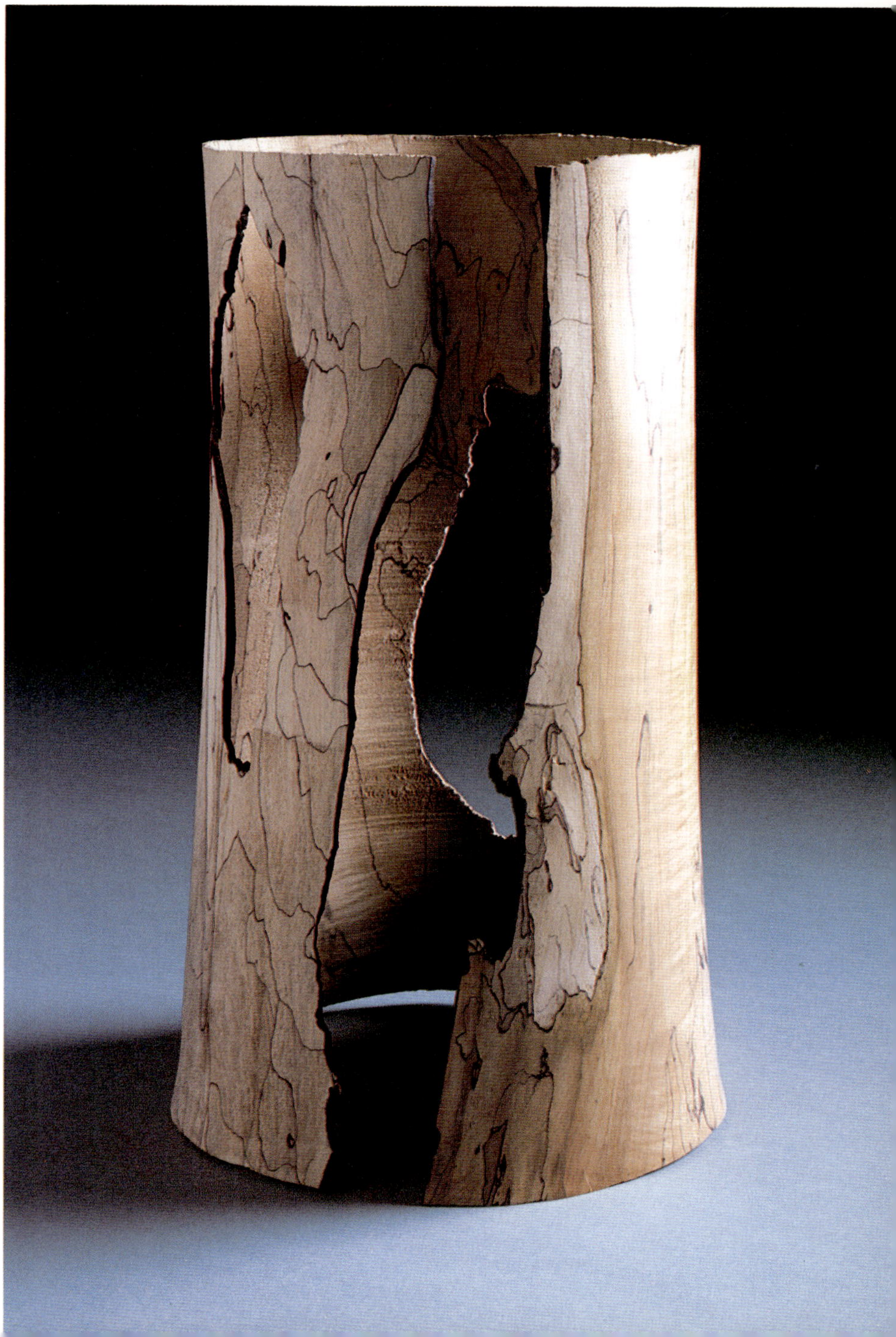

David Ellsworth: Hollow tube. 1984. Spalted sugar maple. H. 15 7/16″–15 11/16″; Diam. (rim) 7 13/16″–8″; Thickness .132″; Base 8⅞″–9¼″.

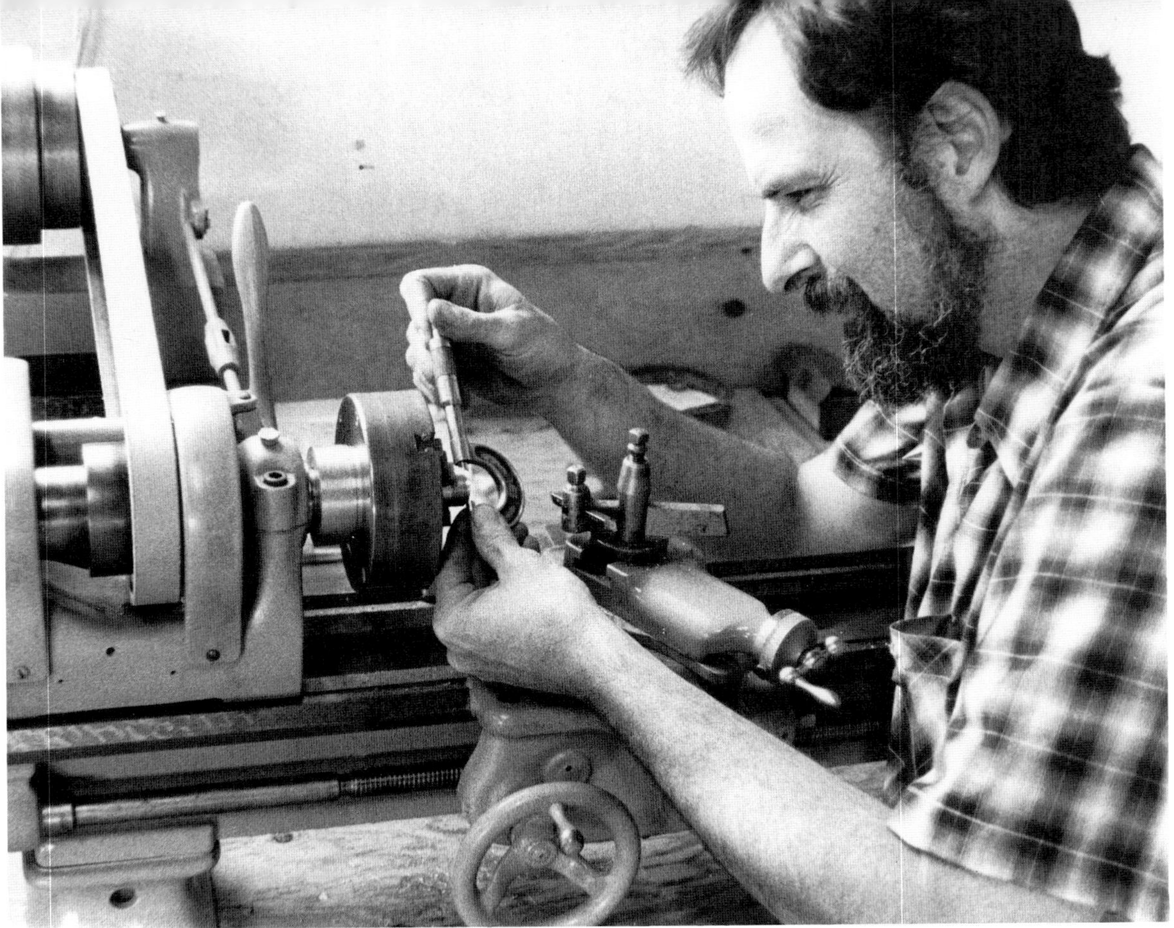

GILES GILSON

766 Albany Street
Schenectady, New York 12307

Born in 1942 in Philadelphia, Pennsylvania, Giles Gilson's interests in art and music have provided him with a unique and diverse self-educational experience. When he was an aerobatic pilot, Gilson received commissions for graphic designs for airplanes, and he worked as a prototype designer and assembler while pursuing a full-time career as a jazz musician. From 1968 to 1973 Gilson played throughout the northeastern states with leading musicians while developing his interest in sculpture and design. In 1979 Gilson began to expand his interests to people and folk cultures, including researching American Indian symbolism in the Southwest. He has developed a lacquer process in combination with wood and is presently working with the design and construction of models and photo-props for commercial advertising art.

Mr. Gilson's work is in the collections of The Metropolitan Museum of Art, New York, and in The Schenectady Museum, Schenectady, New York. The work has been published in several books and in the following magazines: *Craft Horizons, American Craft,* and *Fine Woodworking.* Exhibited in many galleries in the United States and Canada, the work is now to be seen at Holsten Gallery, West Palm Beach, Florida; Snyderman Gallery, Philadelphia, Pennsylvania; and Del Mano Gallery, Los Angeles, California.

STATEMENT FROM THE ARTIST

Turning is a good subject to use as a parallel when training for or discussing many other art forms. It generates more immediate results than some, and the steps in the learning process are more visible. After certain technical levels have been attained, one has then more freedom to express art and/or design forms, but one is also challenged by the existing framework of the art of turning:

1. Traditionally, there have been strong guidelines that dictate the form and function for a turned object.
2. The equipment used dictates that there will be a circular cross section somewhere in the piece.
3. There are many who still dictate how much turning must be used for a piece to be considered as having been "turned."
4. If the piece is "turned," then what type of turned object may be considered "art"?

Contemporary turners are pushing these limitations farther than ever. Essentially, turning is a wonderful tool-technique that can be an exciting part of a larger creative whole in a work of art.

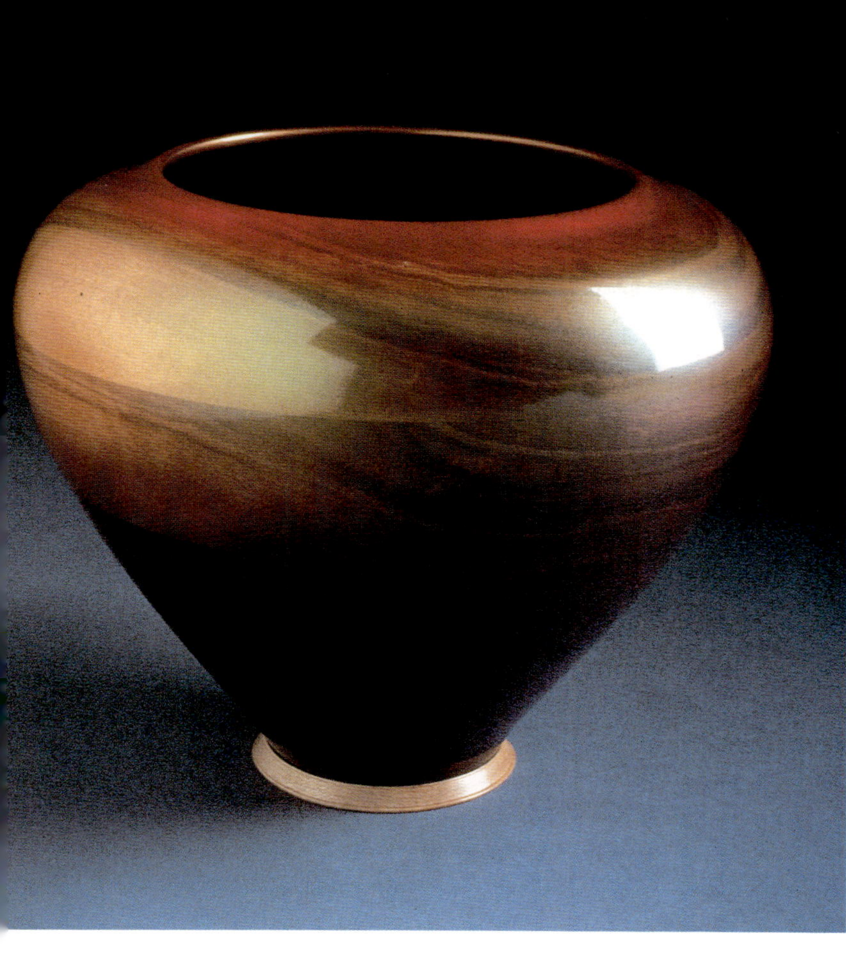

Giles Gilson: Iridescent jar/bowl. 1983. Birch with magenta and blue-purple lacquer. H. $7\frac{3}{8}$″; Diam. $5\frac{5}{16}$″ (mouth)–$8\frac{11}{16}$″ (shoulder); Thickness .185″; Base $3\frac{3}{16}$″.

Giles Gilson: Small, flattened spherical bowl. 1982. Mahogany with peach lacquer, lined with black felt. H. $2\frac{7}{16}$″; Diam. $3\frac{1}{4}$″ (mouth)–$5\frac{9}{16}$″ (belly); Thickness .107″.

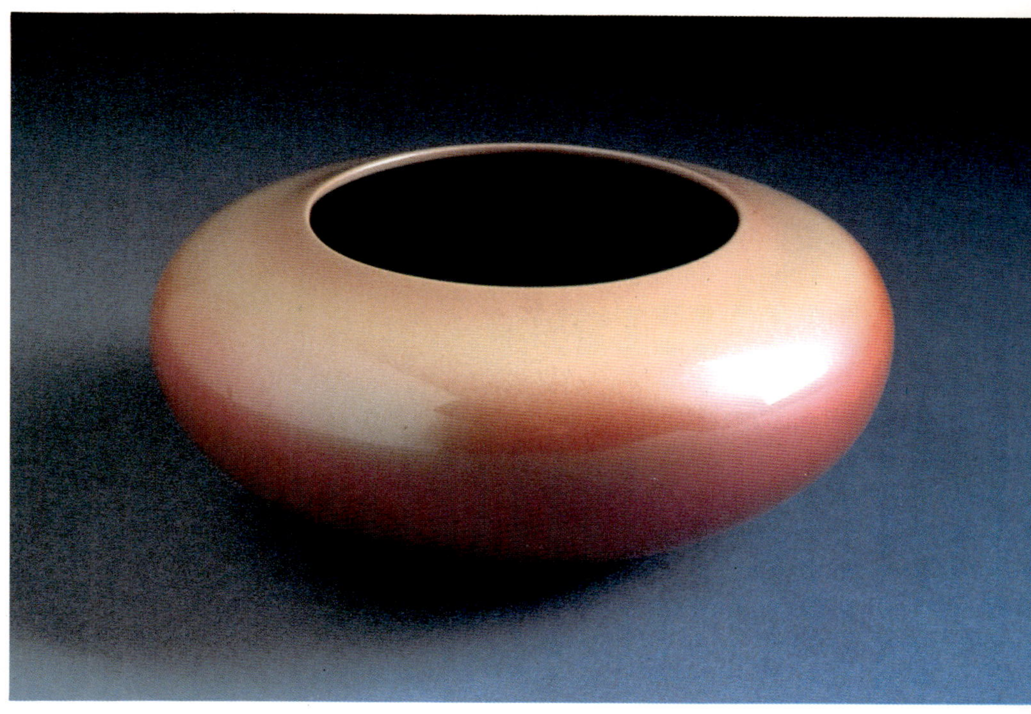

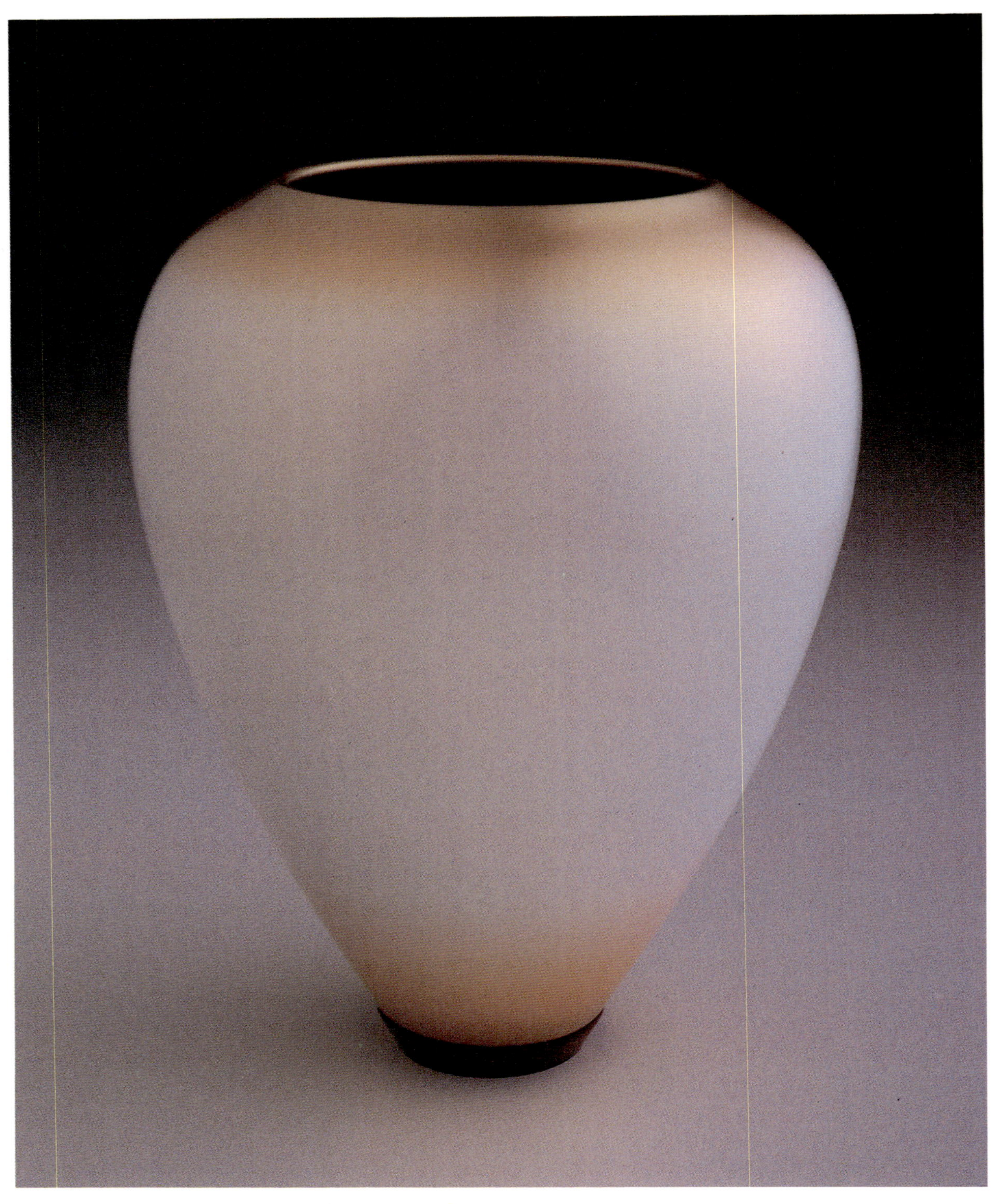

Giles Gilson: Vase-shaped bowl. 1984. Mahogany with pearlescent lacquer, flocked interior, and cocobolo base. H. 8½″; Diam. 12″ (mouth)–21½″ (shoulder); Thickness .188″.

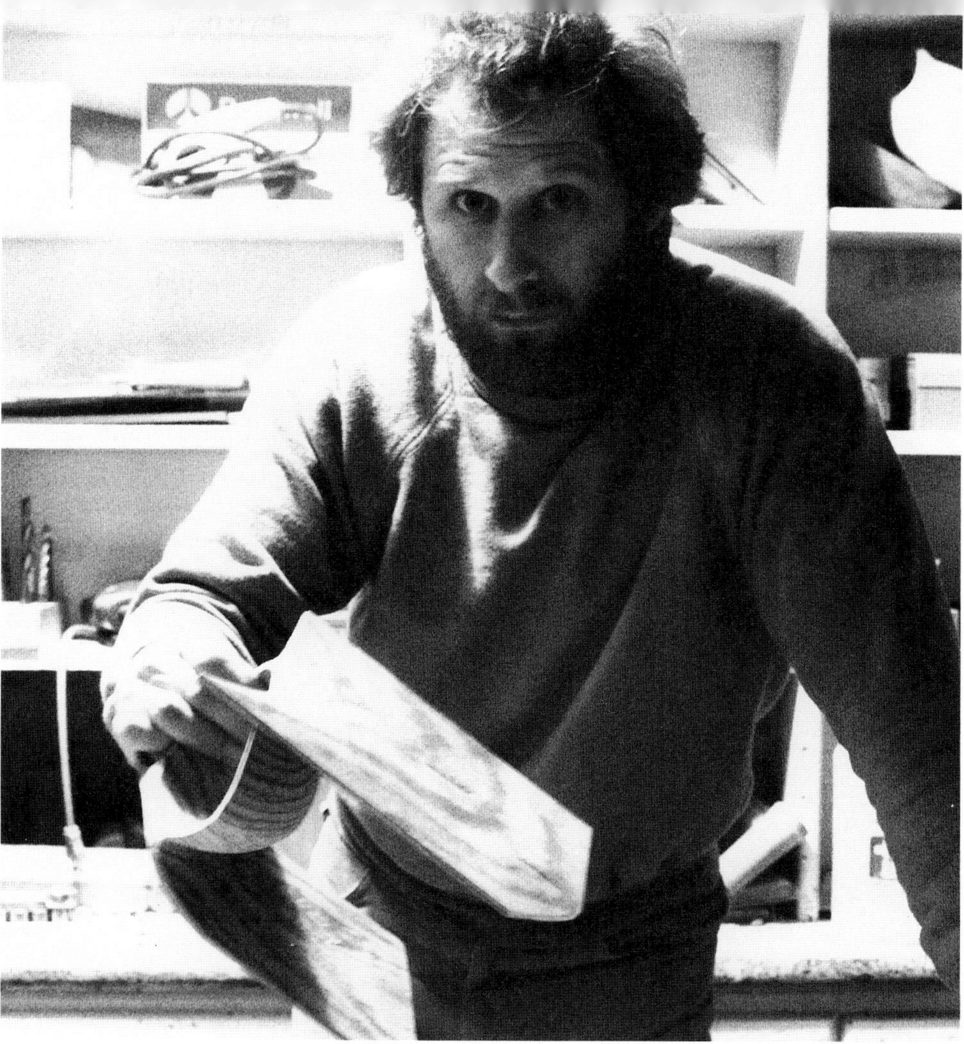

STEPHEN HOGBIN

R.R.3
Owen Sound, Ontario
Canada N4K 5N5

Mr. Hogbin's work has been shown in one-man and group exhibitions at many places in Canada, Australia, and the United States, such as The Craft Gallery, Toronto, Canada; Glendon College, York University, Toronto; Melbourne State College, Melbourne, Australia; Australia Design Centre Art Gallery, Melbourne; National Arts Centre, Ottawa, Canada; Birchfield Center, State University of New York, Buffalo, New York; Parnham House, Dorset, England; Richard Kagan Gallery, Philadelphia, Pennsylvania; American Craft Museum, New York City. His pieces are in such collections as Canadian Guild of Crafts, Toronto; Crafts Association of Victoria, Australia; Melbourne State College, Australia; Massey Foundation, Ottawa. Mr. Hogbin is the author of *Wood Turning* (1981). He has published several articles in the field, and his work has been discussed in articles by other writers. A film was made about Stephen Hogbin by the Australian Crafts Council in 1976.

STATEMENT FROM THE ARTIST

Containers were the first and last elements that I studied during my eleven-year period of using the lathe.

I was also interested in diversification. Some of my other turned forms include a throne for *Ubu Roi*, a bicycle rack, a graffiti board for Melbourne State College, tea tongs, and so forth. The largest wall sculpture created from a single turning is *Binary Spirit*, measuring sixteen by eleven feet. It is located in the Government of Ontario's McDonald Block, Queen's Park, Toronto.

After the initial discovery of cutting and reassembling the turned form, I focused on ritual objects and their functional necessities. These objects ritualized everyday activities through the use of unexpected forms.

My intensive study of wood turning concluded in 1982 with a series of bowls with curved surfaces and polychromed interiors. I am now working exclusively with a variable-arm milling machine whose technical ancestry is found in the lathe, but the forms produced do not bear any special relationship to turned forms.

More detailed analysis of the turned forms may be found in my book *Wood Turning*, published by Van Nostrand Reinhold, or in articles published in *Fine Woodworking* magazine, issues 13 and 21.

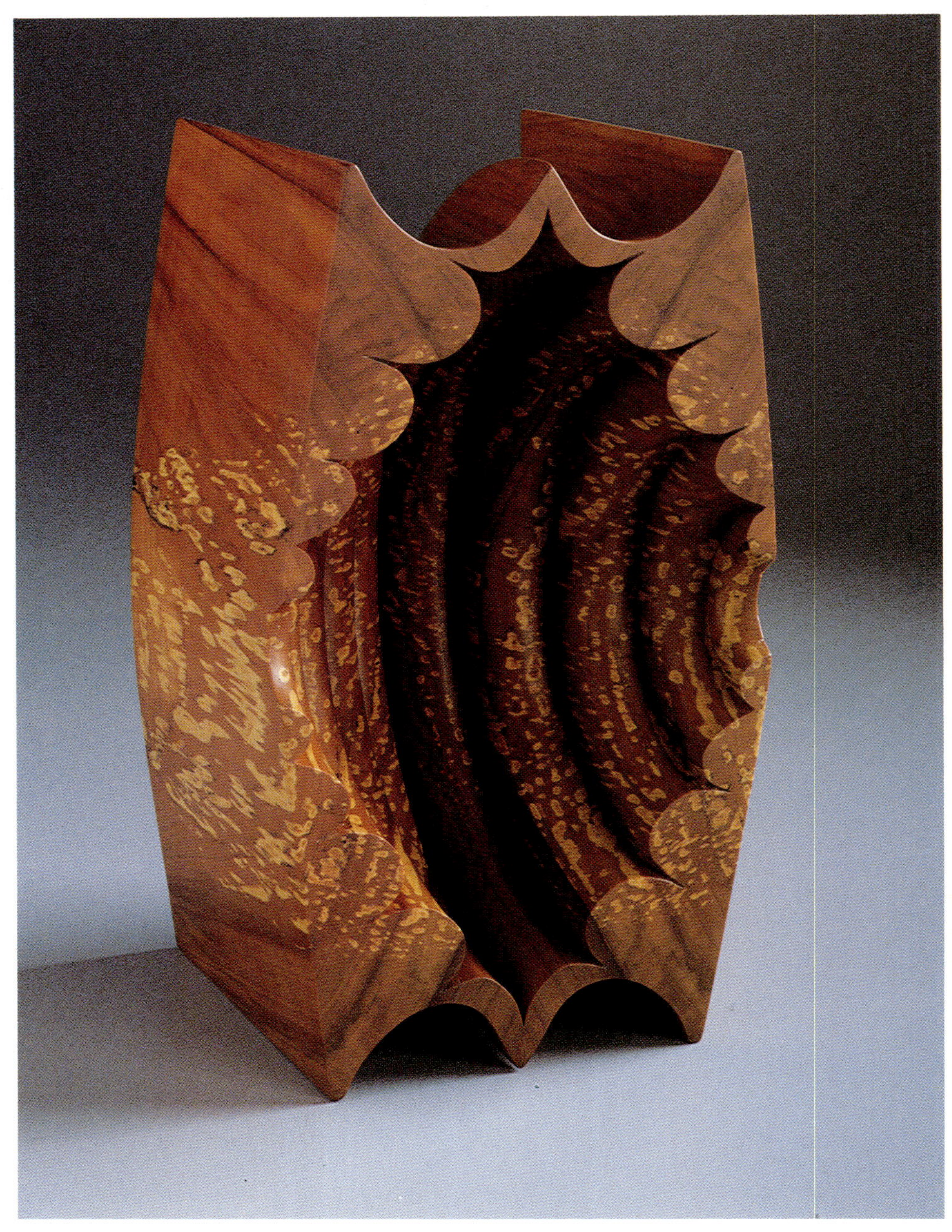

Stephen Hogbin: Suspended coiled bowl. 1978. Spalted apple. H. 4⅛″–4⅜″; Diam. (rim of bowl) 4 15/16″–8 5/16″; L. of frame 8½″; D. of frame 3⅞″–4 5/16″; Thickness .115″.

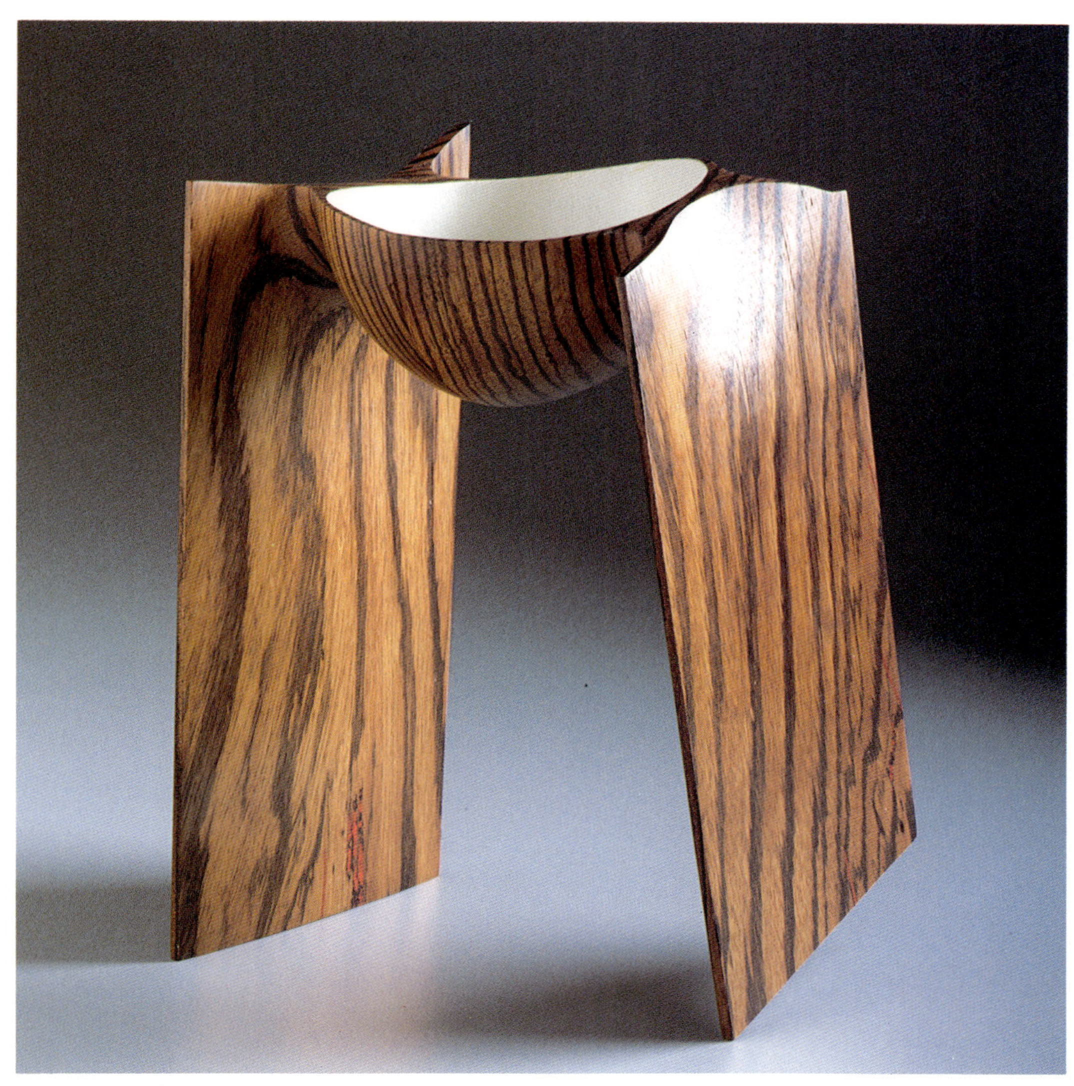

Stephen Hogbin: *Walking Bowl.* 1983. Zebrawood. H. 9¼″–10⅜″ (legs), 9⅜″–10 5/16″ (bowl); Diam. (rim of bowl) 4 9/16″–5″; W. at top 5 1/16″–6 1/16″; D. of legs 5 5/16″; Thickness .146″.

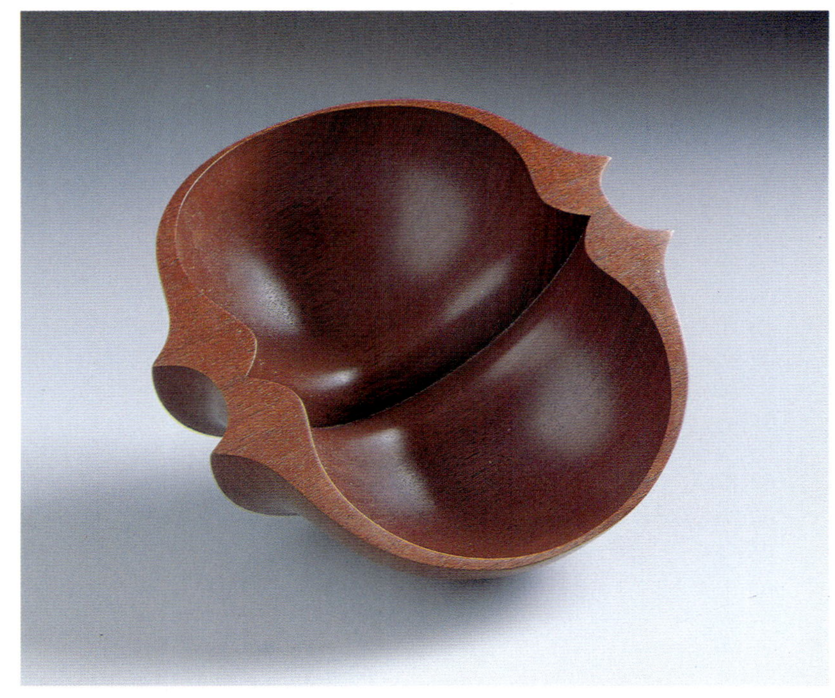

Stephen Hogbin: Rocking Bowl. 1979. Mahogany. H. 3″–3 5/16″; Diam. (rim) 6 9/16″–7⅞″; Thickness .12″.

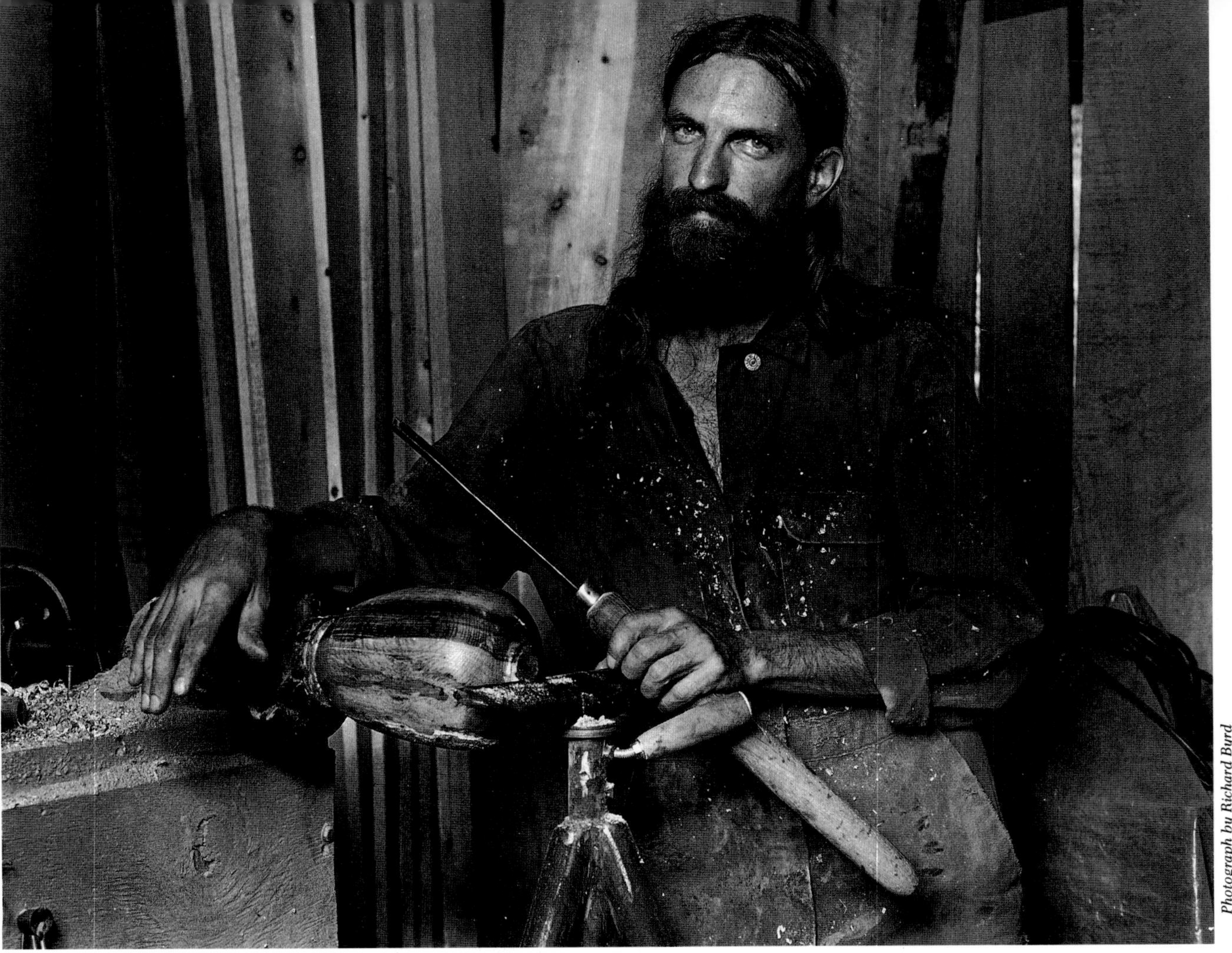

Photograph by Richard Byrd

TODD HOYER

Box 1451
Bisbee, Arizona 85603

Todd Hoyer was educated at Arizona State University, where he majored in Manufacturing Technology and minored in Design Technology. Since his graduation, Mr. Hoyer has focused on wood turning. His work has been exhibited at the American Craft Museum, New York City; the Artisan's Guild Store, Mendocino, California; the Del Mano Gallery, Los Angeles, California; and The Hand and The Spirit Crafts Gallery, Scottsdale, Arizona. Mr. Hoyer is one of three woodturners whose work was exhibited in the "Splendid Bowls" show in 1984 at Mathew Center, Arizona State University, Tempe. His work was published in *Fine Woodworking Biennial #3* (1983), and it can currently be seen at the Contemporary Craftsman Gallery, Santa Fe, New Mexico, and at The Hand and The Spirit Crafts Gallery.

STATEMENT FROM THE ARTIST

Having been involved with metal machining in school and then fibers afterwards, I found wood to be a compromise in texture and workability. The turnings allow me a full three-dimensional perspective of the wood medium, exploring the hidden nature of the tree. This includes knots, holes, and so forth, which are usually removed in flat lumber, and which many people are generally unaware of in terms of colors, textures, and densities.

The use of the lathe as the major instrument of production allows me an uninterrupted focus for working each piece of wood with utmost attention, always seeking a balance between color variations, textures, and form.

I am presently experimenting with turning green wood to the final shape and thinness of the wall and allowing it to dry slowly. This procedure produces an asymmetrical form that allows the life force of the tree to have the final word, thus freeing me from total control over the final form. This freedom permits me to observe and explore many textural and visual qualities not usually found in conventional woodworking.

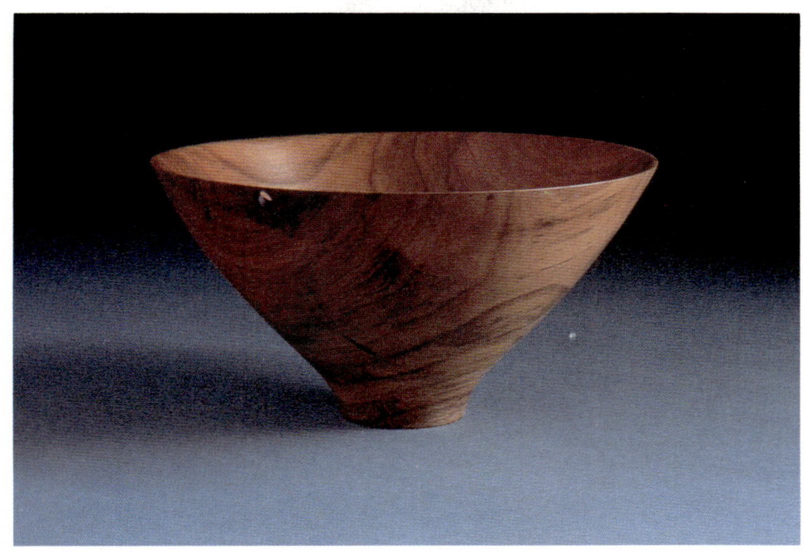

Todd Hoyer: Footed bowl. 1981. Apricot. H. 3⅛″; Diam. (rim) 6″; Thickness .11″; Base (foot) 1⅝″.

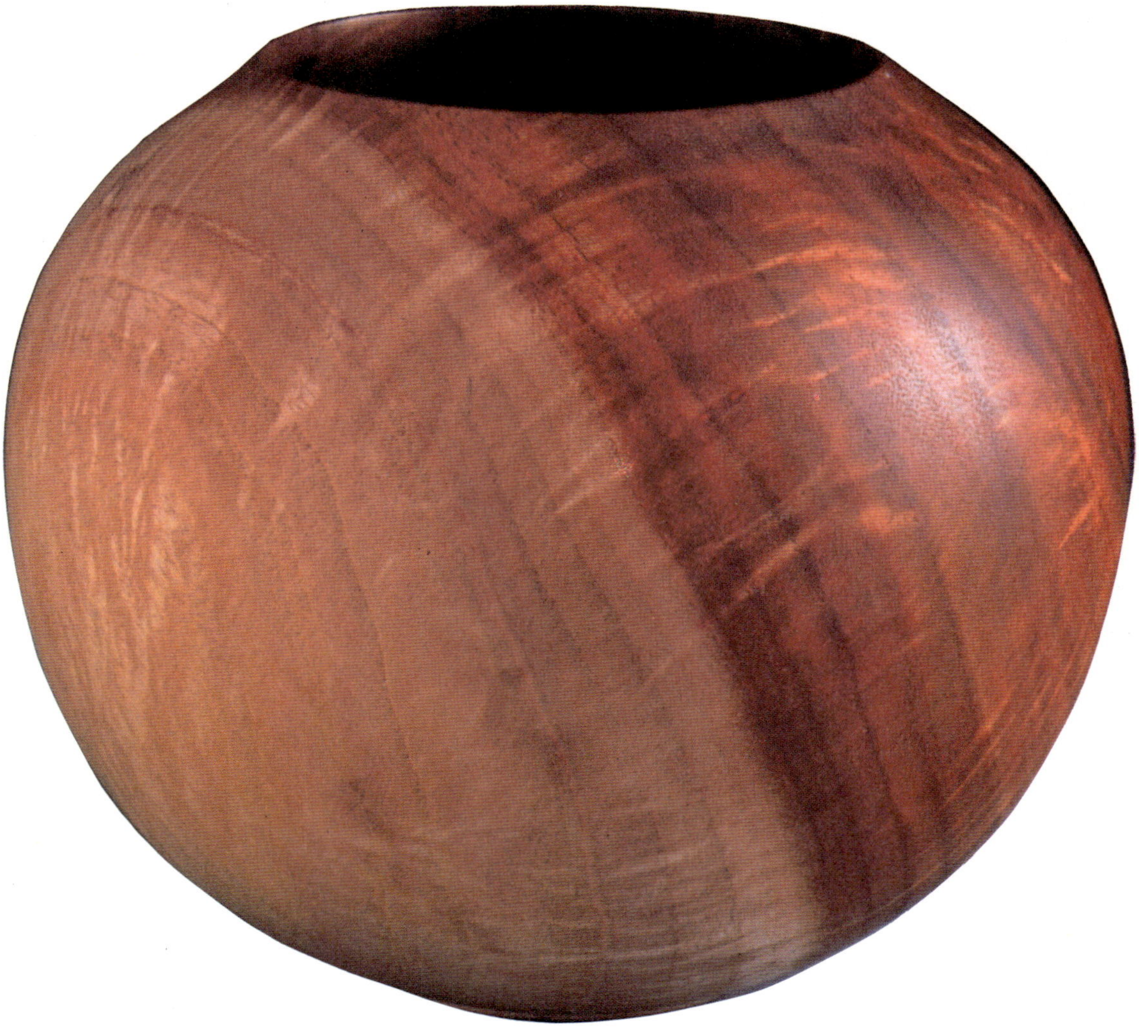

Todd Hoyer: Spherical bowl. 1982. Acacia. H. 4 7/16″; Diam. 2⅞″ (mouth), 5″ (belly); Thickness .143″; Base 2⅛″.

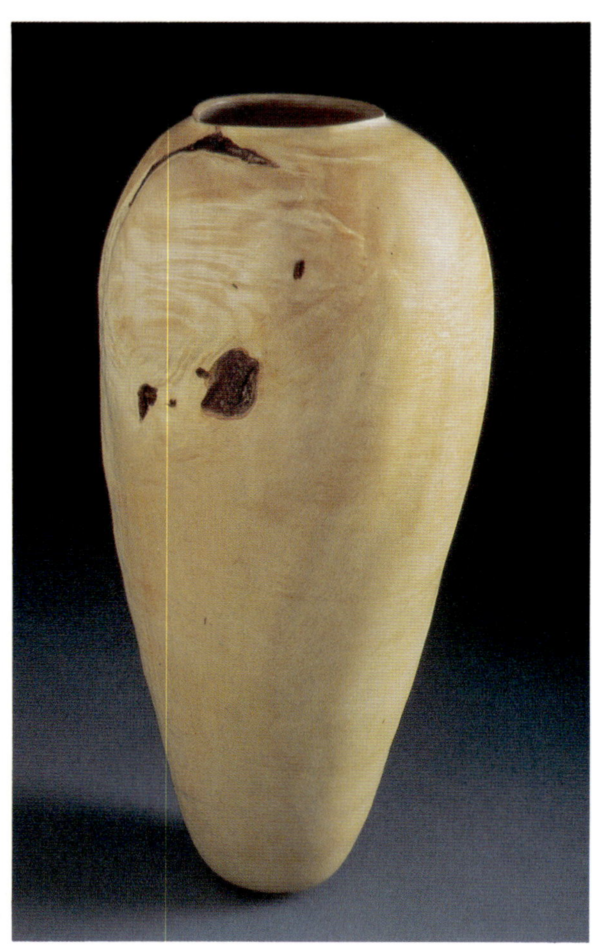

Todd Hoyer: Large, elongated vase. 1983. Arizona paloverde. H. 12⅞″; Diam. 2½″ (mouth)–6⅜″ (shoulder); Thickness .122″; Base 1¼″–1⁷/₁₆″.

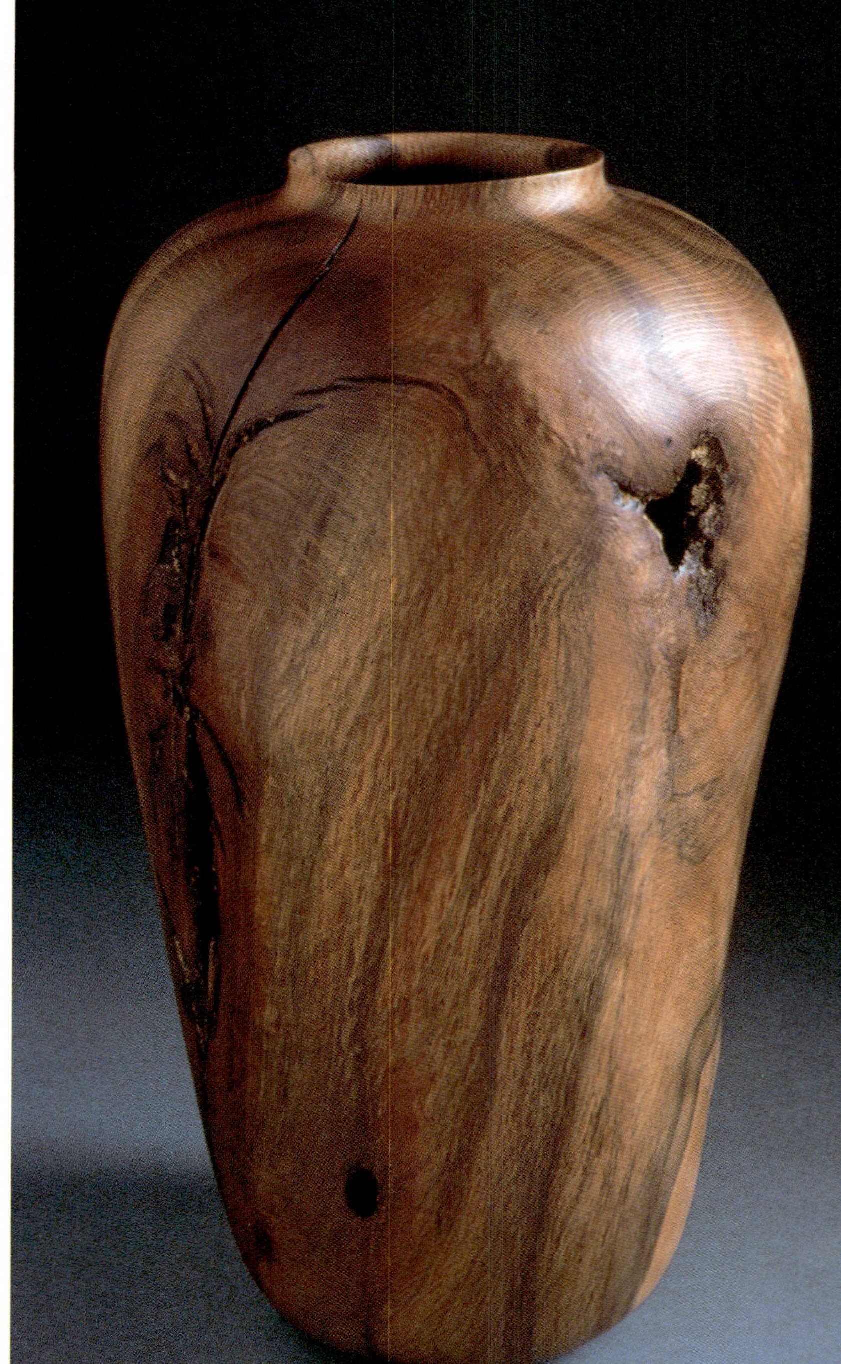

Todd Hoyer: Tall, ellipsoid vase. 1982. Emery oak. H. 12⁹/₁₆″; Diam. 3¹/₁₆″ (mouth)–7¼″ (shoulder); Thickness .112″; Base 2¼″.

Todd Hoyer: Ovoid vase. 1983. Mesquite. H. 8 15/16″; Diam. (mouth) 1½″, (belly) 7⅝″; Thickness .088″.

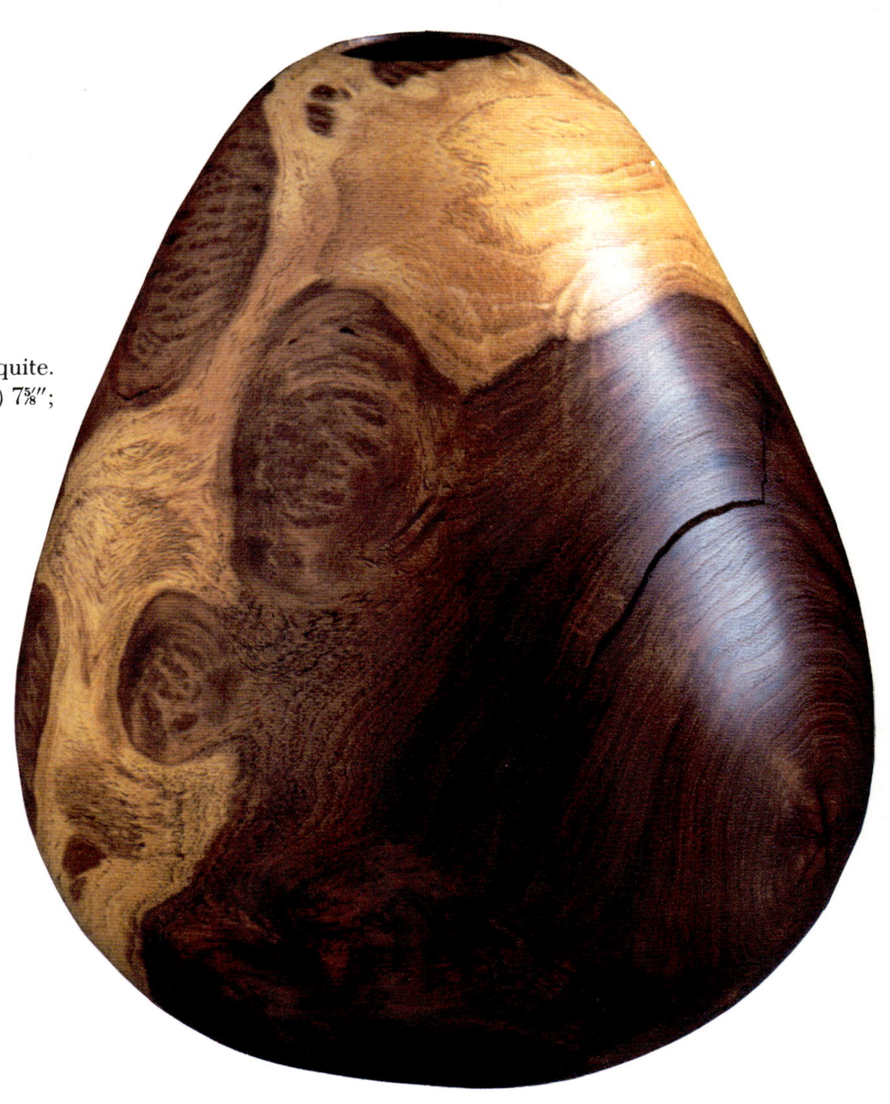

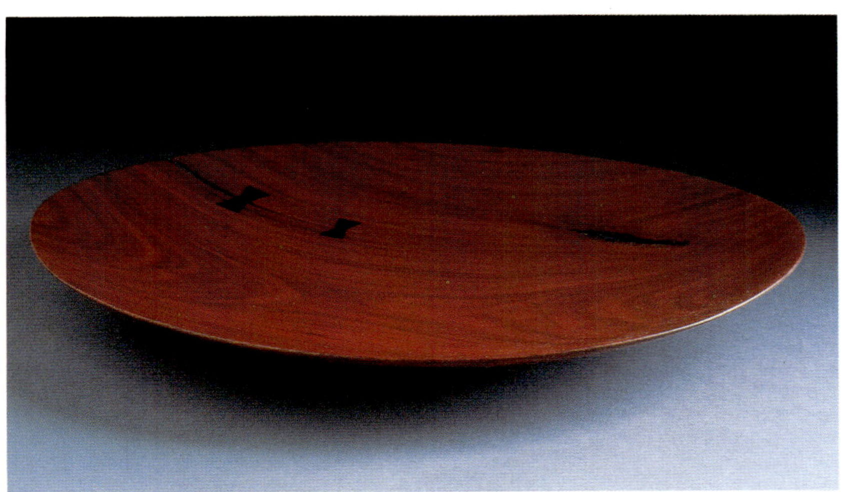

Todd Hoyer: Large plate. 1982. Acacia and ebony. H. 1¾″; Diam. (rim) 16½″; Thickness .134″; Base 7¾″.

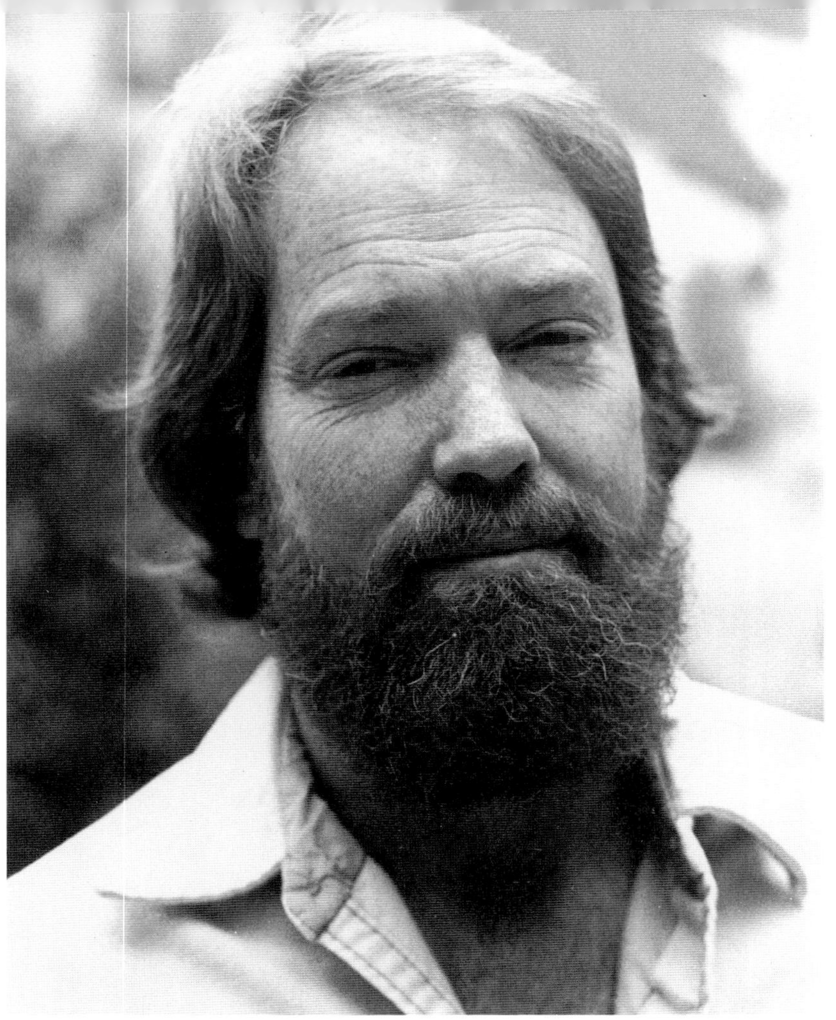

BILL HUNTER

P.O. Box 321
El Portal, California 95318

A native of Long Beach, California, Bill Hunter and his wife built their home and studios overlooking a river near Yosemite National Park in California. While earning his degree in philosophy, Mr. Hunter began wood turning as a means of balancing intellectual paradox with the satisfaction of creation and completion.

Mr. Hunter's work has been exhibited at the following locations: Gallery Fair, Mendocino, California; Del Mano Gallery, Brentwood, California; The Cartwright Gallery, Vancouver, British Columbia; Ten Arrow Gallery, Cambridge, Massachusetts; Signature Gallery, Boston, Massachusetts; The Naples Art Gallery, Naples, Florida. Illustrations of Mr. Hunter's work can be found in *A Gallery of Turned Objects,* in *Design Book III,* and in his article, "Disc Sander Sculpts Spirals," in *Fine Woodworking* magazine.

STATEMENT FROM THE ARTIST

Turning the world's rarest and most precious woods is an engrossing and challenging process. It is workmanship of risk that builds an exciting tension and requires a clear centeredness. That excitement generates new expressions on the lathe as I strive to give my forms movement, balance, and elegance.

The pieces in the Jacobson collection represent variations of the spiral forms in my work. The motion is achieved by sculpturally leading the eye along a journey of exploration around and into the surface of the piece.

Tulipwood Orb is a simple form using the wild color and grain as its principal decoration. The single orbiting line adds dimension to the silhouette as well as to the surface pattern. As it disappears above and below its horizon, the viewer is drawn to investigate its origin and destination.

Rio Vase belies wood's unyielding nature by enfolding a sensuous form with spiraling, draped lines. The solidity of the wood is further disguised by a soft texturing.

The spiral bowl *Autumn Flutes* is defined by forty-eight identically curving lines that form a single rhythm. Although this bowl is the most formally ornamented of all my spiral vessels, its statement is the purest.

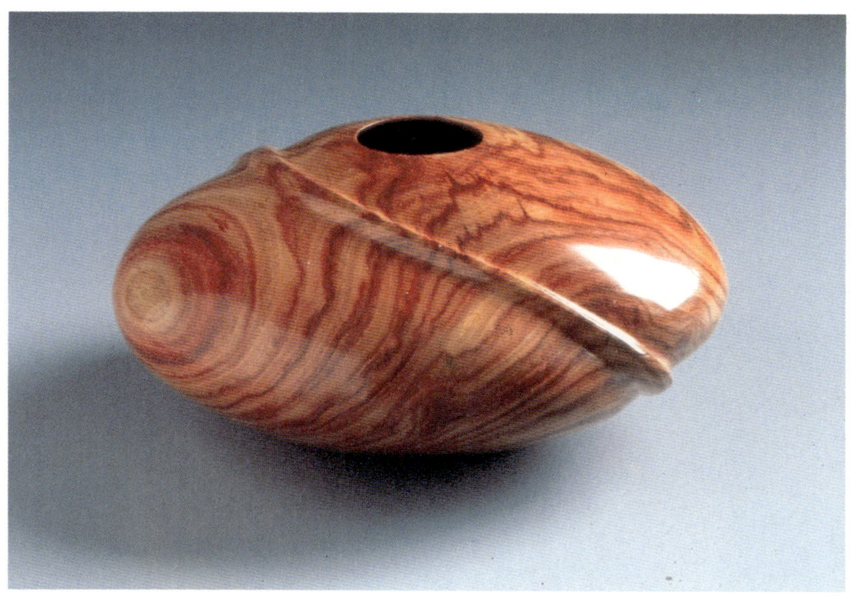

Bill Hunter: ***Tulipwood Orb***. 1982. Tulipwood. H. $3\frac{3}{16}$″; Diam. (mouth) $1\frac{5}{16}$″, (shoulder) $6\frac{1}{2}$″; Thickness .113″; Base $2\frac{1}{16}$″.

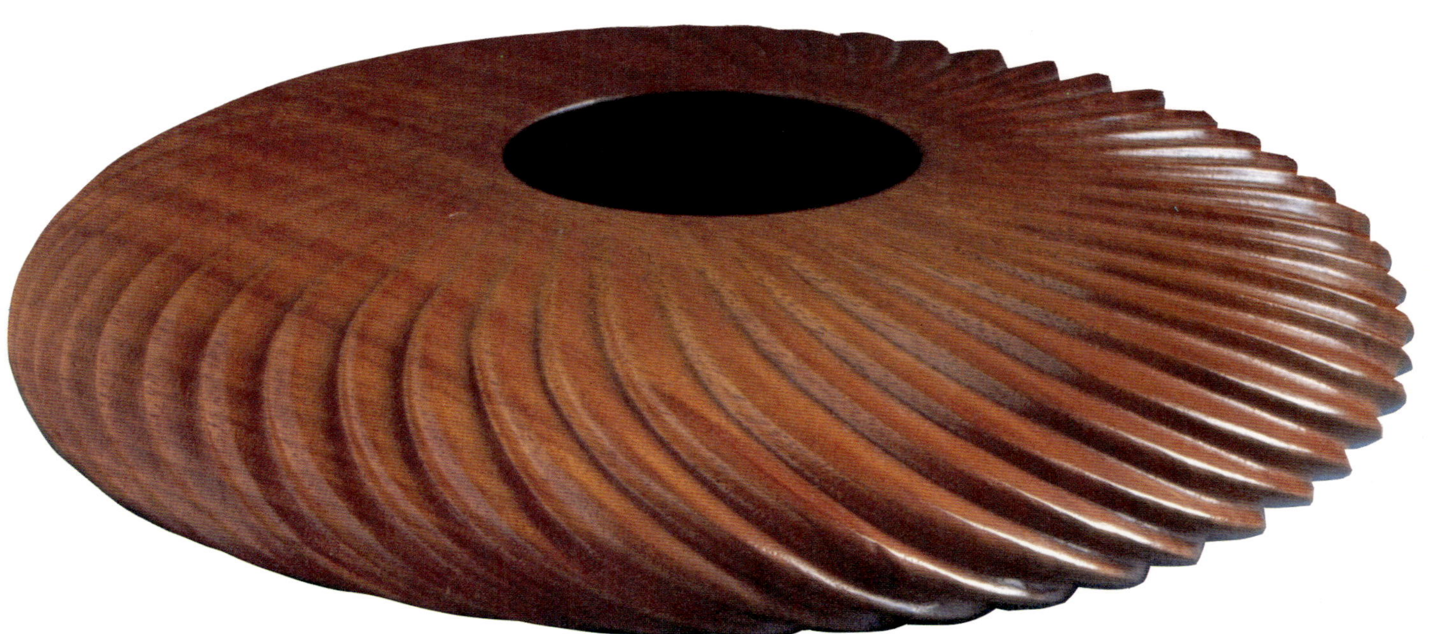

Bill Hunter: ***Autumn Flutes***. 1982. Vinhatico. H. $2\frac{7}{8}$″; Diam. (mouth) $3\frac{1}{16}$″, (shoulder) $10\frac{9}{16}$″; Thickness .181″; Base 3″.

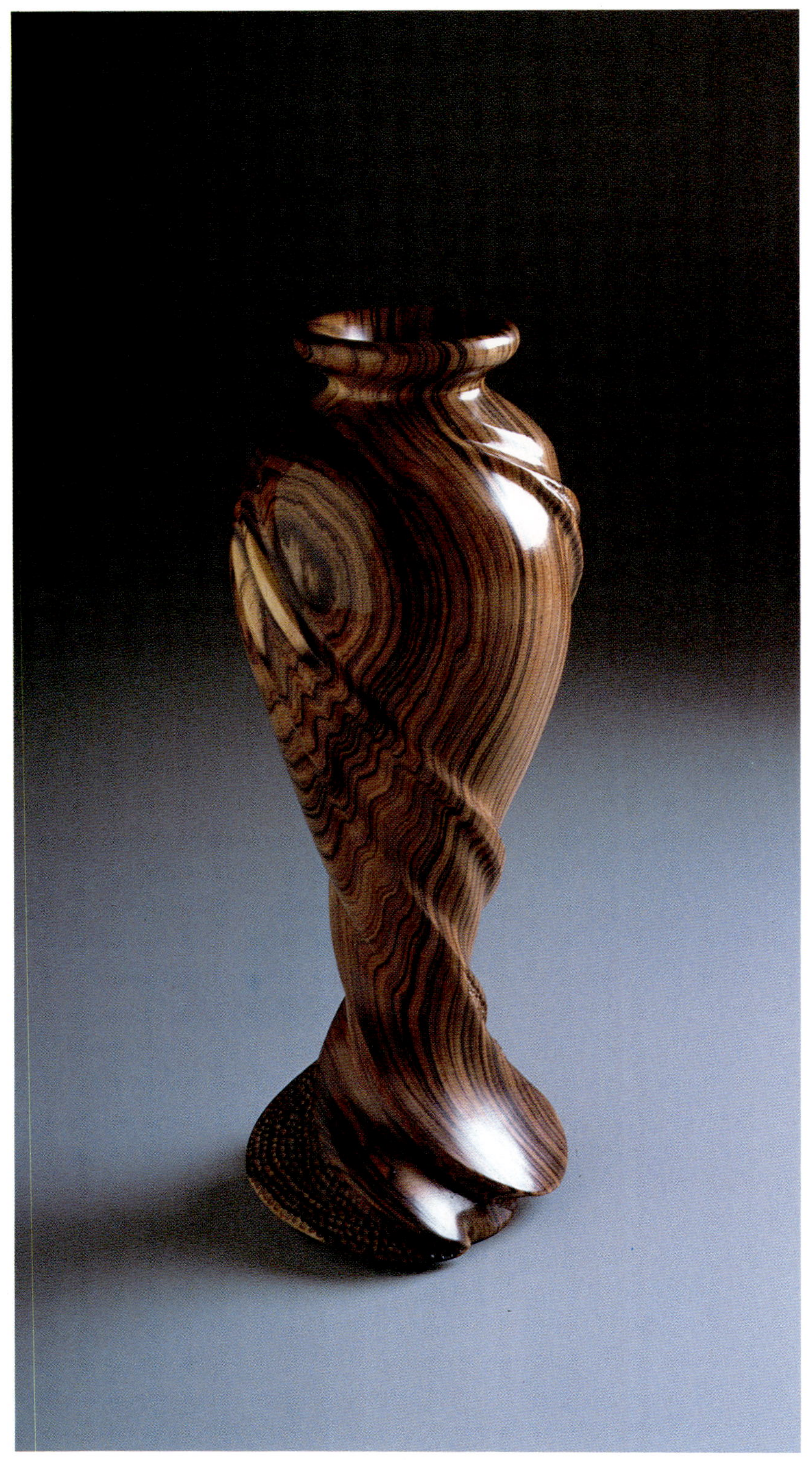

Bill Hunter: *The Rio Vase*. 1983. Kingwood. H. 11⁵⁄16″; Diam. (mouth) 2¹¹⁄16″, (shoulder) 4⅞″; Thickness .364″; Base 3⅝″–3¾″.

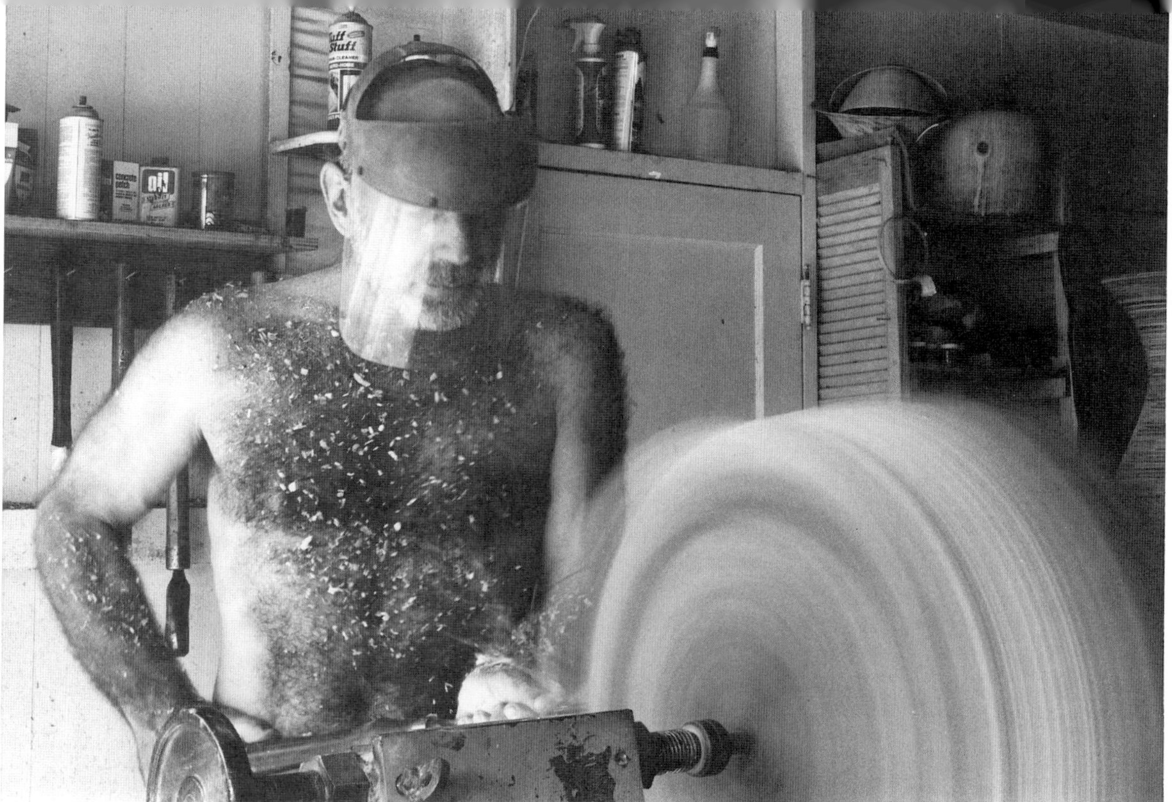

RONALD E. KENT

5329 Kalanianaole Highway
Honolulu, Hawaii 96821

A graduate of the University of California at Los Angeles, Ronald Kent is a stockbroker by profession and a woodturner by avocation. He has been submitting his work to juried exhibitions since 1967 and has consistently had work accepted since that date. Mr. Kent's work is included in the permanent collections of The Metropolitan Museum of Art, New York City; Museum of Fine Arts, Boston; Academy of Art, Honolulu; State Foundation for Culture and the Arts, Hawaii; and American Craft Museum, New York City.

STATEMENT FROM THE ARTIST

My commitment to crafts and art is in no way diminished by my primary commitment to my profession as a stockbroker, nor do I find a conflict in the seeming disparity between the two fields of interest. Business, no less than craft, offers a never-ending variety of creative challenge and fulfillment.

In craft work I have concentrated my efforts on wood, exploring a broad range of experimentation within a narrow range of endeavor. About ninety percent of my work consists of "bottles" and bowls, and almost eighty percent of these are created in one wood—Norfolk Island Pine, a tree that is common throughout Hawaii and other Pacific islands. It is not uncommon for older trees to attain a height of sixty feet and a base diameter of three feet. The "bottles" are nonutilitarian variations on basic bottle/decanter/urn/vase shapes; the bowls also offer broad variations on familiar shapes and proportions. The shape of each bowl is determined by the natural characteristics of the log: size, grain, and knot pattern contribute to the final design. The grain and color are entirely natural; no stain, varnish, or lacquer is used. Instead, I use a finishing process that can take as much as twenty hours spread over more than six months, during which the bowl is repeatedly hand-rubbed with extremely fine sandpaper and colorless sealing oils. It is this repeated saturation that brings out the unique coloration and translucence of the wood, especially when the bowls are eggshell thin.

Because I have had no training at all and. little interaction with other woodturners, many of my techniques are unorthodox. Here are a few examples:

> All of my bowls are turned between centers, rather than with a faceplate. This process leaves stems that are later removed by hand grinding.
>
> I finish the inside of each bowl before shaping the outside.
>
> I use whole logs rather than blocks, and each log is aligned so that the axis of the bowl is the same as the axis of the tree.

My primary challenge is to expose the intrinsic natural beauty of the wood in each log. I enjoy working at the far edge of my ability, for I am constantly trying to create pieces that are a little thinner, a little larger, and a little finer that I have ever made before.

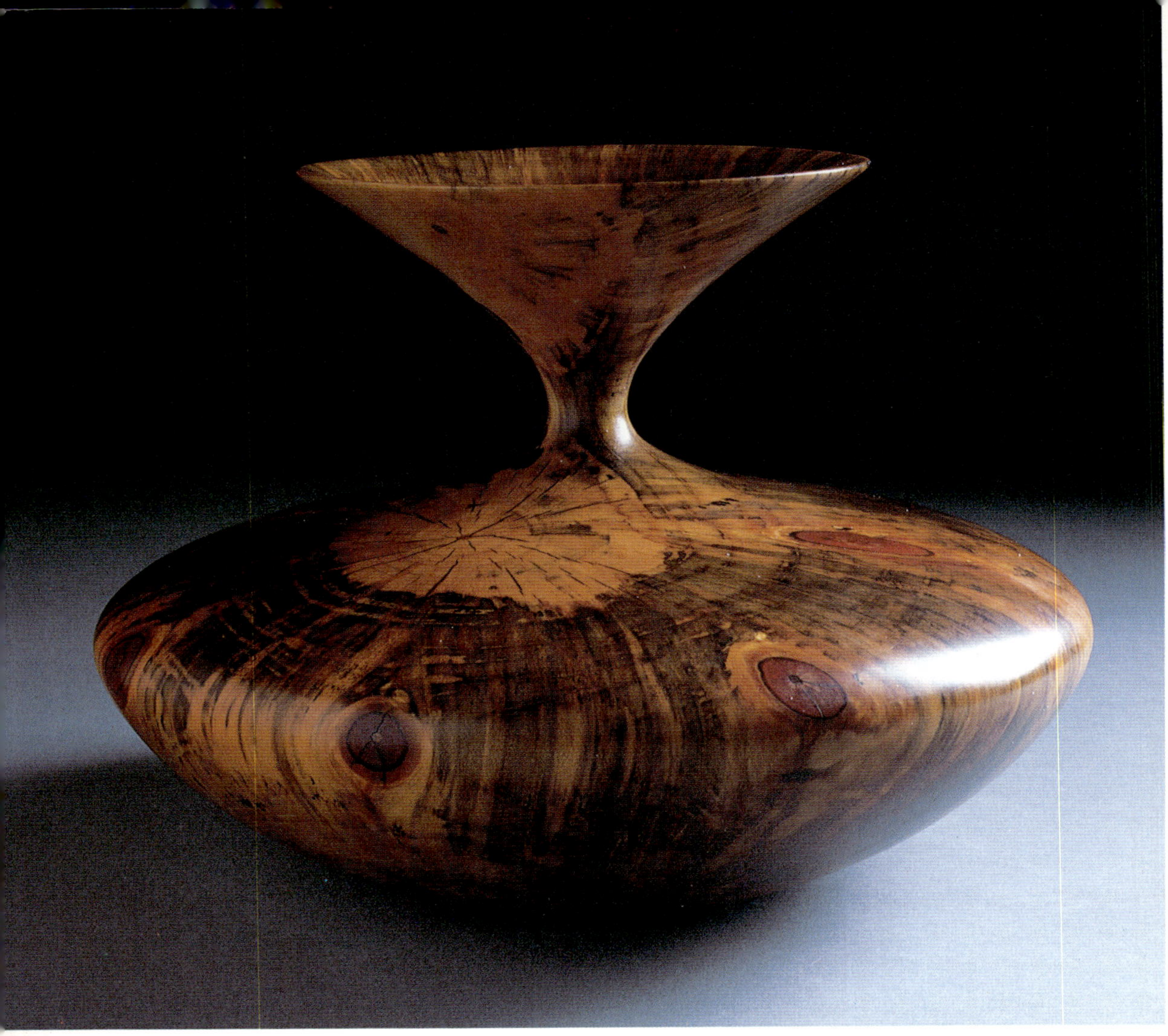

Ronald E. Kent: Large trumpet-mouth bottle. 1983. Norfolk Island pine. H. 10 3/16″; Diam. (rim) 7 15/16″; Thickness (rim) .19″; Waist 14 1/4″; Solid base 13 7/8″.

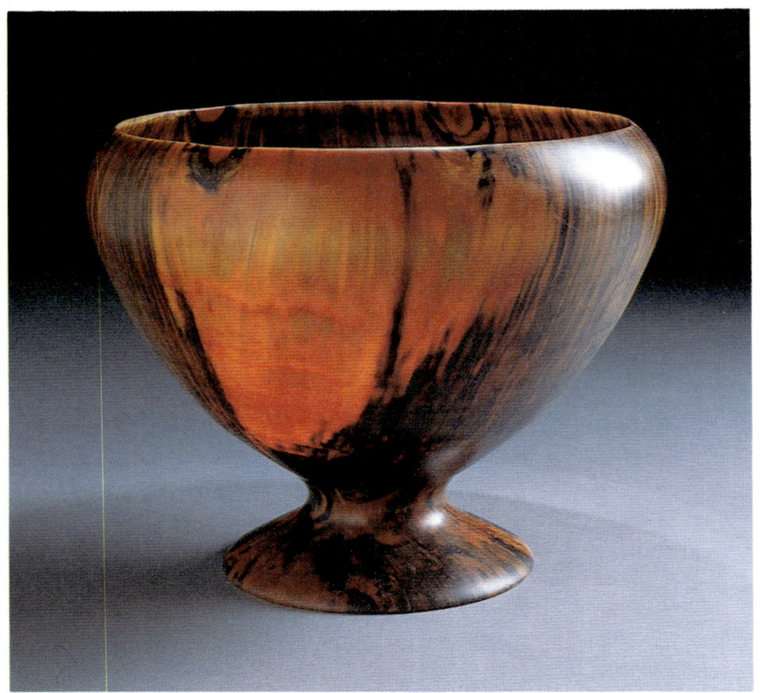

Ronald E. Kent: *Perfect Chalice*. 1984. Norfolk Island pine. H. 8 9/16″; Diam. (rim) 9 1/2″, (shoulder) 10 3/4″; Thickness .141″; Base (foot) 6″.

Ronald E. Kent: Medium-size translucent bowl. 1984. Norfolk Island pine. H. $5\frac{1}{2}$″; Diam. (rim) $6\frac{11}{16}$″, (shoulder) $7\frac{1}{2}$″; Thickness .083″; Base (foot) $2\frac{11}{16}$″.

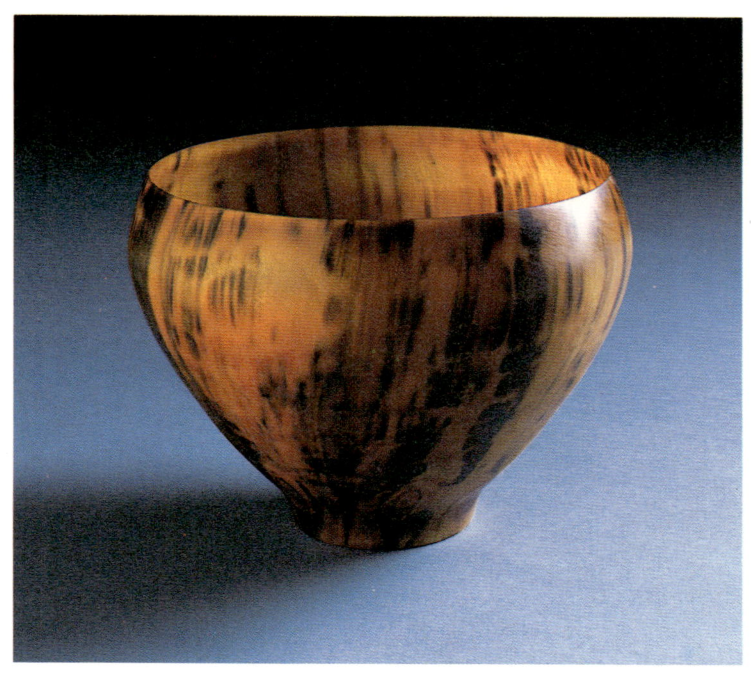

Ronald E. Kent: Very large translucent bowl. 1984. Norfolk Island pine. H. $8\frac{1}{4}$″; Diam. (rim) $18\frac{3}{8}$″; Thickness .170″; Base (foot) $5\frac{15}{16}$″.

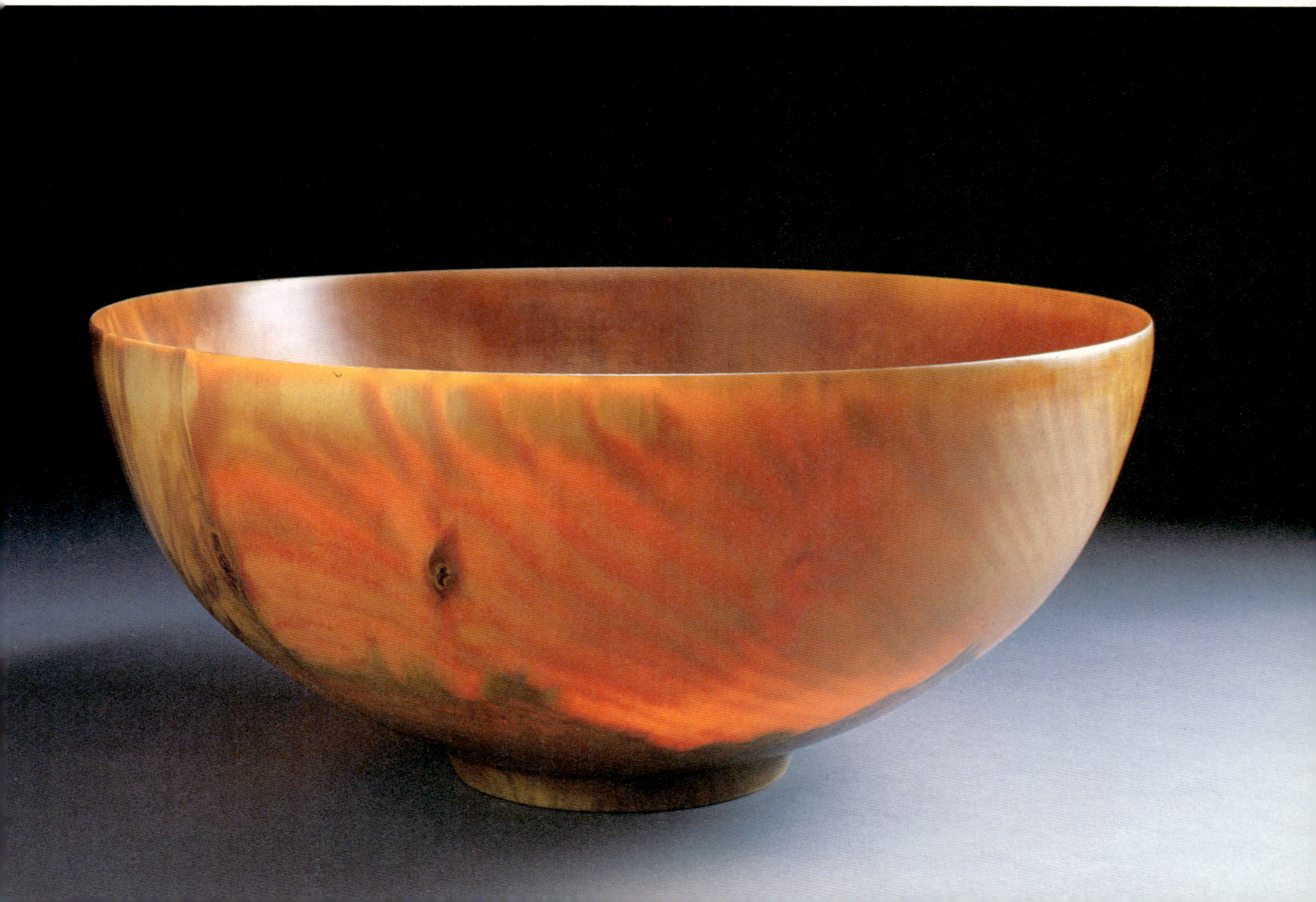

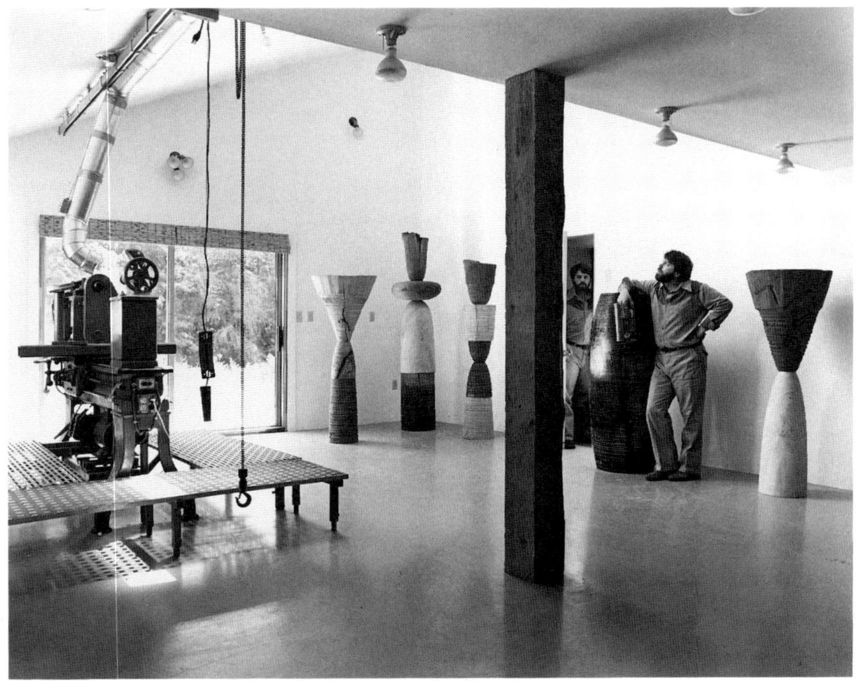

Mark Lindquist in his summer studio at Henniker, New Hampshire, with his current "Totemic Series" works of sculpture within the confines of the bowl. Photograph by Mark Lindquist © 1984.

MARK LINDQUIST

(Summer studio)
Patch Road
Henniker, New Hampshire 03242

(Winter studio)
Rt. 2, Box 247
Quincy, Florida 32351

Educated at New England College and Pratt Institute, Mark Lindquist was apprenticed to a New Hampshire potter 1970–1972 and became a MacDowell Fellow in 1979. Mr. Lindquist began wood turning at the age of ten, being taught by his father, Melvin Lindquist. He was designated in 1983 a "New England Living Art Treasure" by the University of Massachusetts at Amherst. His work is in several museum collections including The Metropolitan Museum of Art, New York City; National Museum of American Art, Smithsonian Institution, Washington, D.C.; Philadelphia Museum of Art; The High Museum of Art, Atlanta, Georgia. Since 1972, Mark Lindquist has exhibited widely throughout the United States in one-man shows, and group and invitational exhibitions at galleries, universities, and museums, including the following: Fairtree Gallery, New York City; The Works Gallery, Philadelphia; The Elements Gallery, Greenwich, Connecticut, and New York City; Greenwood Gallery, Washington, D.C.; The Hand and the Spirit Crafts Gallery, Scottsdale, Arizona; Cornell University; Dartmouth College; DeCordova Museum; Renwick Gallery of the Smithsonian Institution; American Craft Museum; Bowdoin College Museum of Art. In addition to considerable teaching and lecturing experience Mark Lindquist has written articles on the subjects of wood, tools, techniques, and aesthetics for such magazines as: *Fine Woodworking, Studio Potter, Holz und Elfenbein* (Germany), and *Kunsthandverk* (Norway).

STATEMENT FROM THE ARTIST

I am and have been from the beginning of my association with wood concerned about personal expression and growth. Through my involvement with wood and wood turning, I have learned and continue to seek new understandings about myself and about life.

Conceptually, within the frame of reference of fine art (and within a very specifically defined vision, gained through an apprenticeship to a potter and studies with a sculptor), it became my intention to translate ancient ceramic form and sculptural ideology into the medium of wood through the technology of wood turning. I did not then (the late 1960s) care for the time-honored traditions of the craft, and I do not now care about the taboos of the purists. As in any art form, it becomes a duty of those deeply committed to their own visions to be responsible to the "seen unseenness" of the goals that lie immanently beyond current horizons.

Perhaps it has been the stigmas of the traditional field of wood turning that have been so challenging and rewarding throughout the pursuit of these truths. Anyone who challenges the accepted norms or standards by offering new alternatives does so with objects that draw attention away to things already existing that have simply been unperceived. The only way a standard can become one is to make the existing one obsolete, becoming thereby merely a current accepted solution to the problem of circumscribing another seeming finality.

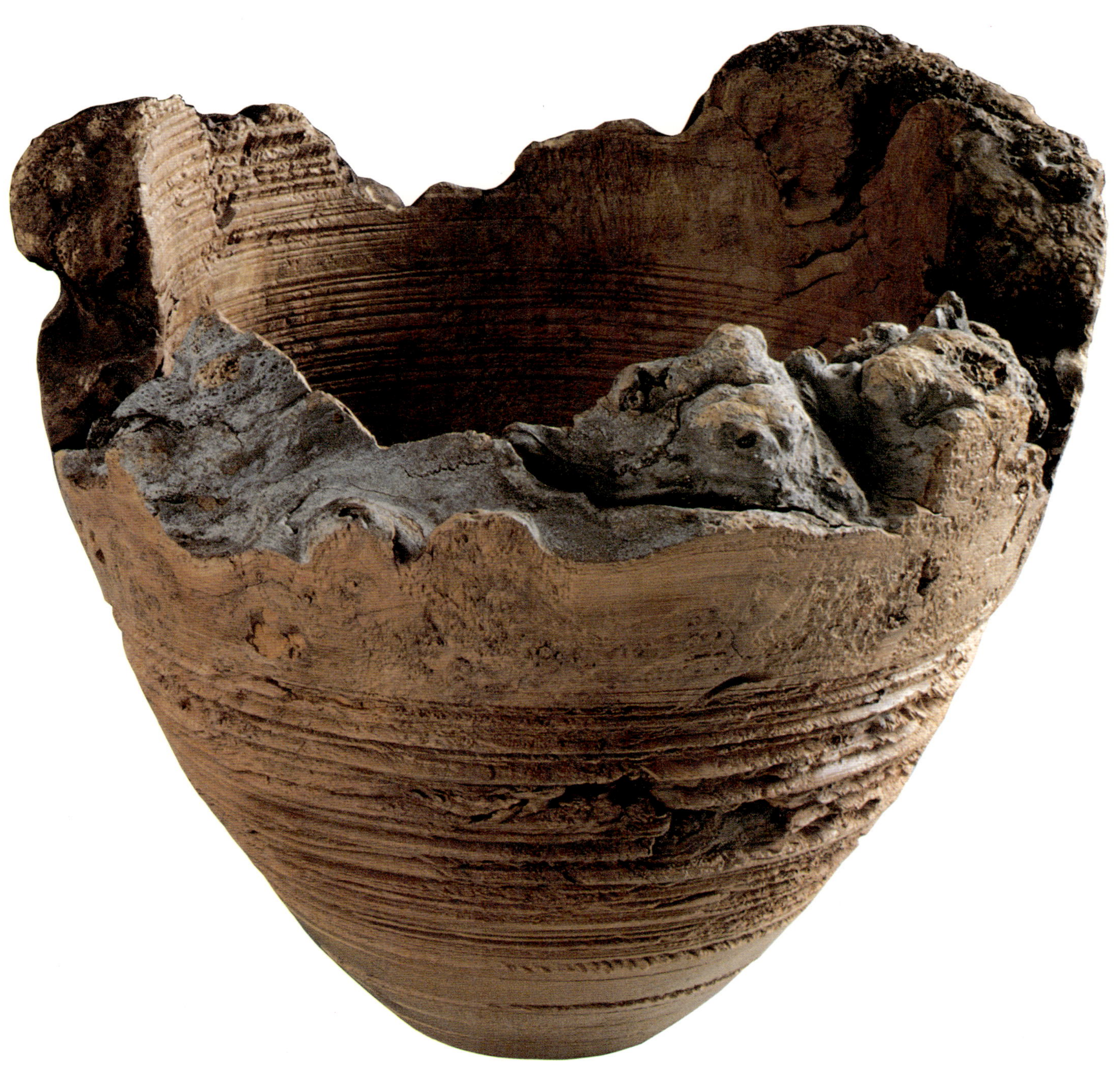

Mark Lindquist: *Unsung Bowl #1.* 1981. Cherry burl. H. 6″–9¾″; Diam. (rim) 10⅜″–10¹¹⁄₁₆″; Thickness 1⁵⁄₁₆″; Base 3⅛″.

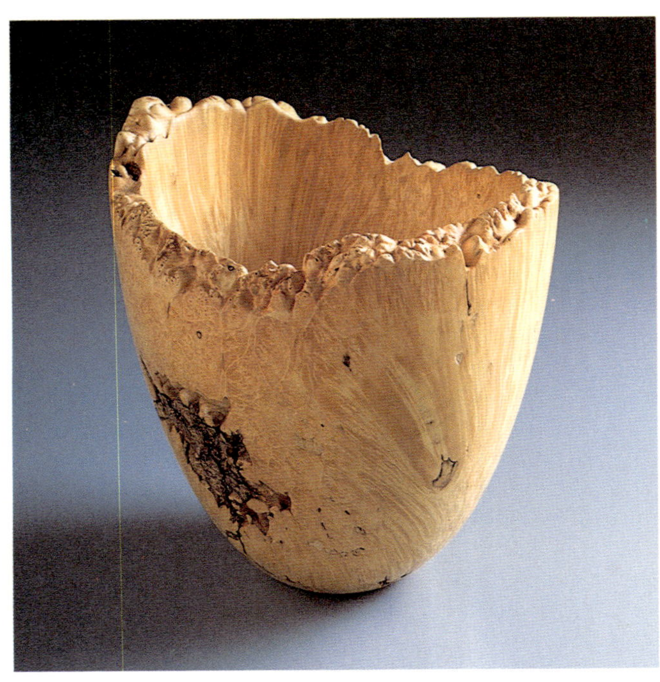

Mark Lindquist: Ellipsoid bowl. 1981. Bay elder burl. H. 6″–7½″; Diam. (rim) 6 13/16″–7⅛″; Thickness .512″; Base 2 1/16″.

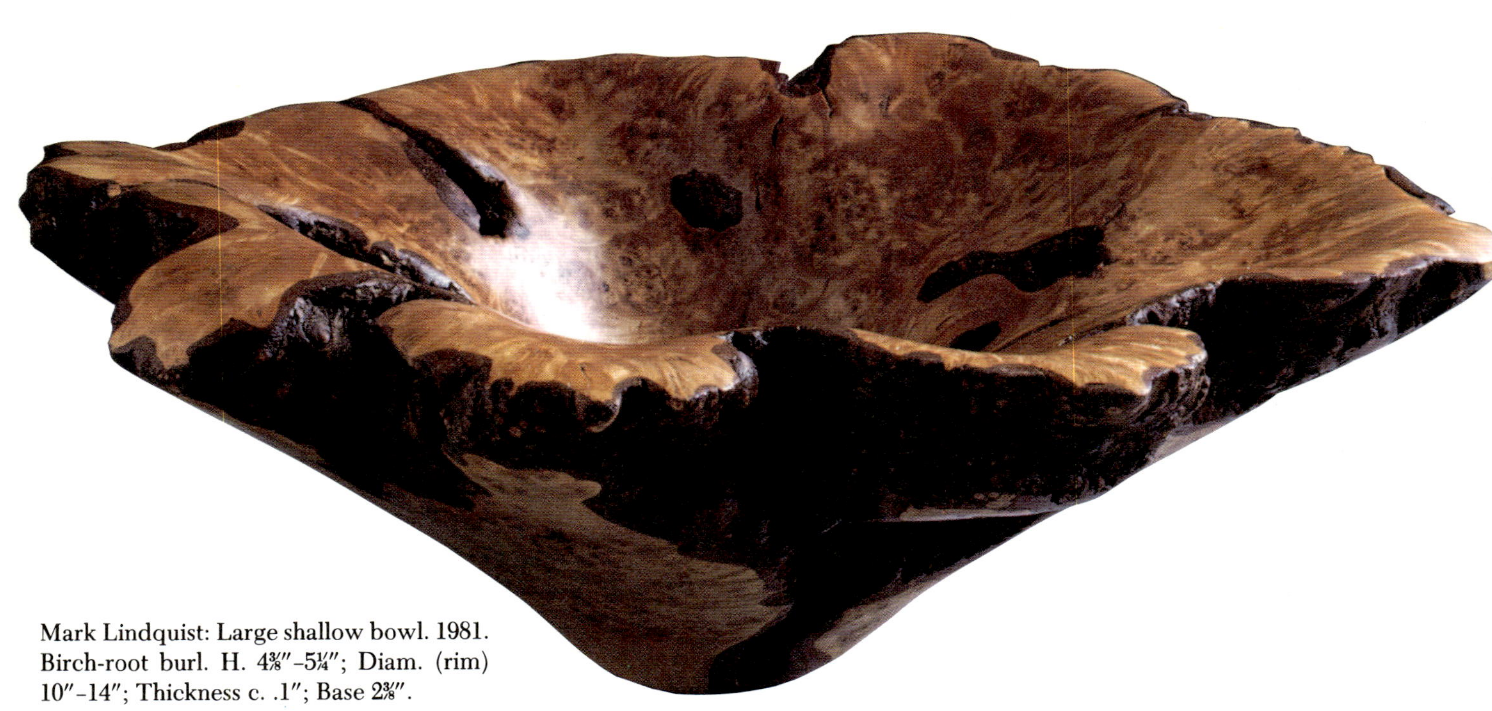

Mark Lindquist: Large shallow bowl. 1981. Birch-root burl. H. 4⅜″–5¼″; Diam. (rim) 10″–14″; Thickness c. .1″; Base 2⅜″.

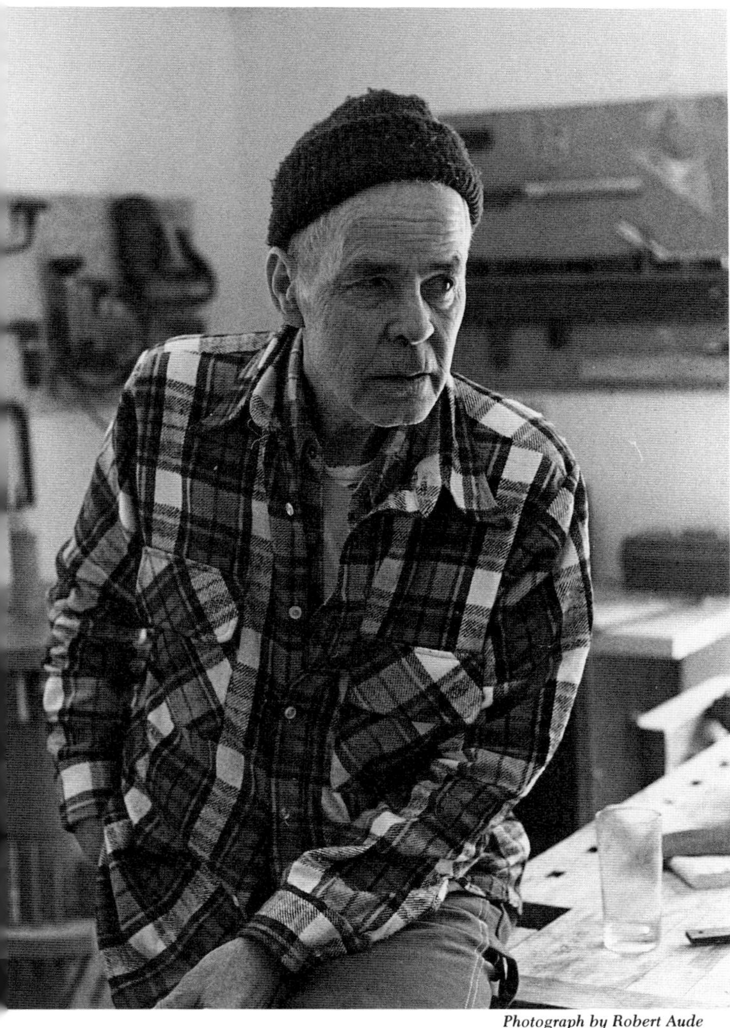

Photograph by Robert Aude

MELVIN LINDQUIST

(Summer studio)
Patch Road
Henniker, New Hampshire 03242

(Winter studio)
Rt. 2, Box 247
Quincy, Florida 32351

Educated at Oakland Polytechnic College of Engineering, Melvin Lindquist began turning in the 1930s as a vertical turret-lathe operator for the General Electric Company. In his shop at home he began an exploration of the vase form that has continued for fifty years through the study of ancient Oriental, Greek, and Indian ceramic vases, and through the development of turning methods such as blind boring (turning hollow forms), reverse turning, horizontal parting, and vertical parting.

Through the years Melvin Lindquist has applied his engineering and machinist's background to the development of new tools, such as carbide-tipped turning tools, and new turning techniques, including the "equilibrial abrasion" method of turning spalted wood, which he and his son, Mark, developed together.

Melvin Lindquist began turning spalted wood in the late 1950s, when he discovered wood on his land in the Adirondack mountains of New York. According to *Fine Woodworking* magazine (January/February 1982), Melvin and Mark Lindquist "unleashed spalted wood upon the world."

After retiring as an engineer in 1967, Melvin Lindquist maintained his shop in Schenectady, New York, until 1981, showing his work through galleries, museums, and the American Craft Council fairs at Rhinebeck, New York, and at Baltimore and San Francisco. In 1981 he moved to Henniker, New Hampshire, where he now has his studio. Mr. Lindquist's work is included in such collections as The Metropolitan Museum of Art, New York City; The Schenectady Museum, New York; Fine Arts Museum of the South, Mobile, Alabama; and the collection of *U.S. News & World Report* magazine, Washington, D.C.

STATEMENT FROM THE ARTIST

For me, the lathe and its accouterments are simply tools that enable me to get to the end result. After all these years of turning I'm still fascinated by being able to find a useless piece of wood and turn it into something worthwhile. I turn wood for the pure enjoyment of it. Tools and machines have been a way of life for me, and I don't think much about them anymore. At the age of seventy-three, I'm getting old and stiff, but turning is for me being young again as each stiff, old, distressed piece of wood comes alive with a refreshing new chance at life. I once heard about how the Japanese potter Hamada felt about his work in his old age. He said that for him throwing a pot was like walking down the hill with the breeze at his back. For me, turning a bowl is like struggling to climb a very difficult mountain, but finally receiving the reward once I've reached the top.

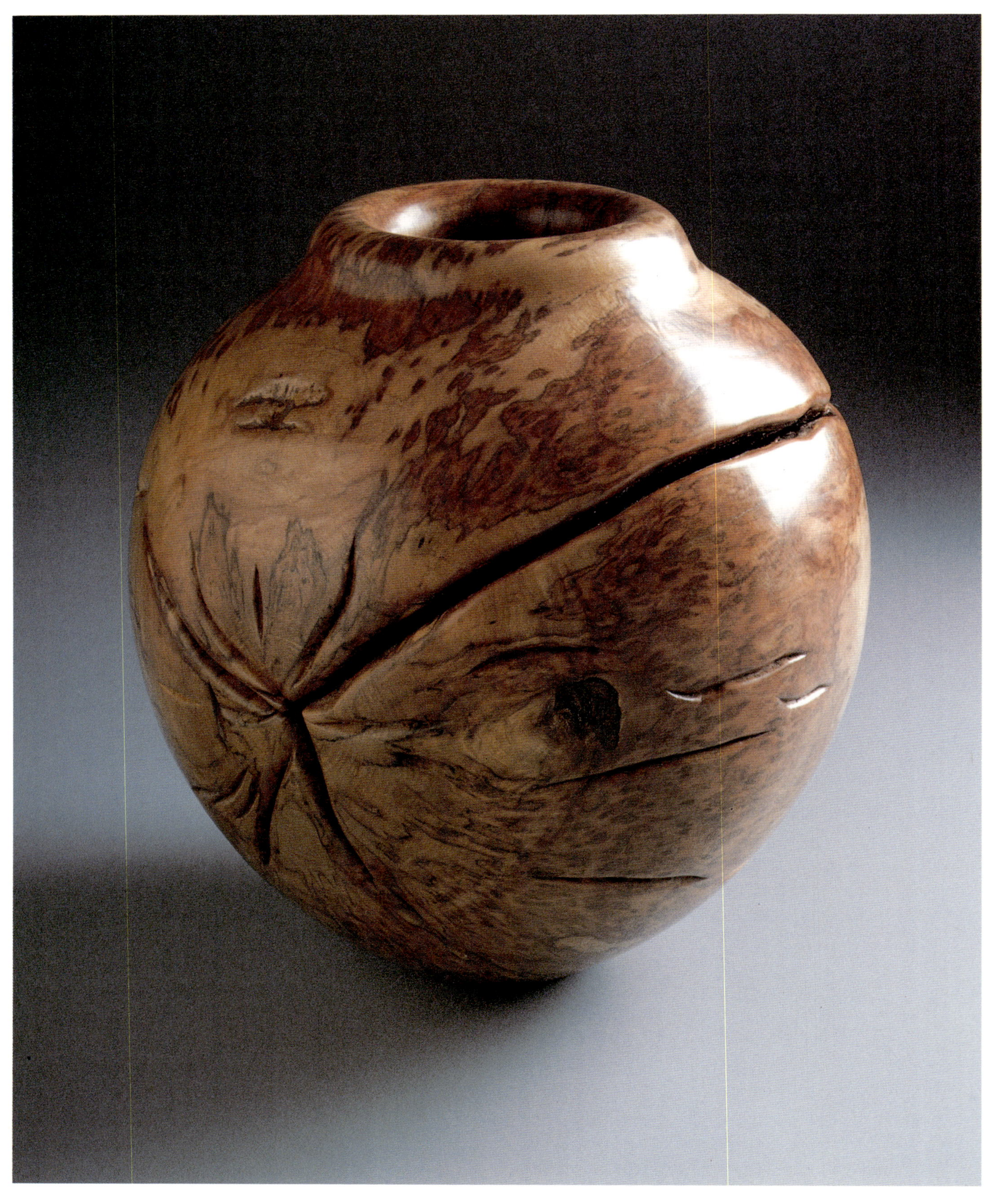

Mel Lindquist: Spherical jar. 1982. Maple burl. H. 10¾″; Diam. (outer edge of mouth) 4⅝″, (shoulder) 10³⁄₁₆″; Thickness 1″; Base 2¹⁵⁄₁₆″.

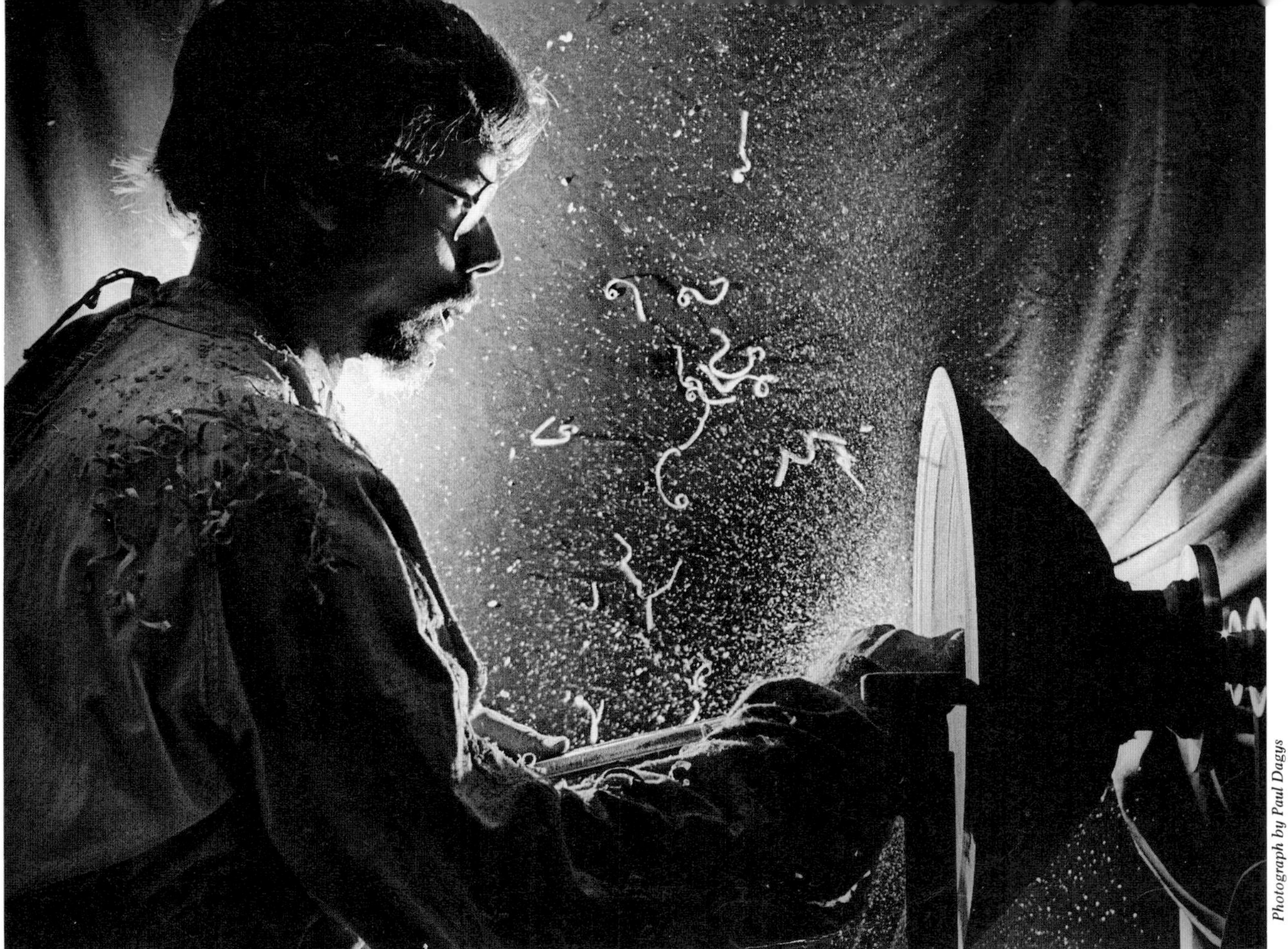

Photograph by Paul Dagys

DAVID LORY

R.R. #2, Box 76
Platteville, Wisconsin 53818

In 1977 David Lory was one of the first two students to take part in a unique apprenticeship-type class at the University of Wisconsin, Platteville. It was in this class that David Lory taught himself to create his thin epoxy-finished bowls in the same technique pioneered by the late Henry Nohr. Mr. Lory's love and appreciation of wood goes back many years, for as a boy his father helped him get started on the lathe, and in 4-H he made lamps and vases so well that he became a leader of the woodworking groups.

David Lory's work has been exhibited at the major Midwest art shows, such as the 57th Street Art Fair in Chicago; Lakefront Festival of the Arts in Milwaukee, Wisconsin; North Shore Art League, Chicago; and Art Fair on the Square, Madison, Wisconsin. Mr. Lory's work is represented at the following locations: Tamarack Gallery, Omena, Michigan; Mindscape Gallery, Evanston, Illinois; The Works, Philadelphia; The Hand and The Spirit Crafts Gallery, Scottsdale, Arizona; Elizabeth Fortner Gallery, Santa Barbara, California; Ten Arrow Gallery, Cambridge, Massachusetts; Appalachiana Gallery, Bethesda, Maryland. Mr. Lory has written for *Fine Woodworking* magazine, and his work was illustrated in *Design Book II*, published by *Fine Woodworking*.

STATEMENT FROM THE ARTIST

All my bowls are finished with an FDA-approved epoxy. The bowls are baked in an oven to remove all moisture. After the baking process the epoxy is applied to penetrate and seal the wood. With this epoxy finish the bowls are durable and usable. Indeed, the bowls are so durable that I give them a lifetime guarantee. For this reason I call them Heirloom Bowls, for they can be passed down from one generation to another.

Most of my bowls are turned from the log, crotches, or stump, with the remainder turned from burls. However, good, sound burls are rare, so the burl bowls account for only a small percentage of my output. The bowls vary in size from three inches in diameter and three inches deep to eighteen inches in diameter and twelve inches deep. All the bowls are simply shaped because: (1) a simple shape shows off the grain best; (2) a simple shape is more usable; (3) there cannot be any sharp edges, for the epoxy will wear off these spots sooner.

A great deal of time and care is put into each of my bowls so that it becomes a work of art that will appeal to those who feel that art should be useful as well as to those who feel that art need only be art.

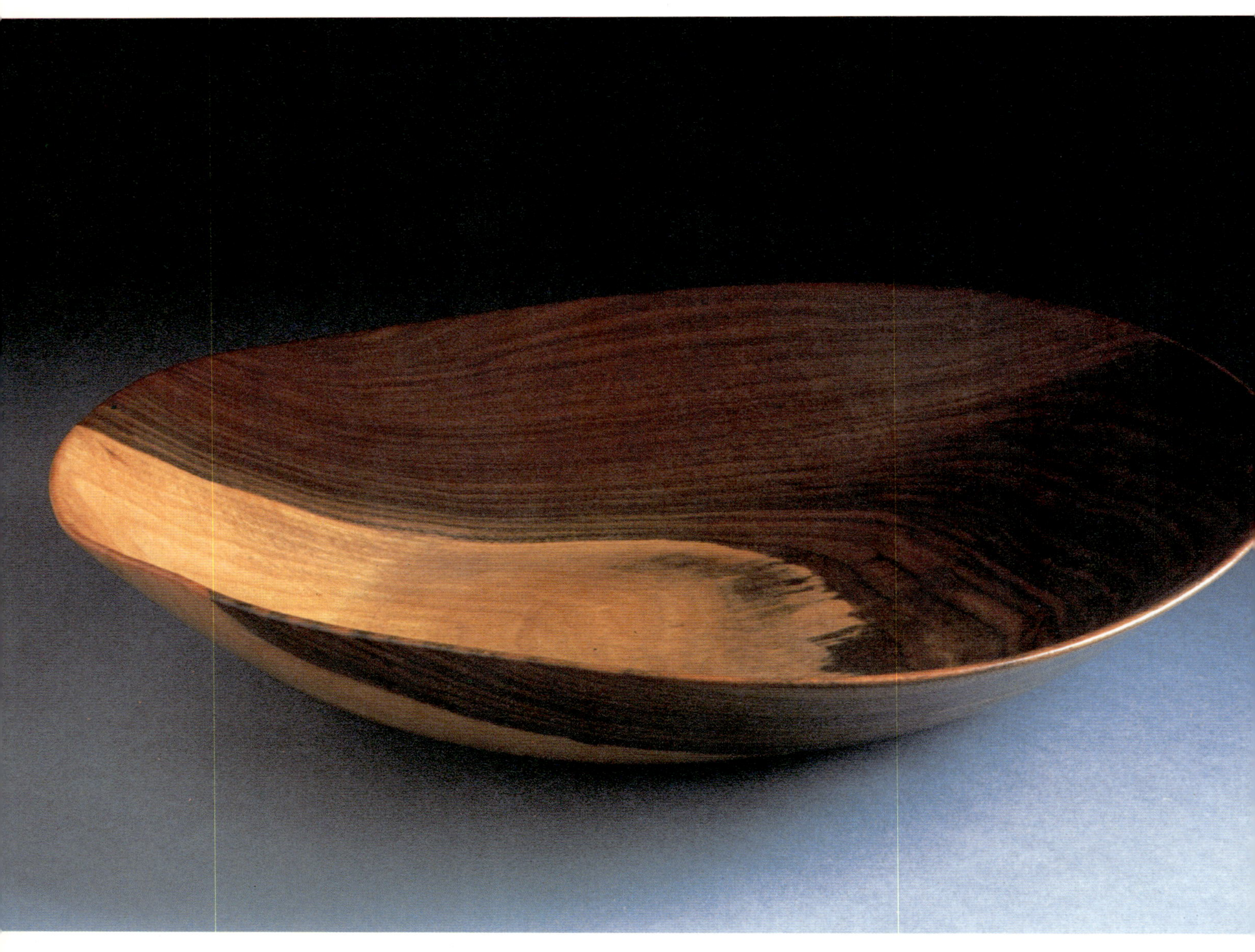

David Lory: Wide shallow bowl. 1981. Black walnut crotch. H. $2\frac{9}{16}$″–$3\frac{1}{4}$″; Diam. (rim) $14\frac{1}{4}$″–$14\frac{13}{16}$″; Thickness .169″.

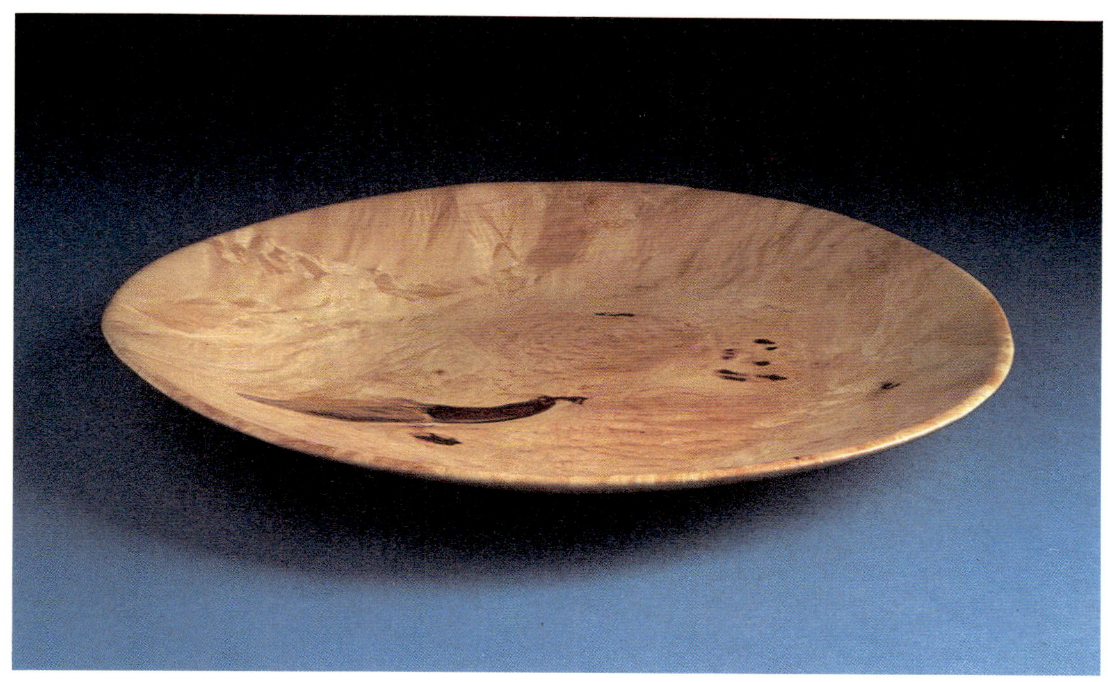

David Lory: Medium-size shallow plate. 1981. Hard maple burl. H. 1″–1 5/16″; Diam. (rim) 10⅝″–11″; Thickness .157″.

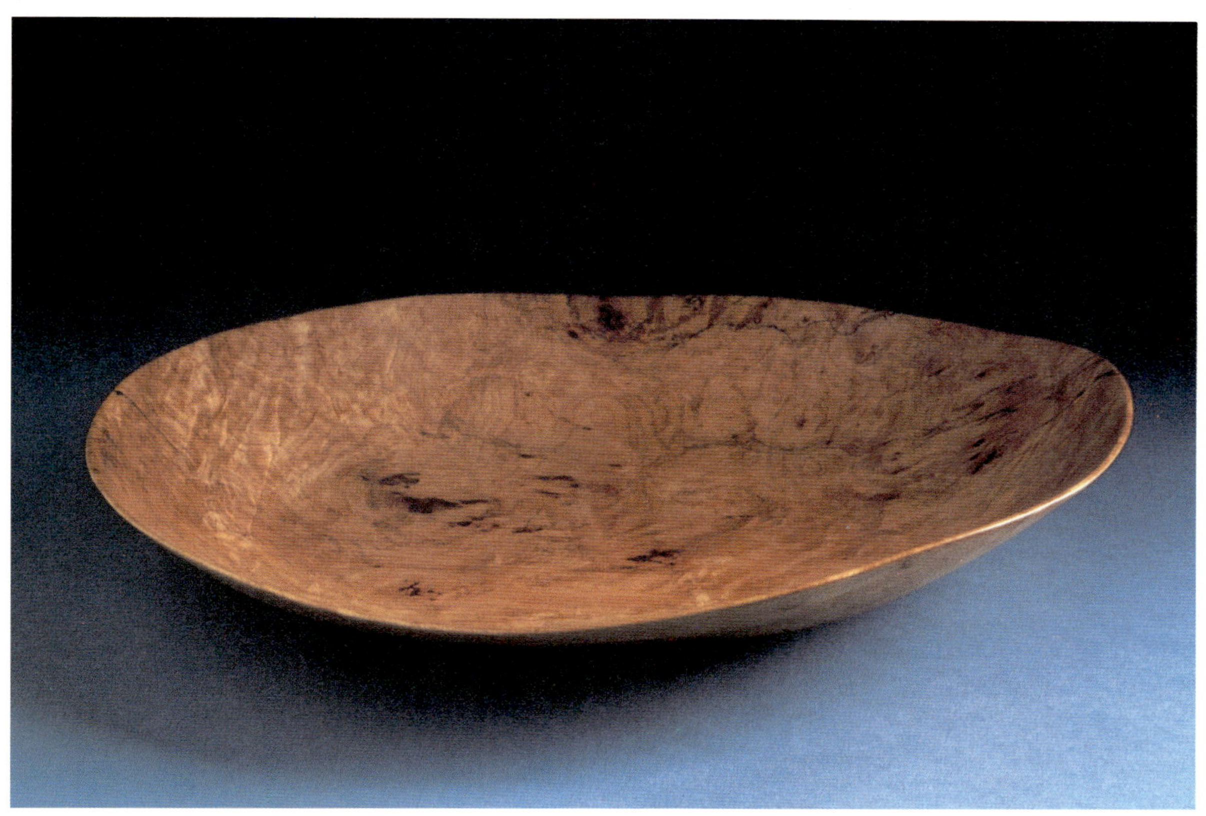

David Lory: Wide shallow bowl. 1981. Hard maple burl. H. 1⅞″–2 11/16″; Diam. (rim) 14 5/16″–14⅜″; Thickness .115″.

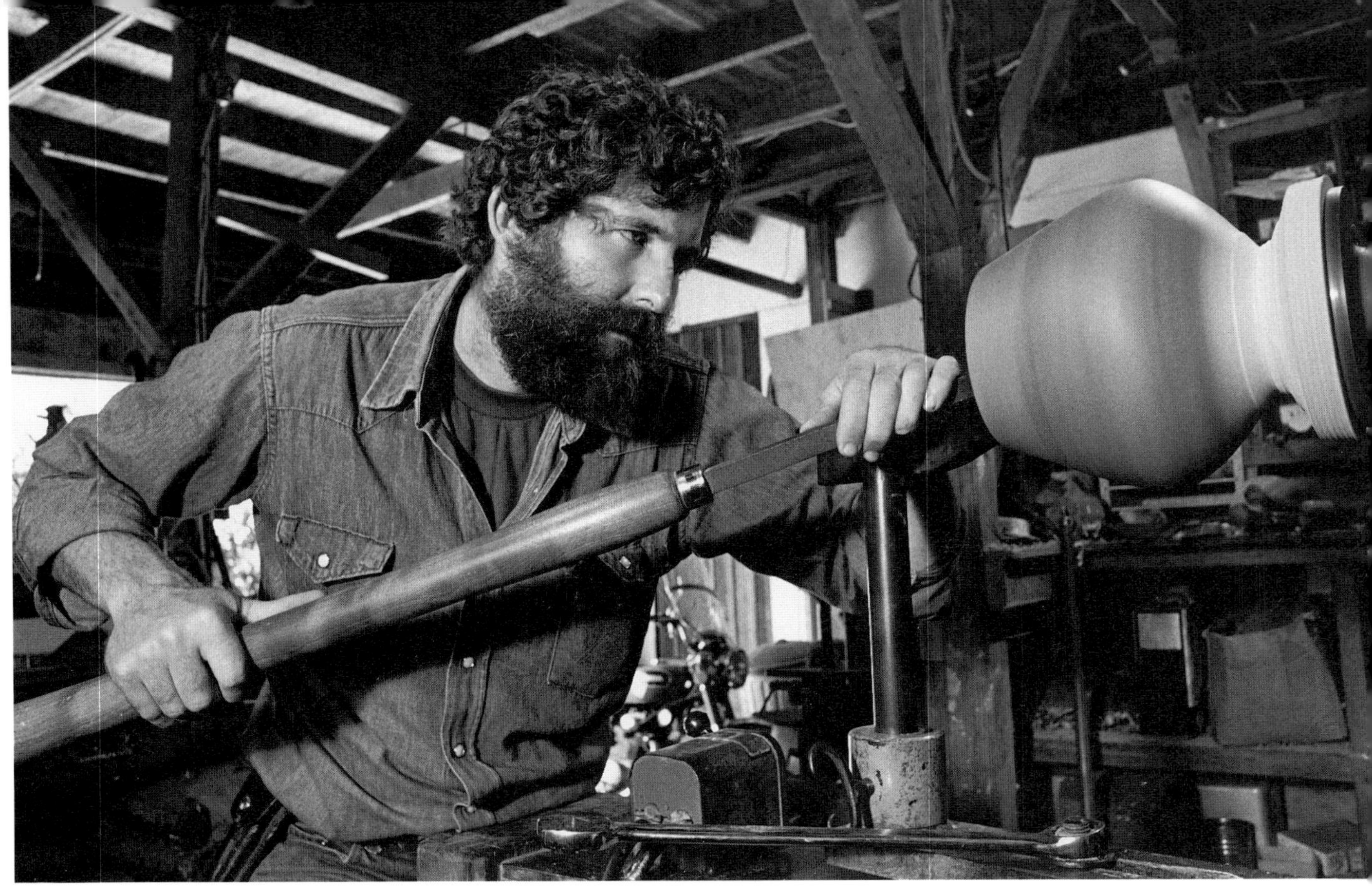

BRUCE MITCHELL

P.O. Box 308
Inverness, California 94937

Bruce Mitchell graduated from the University of California at Santa Barbara in 1970. He studied pre-Columbian pottery, stone carving, metalsmithing, and textiles while traveling for six months in Central and South America in 1976.

Mr. Mitchell served as technical assistant to wood sculptor J. B. Blunk in Inverness, working on numerous public and private commissions from 1969 to 1977. He incorporated the technical and aesthetic aspects from this sculptural background into his approach to turning, and he has been self-taught as a woodturner since 1977. He acquired additional training through participation in several invitational national wood-turning symposia. Mr. Mitchell was originally accepted as a student participant in 1979 and 1980, and then was invited to return as a teacher in 1980, 1982, and 1984.

Bruce Mitchell's work is currently represented by: Pritam & Eames, East Hampton, New York; The Hand and The Spirit Crafts Gallery, Scottsdale, Arizona; Cole-Wheatman, Inc., San Francisco; Gillette-Futchey Gallery, Ltd., Atlanta, Georgia; Gallery Eight, La Jolla, California; Following Sea, Honolulu; Del Mano Gallery, Los Angeles; A Singular Place, Santa Monica, California; David Cole Gallery, Inverness, California; Snyderman Gallery, Philadelphia.

STATEMENT FROM THE ARTIST

My primary concern is to explore the expressive qualities of wood in order to create objects that transcend traditional functions of utility. The contemplative, conceptual forms allow me complete improvisational freedom throughout the design process.

As the rough-sawn blank begins to take shape on the lathe, new layers of grain and color are revealed. The emerging form suggests itself through an interplay of hard edges and curved surfaces. My artistic feelings are integrated into the process with a focused control of eye, hand, and tool. The transformation that occurs becomes a ritual exchange of ideas and possibilities between myself and the wood.

I prefer working with green, uncured wood. In this state the fibers are soft and elastic, allowing easy removal of excess material. Some shapes require thorough drying before they can be completed, but I experiment with many forms that may be finished while still in the green state. As these finished pieces continue drying, the wood shrinks and distorts across the entire surface of the piece, giving it a tactile, fluid texture. Both techniques offer many variations to play with in my pursuit of new forms.

The essential effort in my current work is to incorporate the full range of potential in the woods I use. The function of the work flows from the response it receives from those who see and touch it.

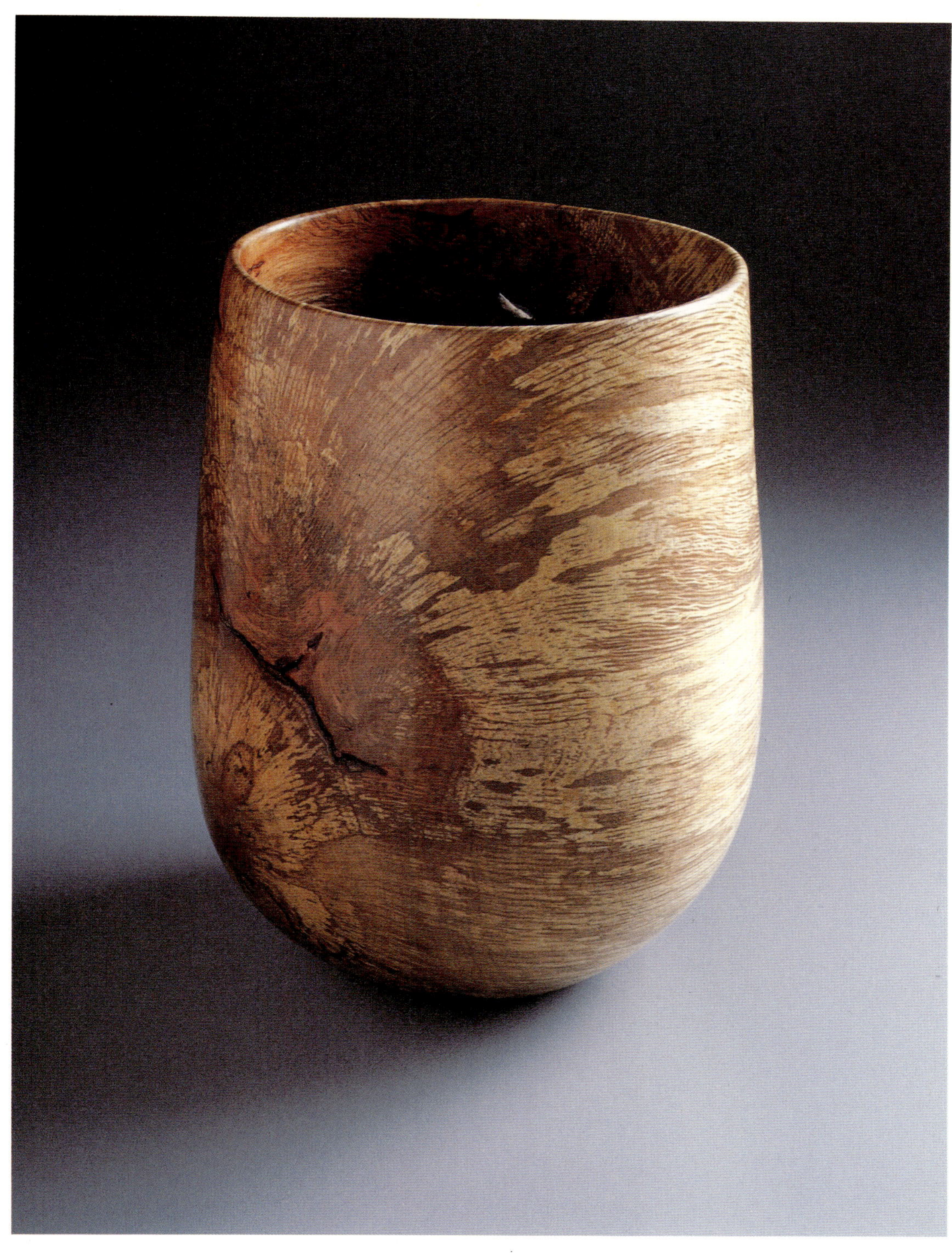

Bruce Mitchell: *Acorn Urn*. 1981. Spalted tanbark oak. H. 10⅜″; Diam. (rim) 6⅝″–6 15/16″; Thickness .206″; Base 3 3/16″–3 15/16″.

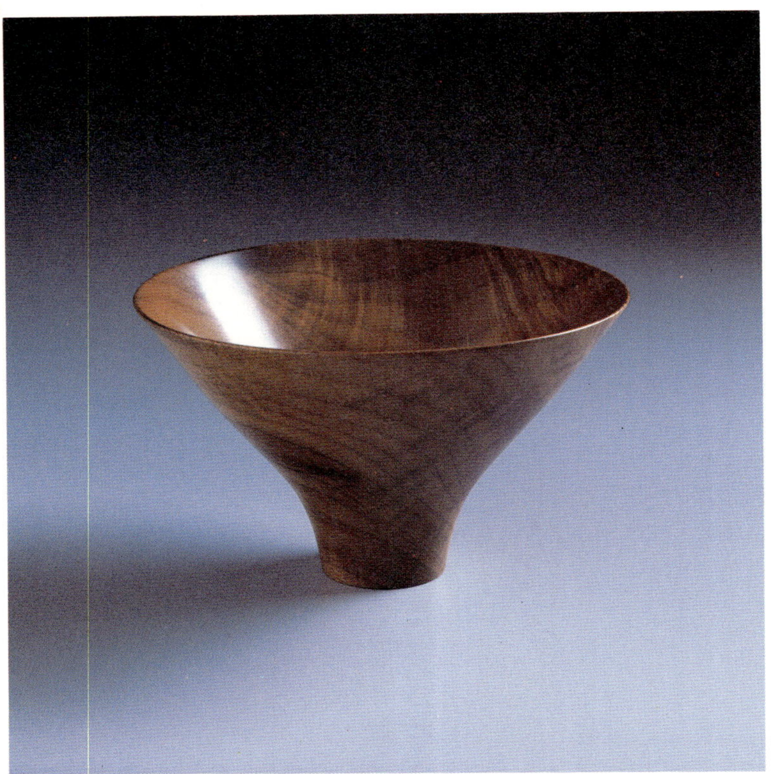

Bruce Mitchell: Medium-size tapering bowl. 1982. Bay laurel. H. 3⅜″; Diam. (rim) 5¾″; Thickness .92″; Base (foot) 1½″.

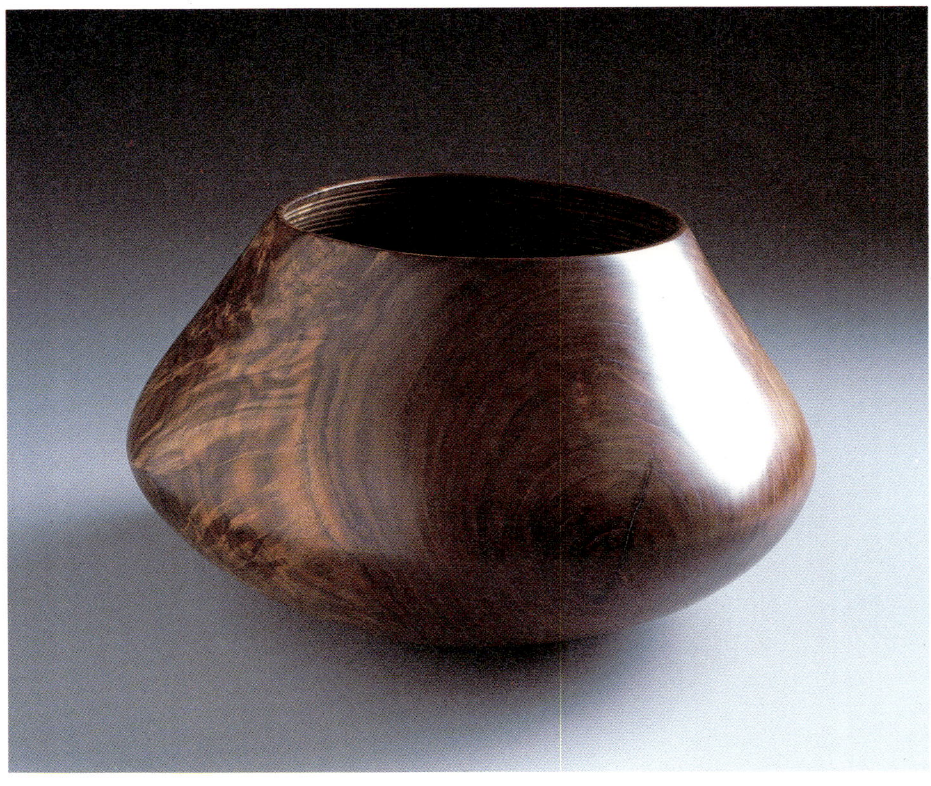

Bruce Mitchell: *Calabash Urn*. 1982. Claro walnut root. H. 6³⁄₁₆″; Diam. (rim) 6¹¹⁄₁₆″–6⅞″, (shoulder) 11¼″; Thickness .225.

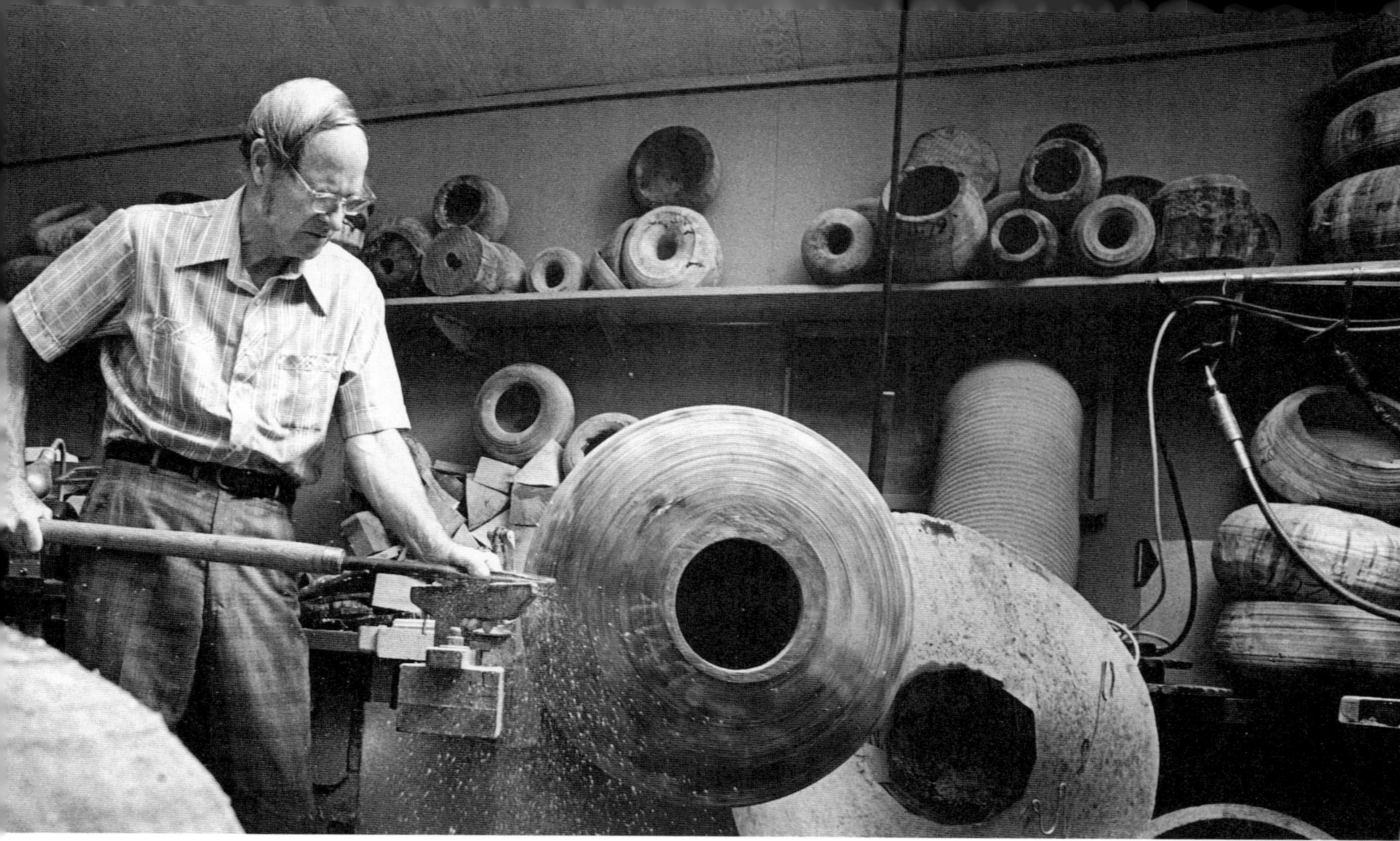

Photograph by Louis Favorite

ED MOULTHROP

4260 Carmain Drive, N.E.
Atlanta, Georgia 30342

Educated at Case Western Reserve University and Princeton University, Ed Moulthrop taught both architecture and physics at Georgia Institute of Technology and was also a practicing architect for many years. His love of wood turning began at the age of thirteen, and he first exhibited his work in 1963. Mr. Moulthrop began wood turning as a full-time profession in 1976. In addition, he was chairman of the Georgia State Arts Commission 1954–1965. Ed Moulthrop's work is represented not only in many notable private collections, but also in the collections of The Museum of Modern Art, New York City; The Metropolitan Museum of Art, New York City; and The High Museum of Art, Atlanta, Georgia.

STATEMENT FROM THE ARTIST

For me, wood is the most exquisite of all materials; I sense that nature herself has created fantastic visual and sensual beauty in wood.

I try to reveal this beauty hidden in the wood and attempt to employ only those utterly simple shapes or forms that will display this beauty without distracting from it, or without imposing my own conflicting shapes or designs upon the beauty that is already there.

I often say that each bowl already exists in the tree trunk and my job is simply to uncover it and take it out. Thus, not only my simple shapes, but also my search for a crystal-clear finish, and my final polishings are all aimed at best revealing the myriad complexities, the subtle or exotic range of colors, and the etchinglike patterns of growth rings that nature has placed there.

Working with the larger bowls is terribly exciting. It is just thrilling to behold that huge block of almost homogeneous material that has all grown miraculously as a living material. I love the heft and the solidness of those huge blocks. I love to feel their weight as they resist the leverage of a big cant hook, or to sense the tug of gravity as the electric hoist slowly separates a fifteen-hundred-pound block from the ground.

How I feel about wood has everything to do with what I produce in wood. The lathe and the tools are only means to accomplish the expression of my feelings about wood, feelings I desire to share with others through the medium of my work.

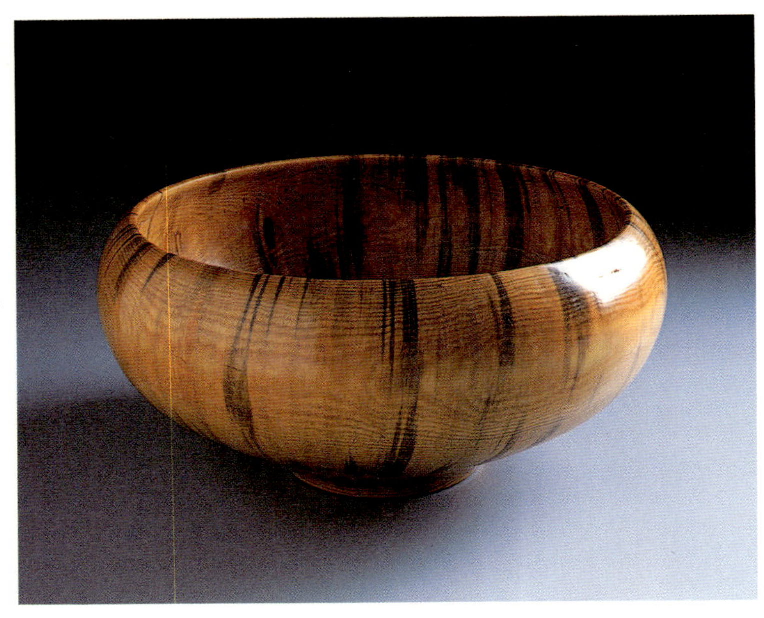

Ed Moulthrop: Large footed bowl. 1979. Georgia pine. H. 7 1/16″; Diam. (rim) 12 5/8″, (belly) 14 7/8″; Thickness .269″; Base (foot) 5 5/16″.

Ed Moulthrop: Flattened spherical bowl. 1979. Orangewood. H. 5 1/2″; Diam. (mouth) 4″, (belly) 8 7/8″; Thickness 2 15/16″; Base 4 3/16″.

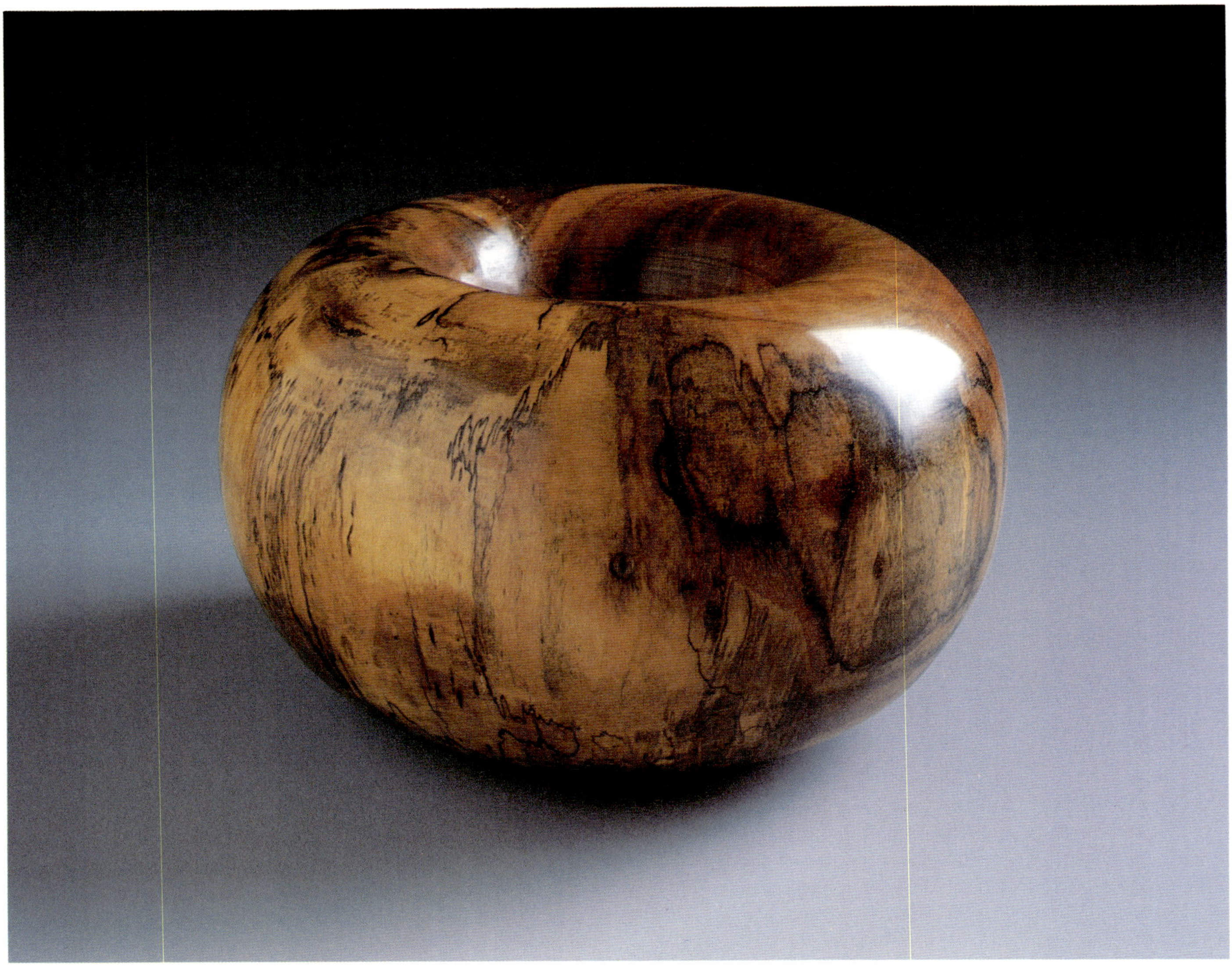

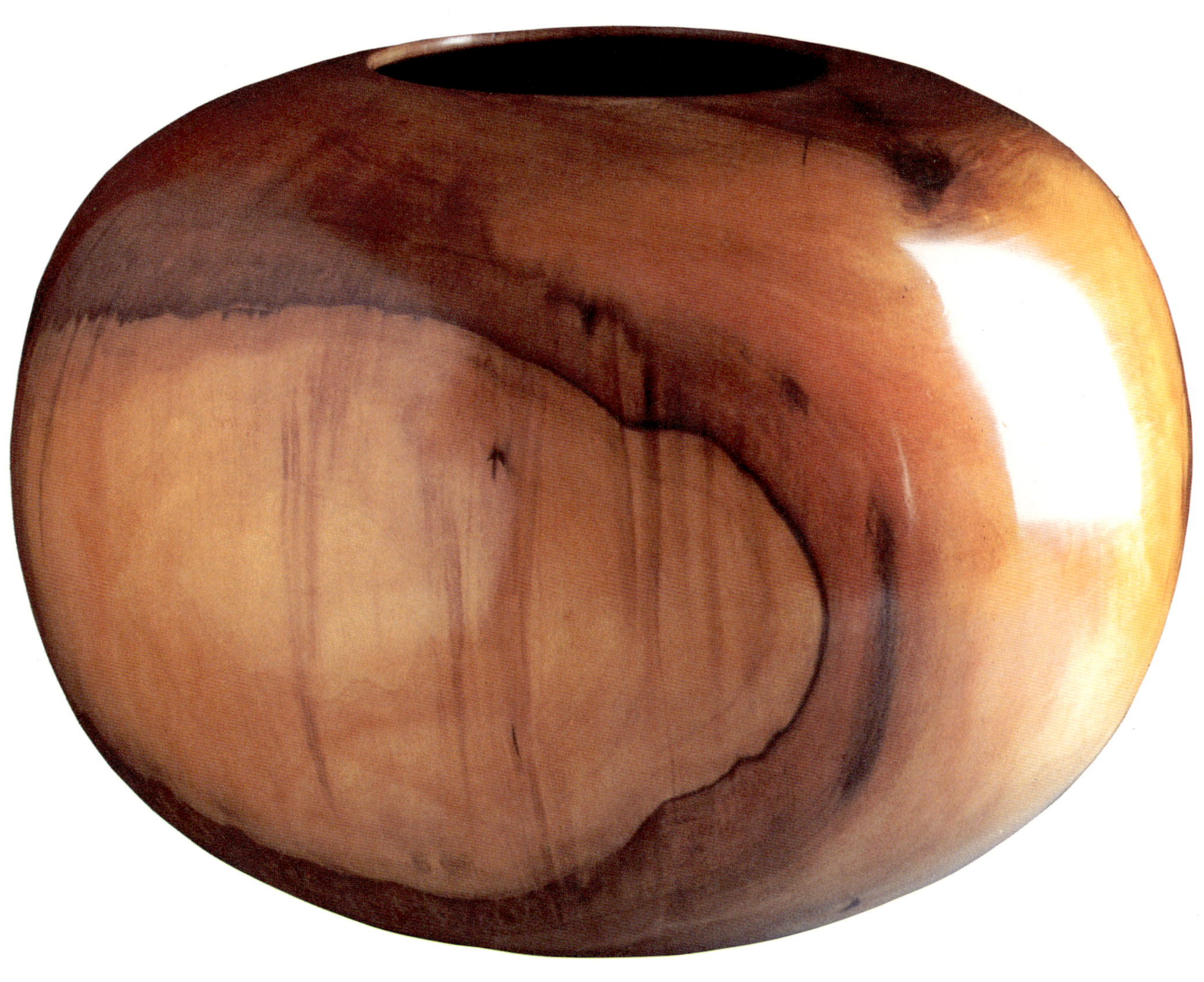

Ed Moulthrop: Large spherical bowl. 1978. Tulip poplar. H. 15″; Diam. (mouth) 7⅞″, (belly) 20⅝″; Thickness .347″; Base 7⅝″.

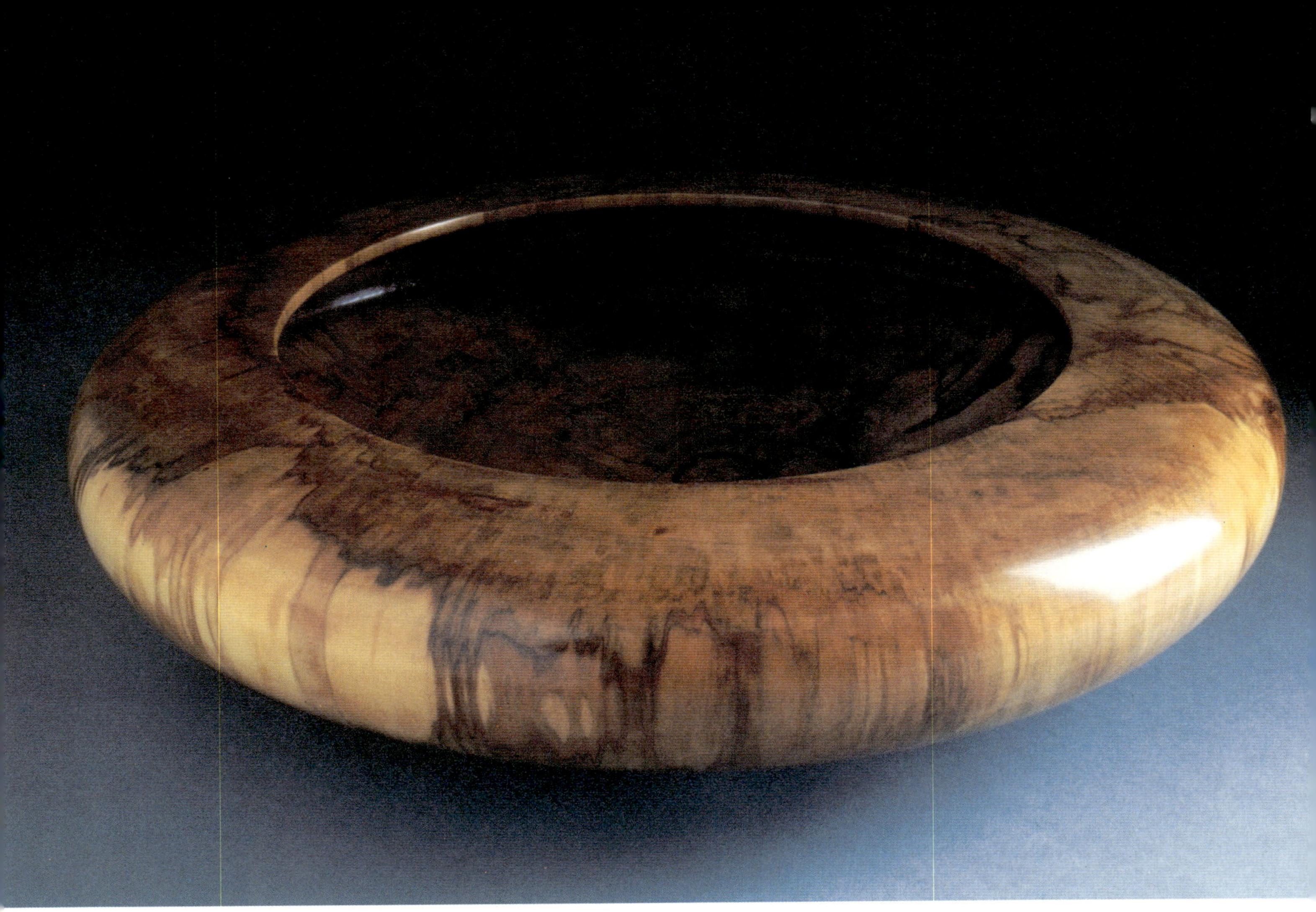

Ed Moulthrop: Large, flattened spherical bowl. 1981. Figured sweet gum. H. 6″; Diam. (mouth) $11\frac{5}{16}$″, (belly) $17\frac{9}{16}$″; Thickness .321″; Base $6\frac{1}{2}$″.

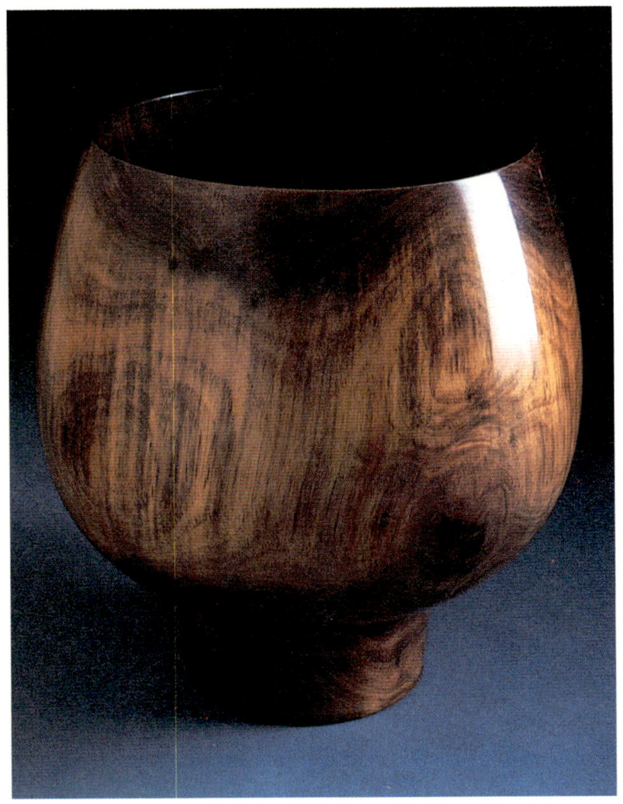

Ed Moulthrop: Tulip-shape footed bowl. 1981. Black walnut. H. $9\frac{1}{4}$″; Diam. (rim) $6\frac{11}{16}$″, (belly) $8\frac{7}{8}$″; Thickness .201″; Base (foot) $4\frac{1}{8}$″.

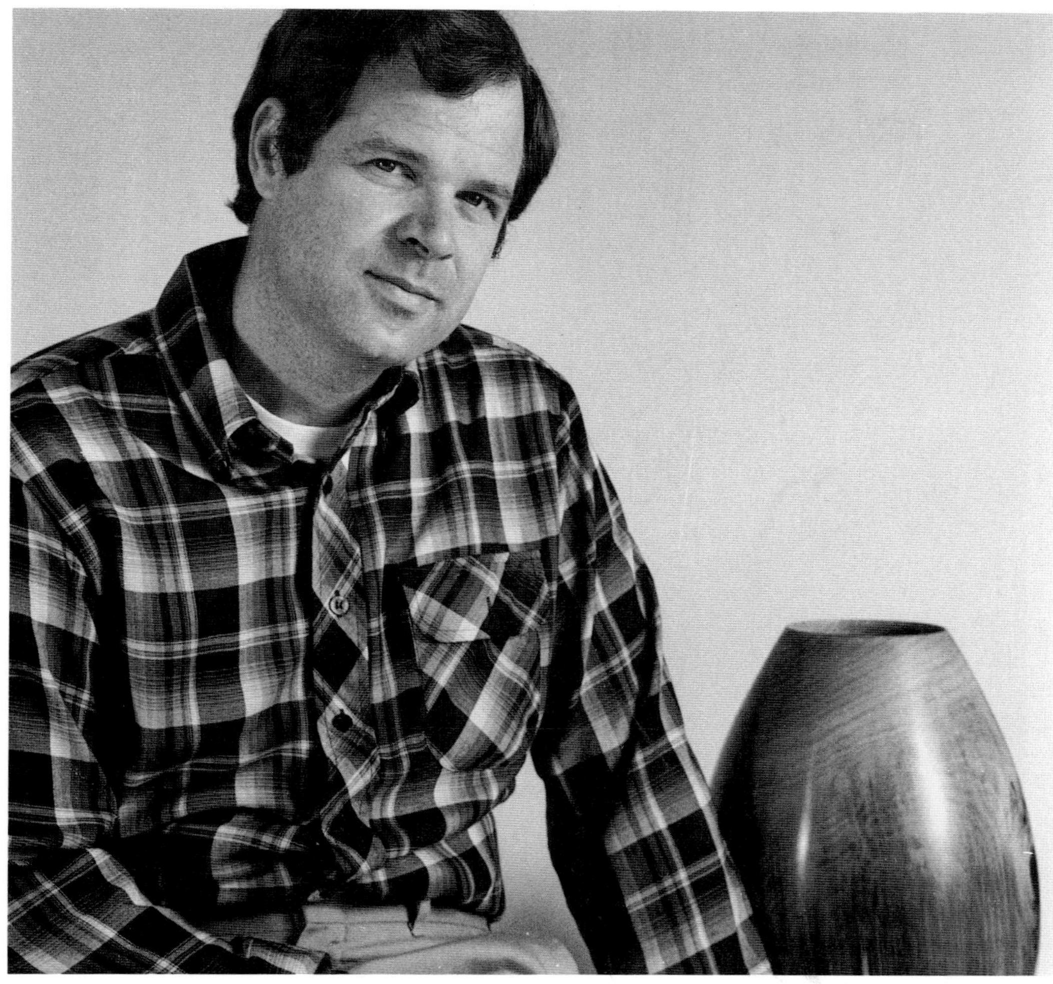

PHILIP C. MOULTHROP

3469 Fox Hollow Drive
Marietta, Georgia 30067

Educated at West Georgia College, Philip Moulthrop worked for a while as a biologist and a chemist and later in real estate. He then attended law school and is now a member of the Georgia Bar Association.

Mr. Moulthrop's time is now divided between his legal profession, his craft work, and his interest in photography. He began wood turning in 1980 and has even made most of his own tools and equipment. Mr. Moulthrop's pieces have been displayed in numerous regional and national shows and competitions, including the international wood-turning exhibition held in Vancouver, British Columbia, 1983–1984.

Philip Moulthrop's work is represented at the Signature Shop, Atlanta, Georgia; Gallery Eight, La Jolla, California; Magic Mountain Gallery, Taos, New Mexico; Netsky Gallery, Miami, Florida; and Elements Gallery, Greenwich, Connecticut.

STATEMENT FROM THE ARTIST

I have always enjoyed working with my hands and find that wood turning is very satisfying in that respect. No two pieces of wood are ever identical, which makes each piece new and exciting in its own way. I use simple shapes with smooth, flowing lines in order to accentuate the grain and patterns in the wood. The shape and finish enable the viewer to get a feel for the wood, just as they also enhance the color and grain.

My piece in the Edward Jacobson collection is one of the largest cylindrical vases I have turned. It is created from a rare piece of highly figured tulip poplar from Georgia. Wood of this color and pattern is extremely hard to find and highly desirable for the beauty of the turnings one can achieve with it.

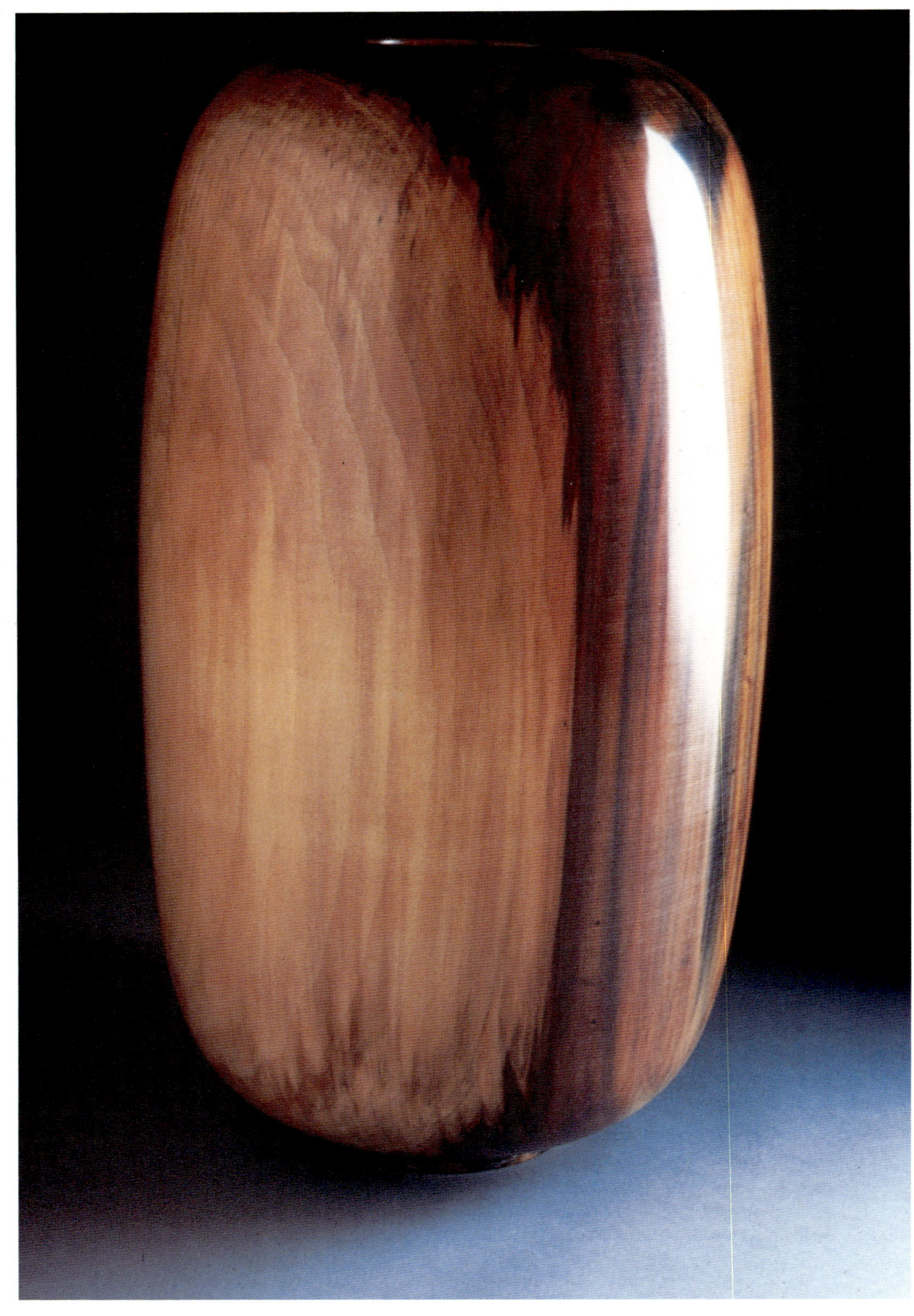

Philip C. Moulthrop: Tall ellipsoid vase. 1983. Tulip poplar. H. 23⅞″; Diam. (mouth) 4⅞″, (belly) 13¼″; Thickness .373″; Base (foot) 6 3/16″.

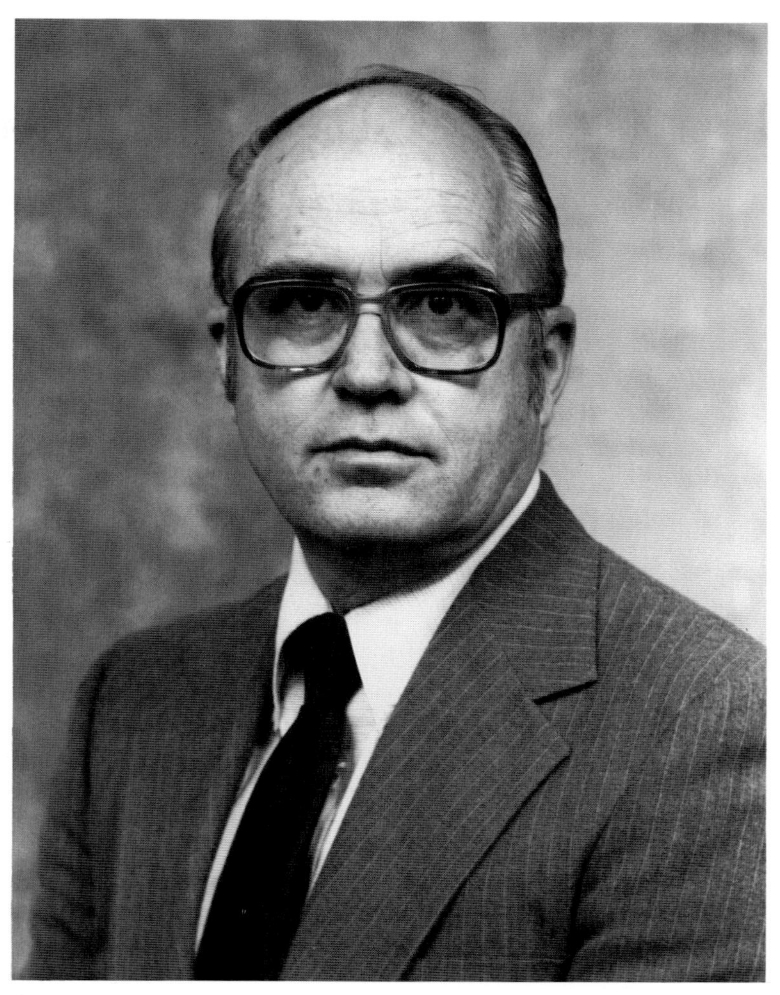

DALE L. NISH

3107 Foothill Drive
Provo, Utah 84604

Dale L. Nish is nationally known as a producing craftsman, writer, and teacher. He is currently a professor of Industrial Education at Brigham Young University, as well as the author of *Creative Woodturning* (1975) and *Artistic Woodturning* (1980).

Mr. Nish has conducted numerous lectures and demonstrations at woodworking shows, universities, and symposia throughout the United States, as well as being a guest instructor at such schools as the Arrowmont School of Crafts in Tennessee, Berea College in Kentucky, and Anderson Ranch in Colorado.

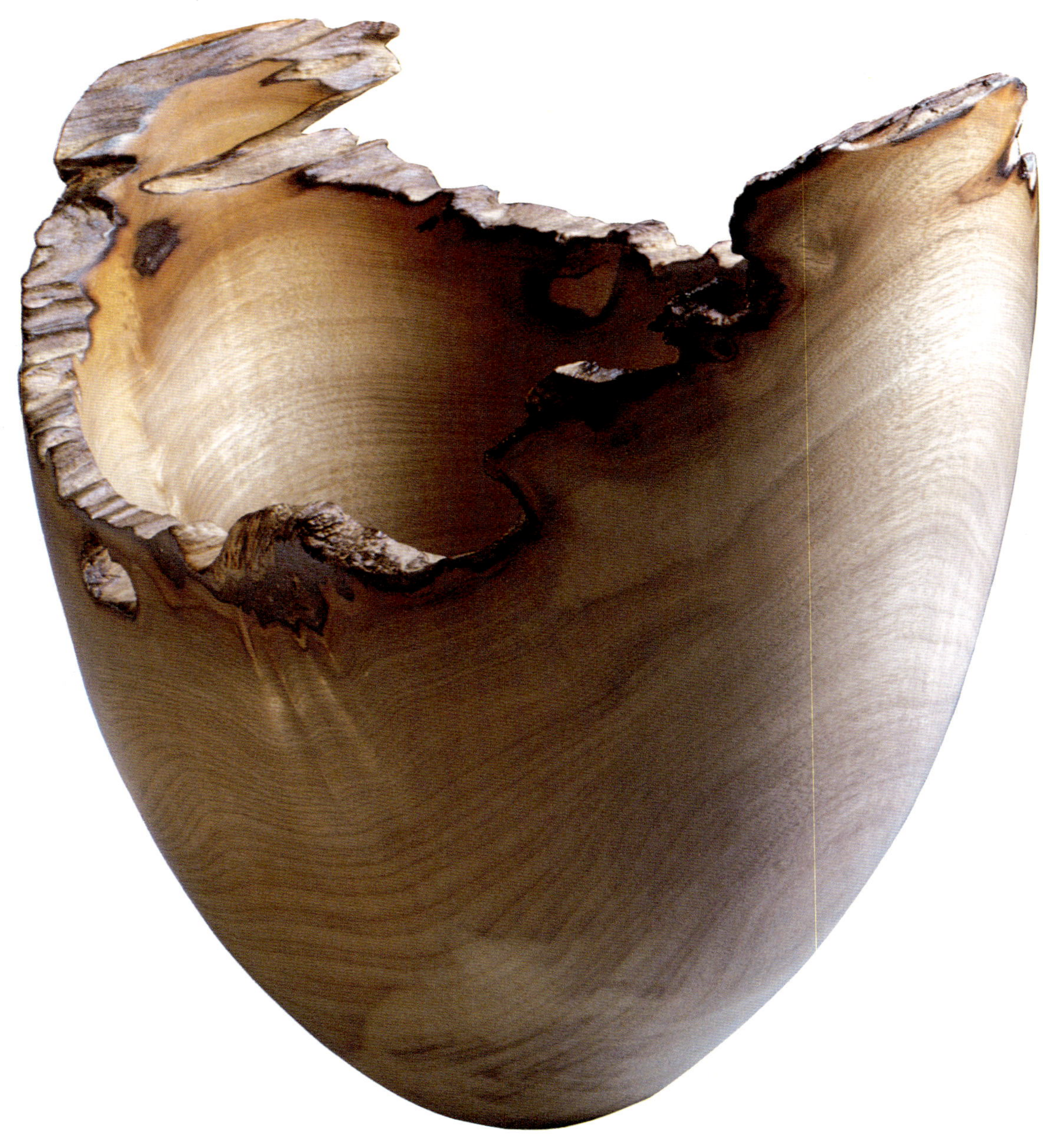

Dale L. Nish: Large ellipsoid bowl. 1984. Myrtlewood. H. 7 1/16″–10 3/4″; Diam. (rim) 9 11/16″–9 3/4″; Thickness .478″; Base 3″.

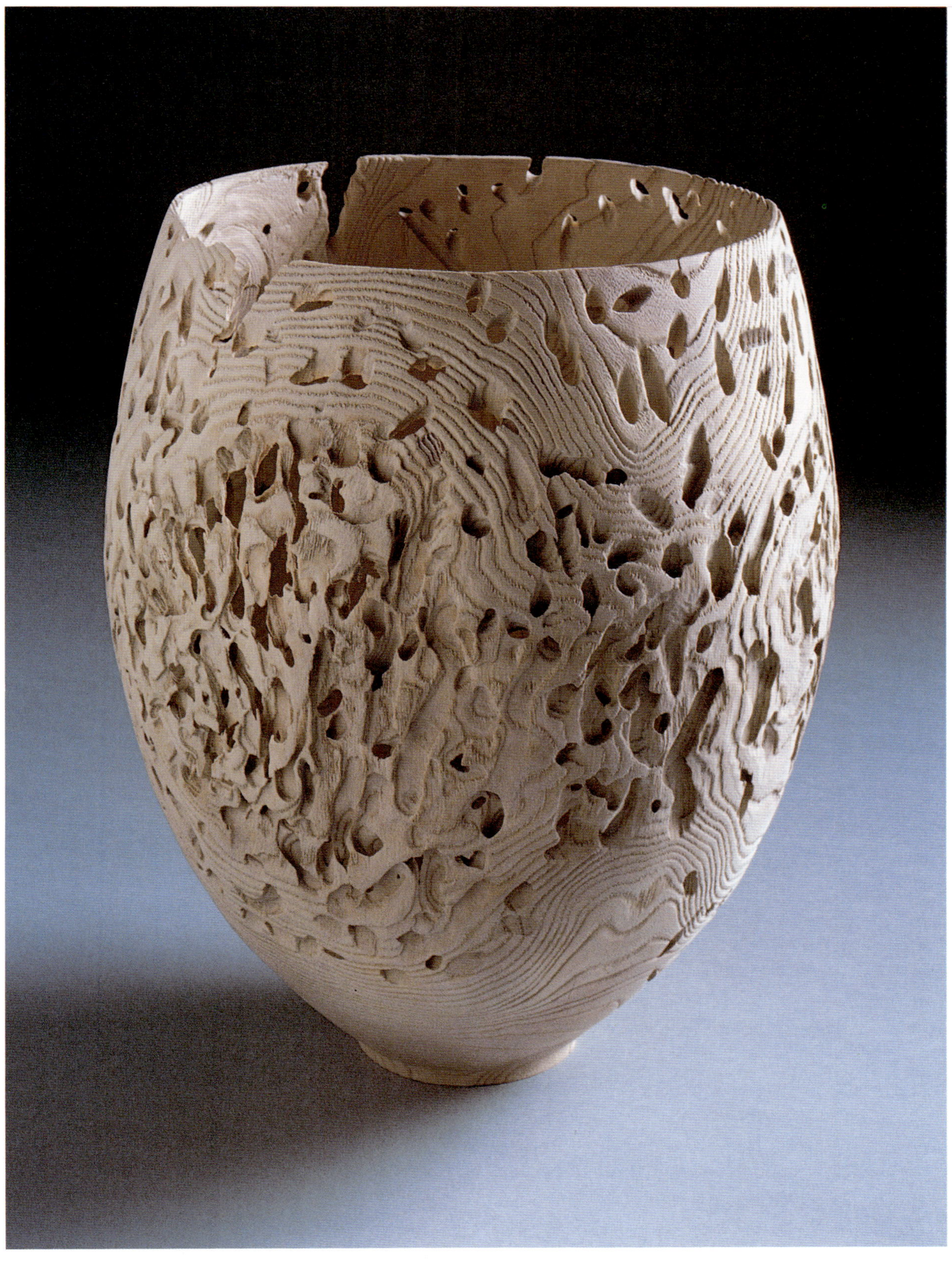

Dale L. Nish: Ellipsoid "sponge" bowl. 1984. Wormy ash. H. 12⁵⁄₁₆″–12⁷⁄₁₆″; Diam. (rim) 8¼″–8½″; Thickness .162″; Base 3¼″.

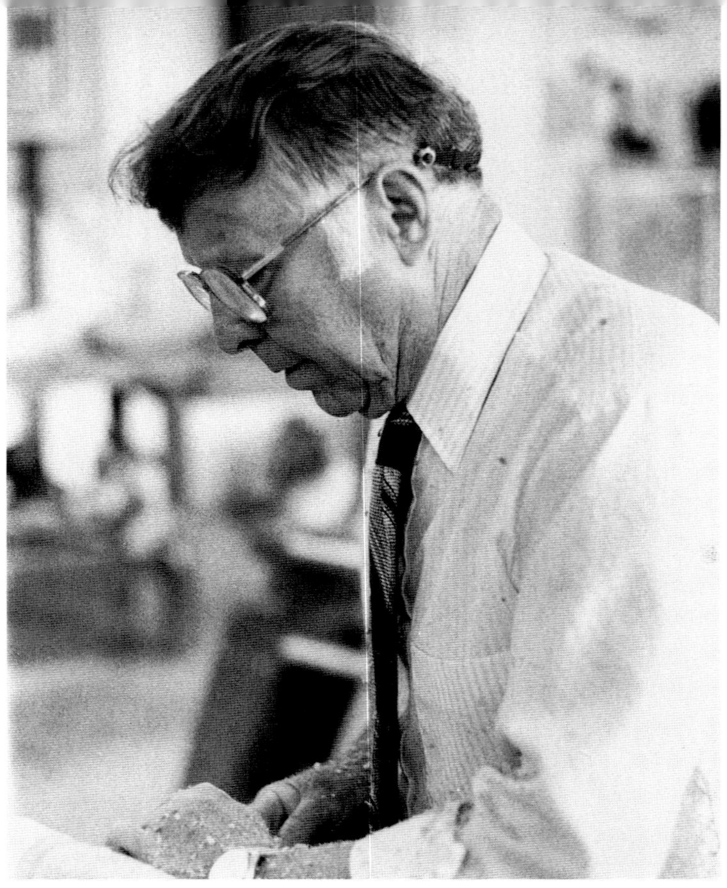

RUDE OSOLNIK

Scaffold Cane Road
Berea, Kentucky 40403

It was at high school in Johnston City, Illinois, that Rude Osolnik developed his interest in woodworking through the influence of a shop teacher. His fascination with wood and what could be made from it continued at Bradley University and really flowered with the beginning of his teaching career at Berea College in 1937. During 1975–1977 Mr. Osolnik headed the Berea College Woodcraft Industry. He brought to this Industry more interest in design and in the quality of production of furniture and other wood items. He also improved the quantity and quality of student work in the Industry and introduced more effective business practices.

Rude Osolnik's work has been exhibited at the Smithsonian Institution and is on permanent exhibition at the Museum of Science and Industry in Chicago. His pieces are represented chiefly at the Benchmark Gallery, Berea, Kentucky, and at the American Gallery, Atlanta, Georgia. Among the publications that have featured Mr. Osolnik's work are *Fine Woodworking, Kentucky Arts and Crafts Magazine, Shopsmith,* and the *Vancouver Sun.*

STATEMENT FROM THE ARTIST

My basic philosophy of wood has developed during a period of almost fifty years. It comes from a deep and abiding love of wood: its diversity, color, grain, and texture are constantly fascinating. Each piece is like human fingerprints: no two pieces are alike.

In the beginning we thought we had to use wood without defects. I turned more of the traditional forms and shapes, creating thick and heavy pieces.

In the early 1940s I found a source of wood at a large veneer mill. I rummaged through their scrap pile and found the spurs from the logs they had cut for veneer. These spurs are the enlarged areas of the tree next to its roots. The spurs would range from two inches to ten inches in thickness. Generally this was green wood, but I could not wait to put it on the lathe to see the beauty of each piece. From these irregular shapes of wood came the bowls I called *free form,* but which are now termed *natural edge.* The more knotty, craggy, and knurly the piece the more it excited me. I discovered while turning some of this green wood that the thinner I turned it the less likely it was to crack. The drying period would also cause the turned vessel to become distorted, resulting in some very unusual shapes.

I decided that the design of a piece need not be modern or traditional for its own sake. Instead, design should be a simplified whole that balances ornament against plain surface. Over the many years I have been working in wood, I have steadily moved in the direction of achieving a pure, simple, unadorned style containing a sense of proportion and perfect balance between material, purpose, and contour.

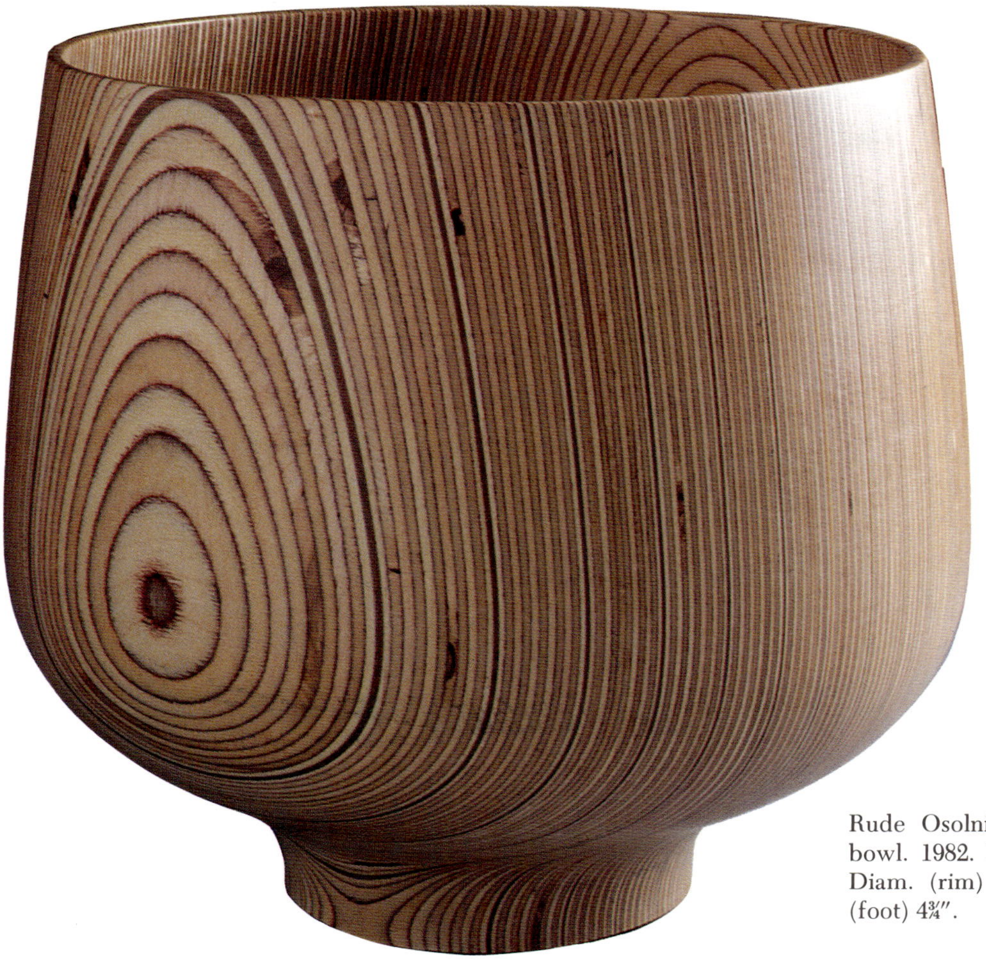

Rude Osolnik: Deep footed "artichoke" bowl. 1982. Laminated wood. H. 9 13/16″; Diam. (rim) 9¾″; Thickness .212″; Base (foot) 4¾″.

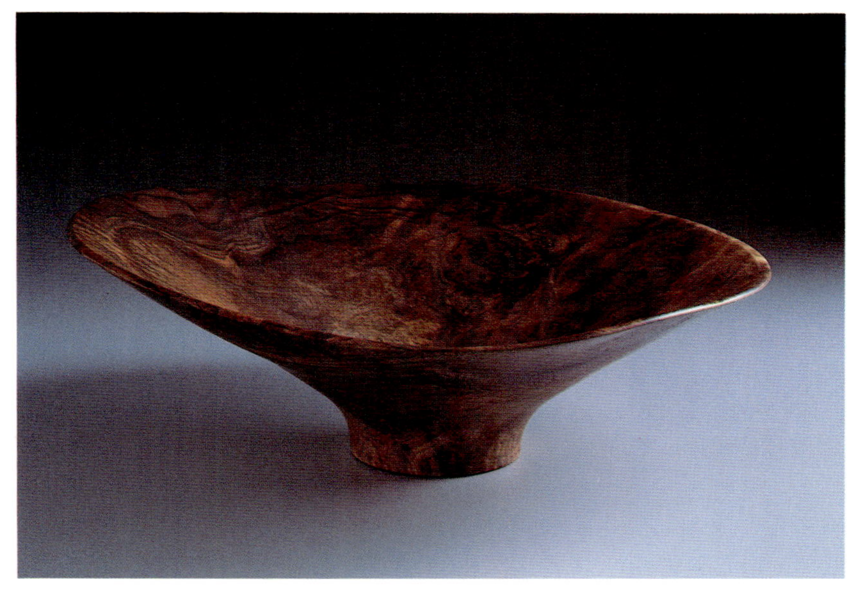

Rude Osolnik: Large footed bowl. 1982. Walnut burl. H. 4⅛″–5¼″; Diam. (rim) 15 1/16″–15 11/16″; Thickness .157″; Base (foot) 3 13/16″.

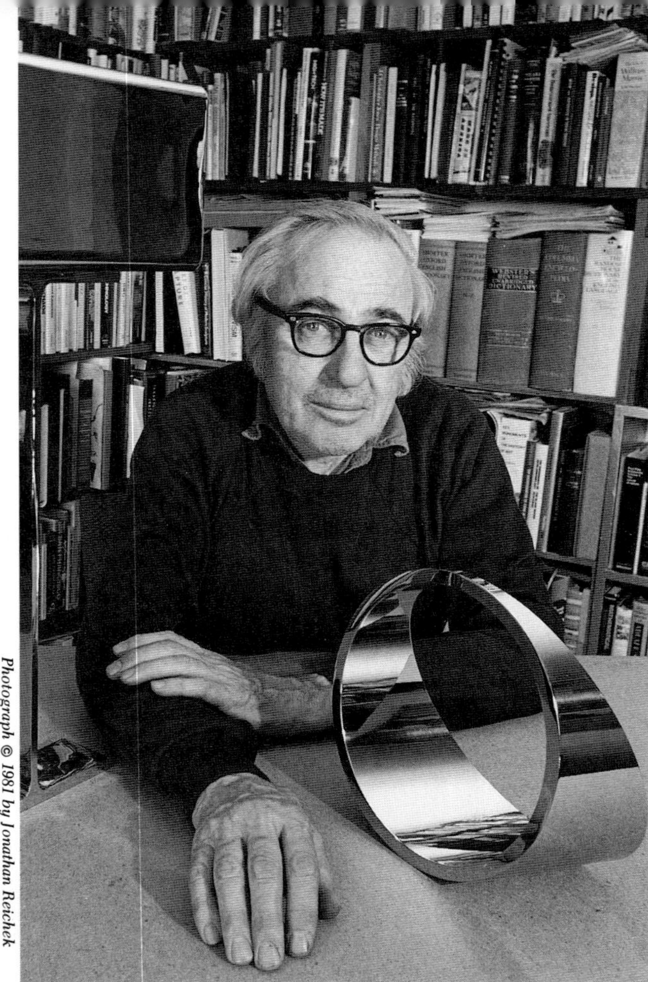

Photograph © 1981 by Jonathan Reichek

JAMES PRESTINI

2324 Blake Street
Berkeley, California 94704

Universally acknowledged as one of the greatest masters of wood turning, James Prestini has spent a lifetime in the field of engineering, design, art, wood turning, and sculpture. Mr. Prestini took his B.S. in Mechanical Engineering at Yale University in 1930, and has taught in several fields. During the years 1939–1946 he was instructor of Design, Institute of Design at Illinois Institute of Technology, Chicago; from 1943–1946 he was assistant research engineer at the Armour Research Foundation, Illinois Institute of Technology; from 1956–1975 Mr. Prestini was first lecturer in Design and then professor of Design (and now professor emeritus) at the University of California, Berkeley. It was during the years 1933–1953 in Chicago that Mr. Prestini concentrated on wood turning. His pieces are included in innumerable public, private, and corporate collections throughout the United States, including The Cleveland Museum of Art, Cleveland, Ohio; Albright-Knox Art Gallery, Buffalo, New York; The Museum of Modern Art, New York City; The Metropolitan Museum of Art, New York City; Walker Art Center, Minneapolis, Minnesota; The Art Institute of Chicago; Museum of Fine Arts, Boston; Philadelphia Museum of Art; National Collection of Fine Arts, Smithsonian Institution, Washington, D.C. His work has been included in many one-man and group shows through the years. The most recent solo show was held in 1983 at Lake Forest Academy, Lake Forest, Illinois; and his work was also shown in 1983 in several group shows at The Brooklyn Museum, The Art Institute of Chicago, The Metropolitan Museum of Art, and Philadelphia Museum of Art. Mr. Prestini's art has been the subject of a great many articles through the years, and he has been the author of many articles based on his several fields.

STATEMENT FROM THE ARTIST

Ideas and Crafts. The ultimate in human performance is the making of ideas. Makers are the all-important segment of all cultures. Makers make. They make ideas, make understanding, make themselves. In addition to contributing to society, makers benefit the most from the making process. Are you working to live? Or are you living to work? Makers live to work!

The three H's make man:

1. Heart
2. Head
3. Hand

The more the integration, the more the man. *Heart* has to do with the spirit. What good is it if you are the world's greatest craftsman without being socially responsible? *Head* has to do with ideas that develop understanding. *Hand* is the implementation of the spirit through ideas by making. Making makes possible the use of all your human resources: Spirit, Mind, Body. These are three different factors for making understanding—understanding your work, understanding you. Totality of development can come only through the integration of all three factors.

By way of analysis, there are three types of artists:

1. Photographer
2. Painter
3. Sculptor

The *photographer* sees his making. The *painter* draws his making. The *sculptor* makes his making. Therefore, the *sculptor*, the master maker, can develop more fully all his resources.

Wood turning was utilized as an important stage in my development. My approach to wood turning was making through sculpture. Wood turning limited my sculpture to making circles. I left the lathe to be freer in exploring more fully the development of form (content), the structure of art. Wood turning served an important generic step for fuller development of ideas.

Nothing can express the aim and meaning of our work better than the profound words of St. Augustine: "Beauty is the Splendor of Truth."

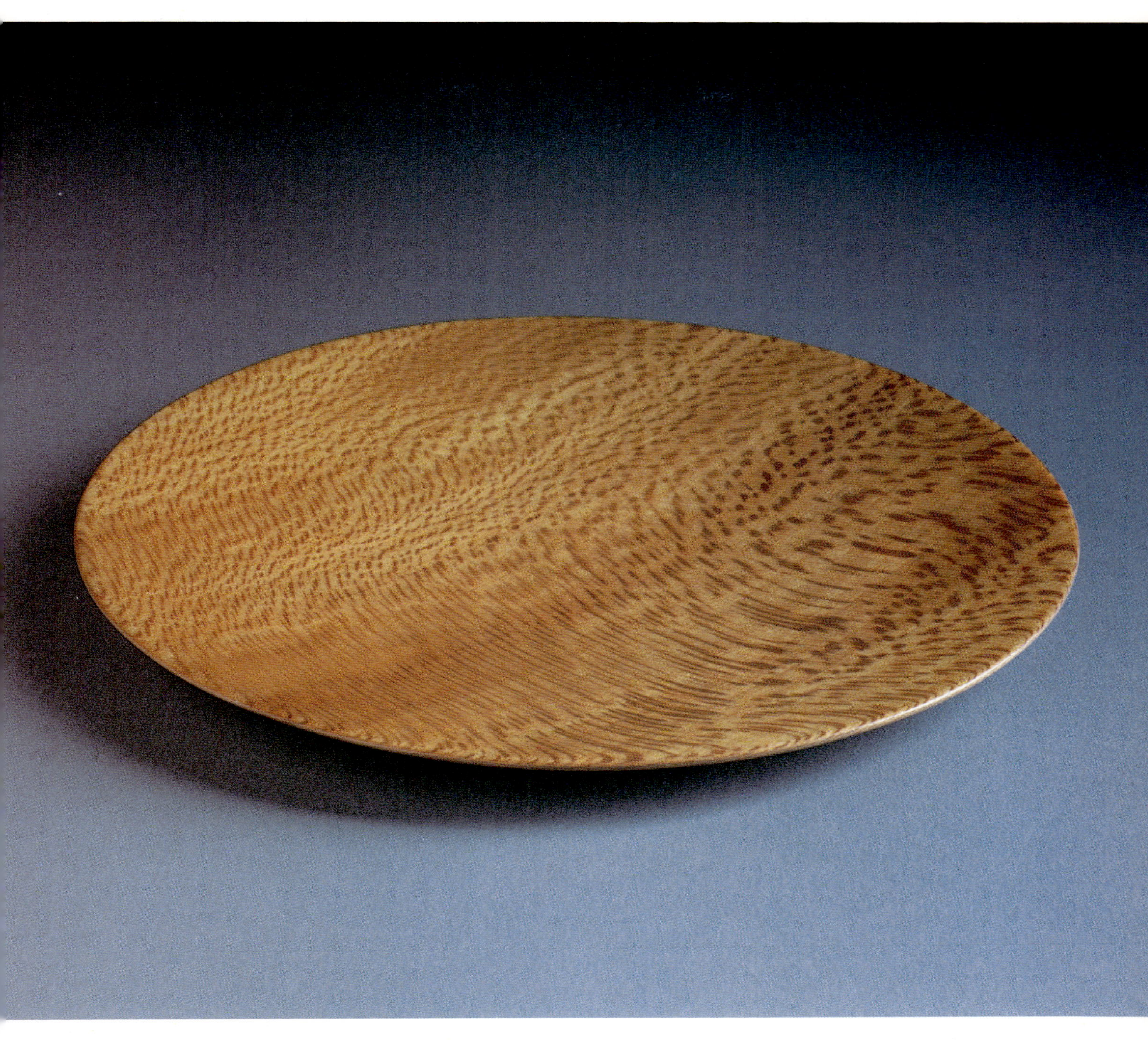

James Prestini: Small plate. 1933–1953 (Chicago). Sycamore. H. ½″; Diam. (rim) 6⁵⁄₁₆″; Thickness .09″.

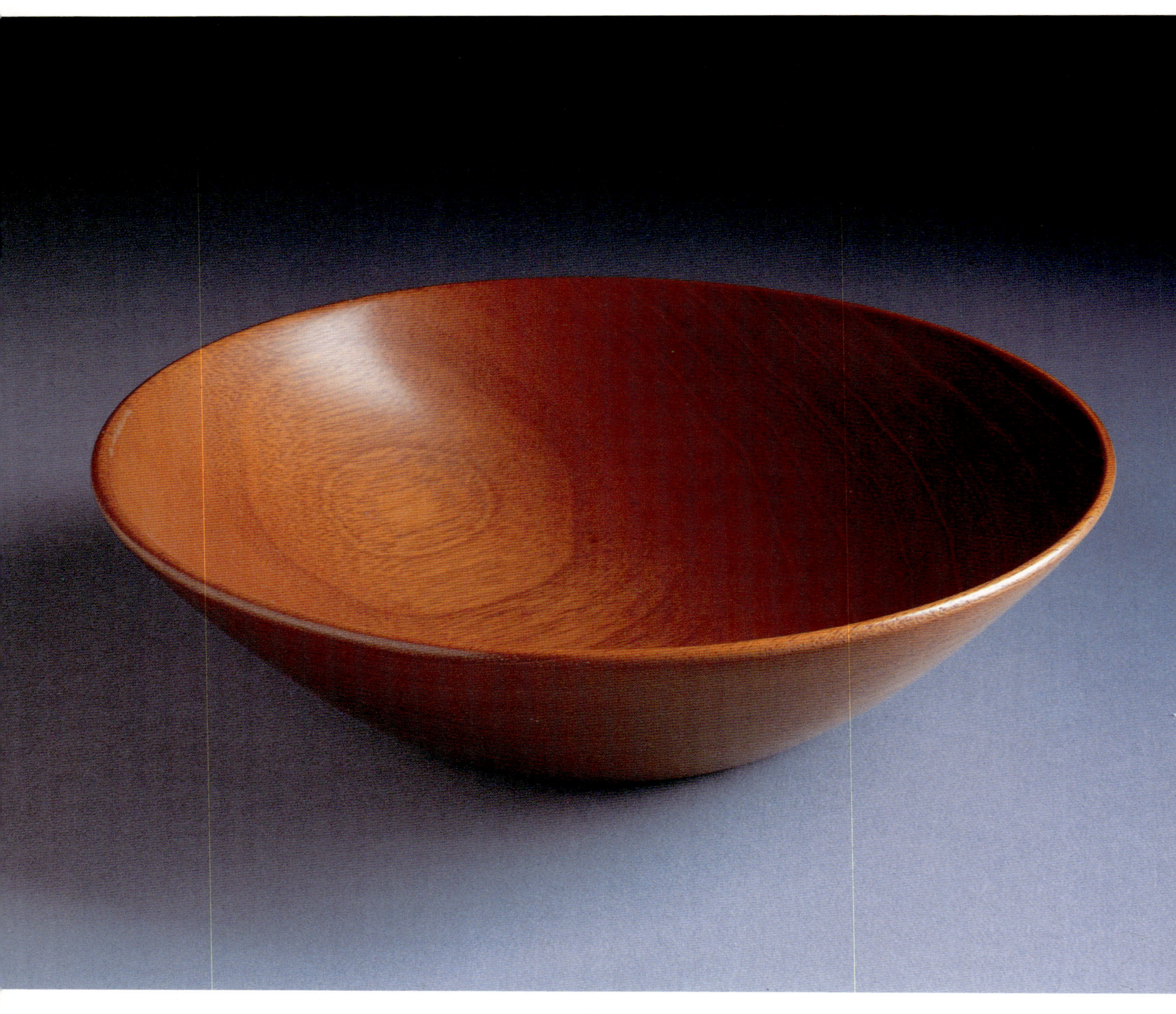

James Prestini: Medium-size round bowl. 1933-1953 (Chicago). Mexican mahogany. H. 1¹⁵⁄₁₆″; Diam. (rim) 7½″; Thickness .158″; Base 3⁹⁄₁₆″.

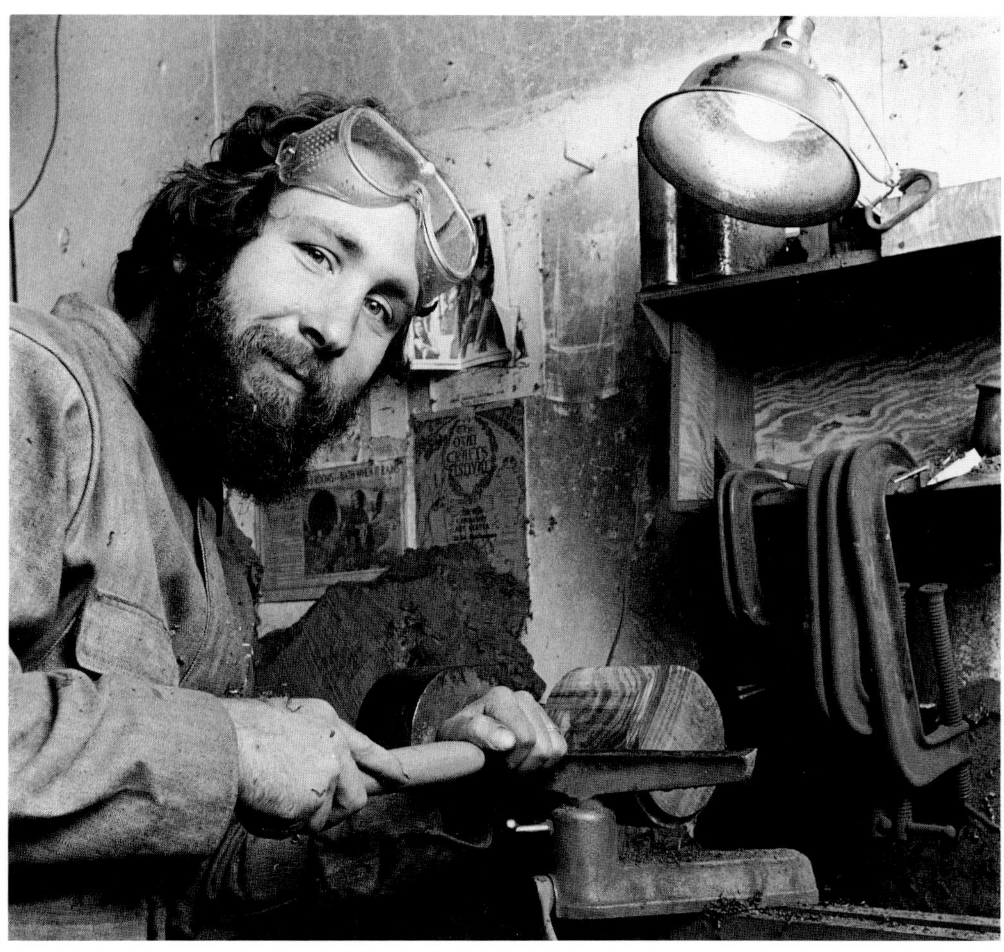

HAP SAKWA

1330 8th Street
Baywood Park, California 93402

In the mid-1960s Hap Sakwa attended the Hershey Industrial School, where he first acquired the skills of craftsmanship and self-discipline. While attending the University of Maryland, Mr. Sakwa became interested in the craft movement and began working in leather, opening his first shop in 1970. His interest in crafts increased after his return to California in 1972, and in 1975 he began working in wood. First concentrating on small lathe-turned objects, he later employed direct-carving techniques, exploring new ways of combining technology and the natural beauty of the material to create lasting and beautiful works of art.

Hap Sakwa's pieces have been exhibited widely, including the following: California State Exposition, Sacramento; Monterey Peninsula Museum of Art; Makers Gallery, New York City; Craftsman's Gallery, Scarsdale, New York; Westlake Gallery, White Plains, New York; Gallery Eight, La Jolla, California; Works Gallery, Philadelphia; Detroit Gallery of Contemporary Crafts; Craft Alliance Gallery, St. Louis, Missouri; Great American Gallery, Atlanta, Georgia; Artisans Guild Gallery, Mendocino, California; The American Artisan Gallery, Nashville, Tennessee; Cooper-Hewitt Museum, New York City. His work has also been published in *Fine Woodworking, American Crafts: A Source for the Home,* and *American Craft.*

STATEMENT FROM THE ARTIST

It's funny (for me) that all this energy about turning is happening at the time when my own interests are moving in a different direction. For the past year and a half I have been focusing most of my energy into sculpture, for I am finding the creative possibilities of turning very limited. This may be my own self-imposed limitations, but they are there nonetheless. I am still turning, but I am finding a great deal of satisfaction in the more sculptural work I'm doing.

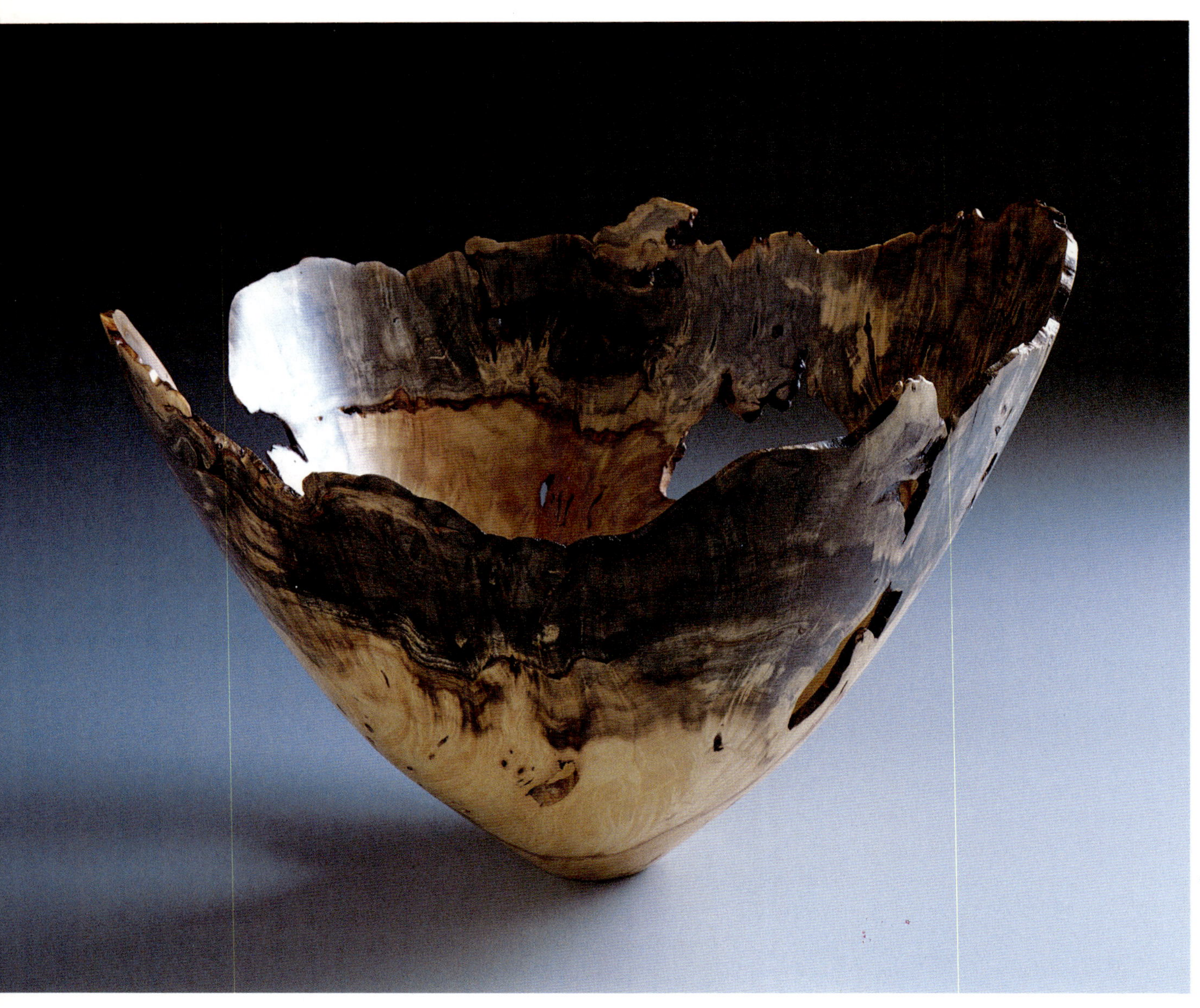

Hap Sakwa: Tapering bowl. 1983. Buckeye. H. 6¾″–9¼″; Diam. (rim) 12⁹⁄₁₆″–13⁷⁄₁₆″; Thickness .050″; Base 1⅞″.

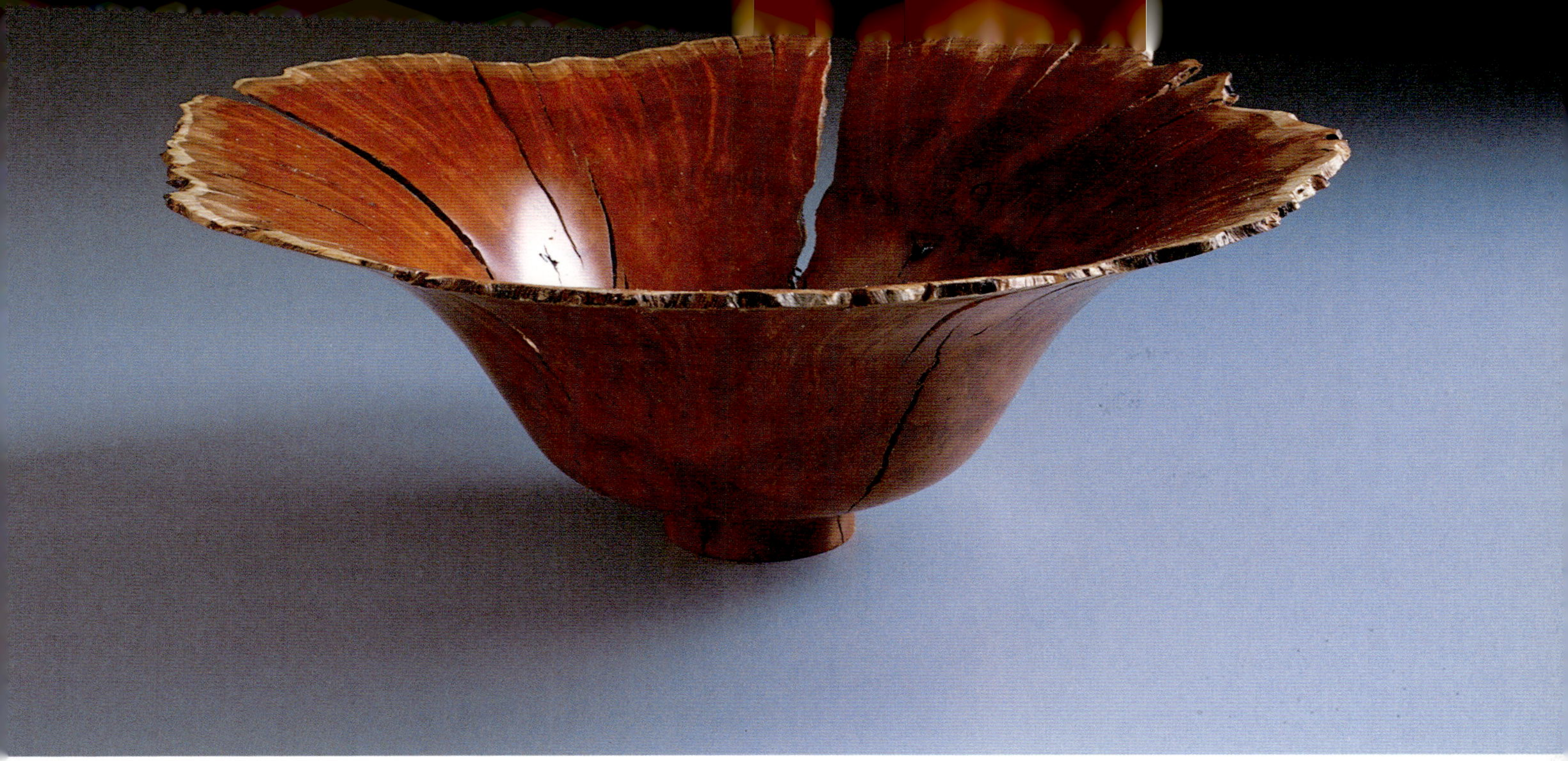

Hap Sakwa: Flower-shaped bowl. 1982. Wild lilac. H. 4¼″–4⅝″; Diam. (rim) 12″–13¼″; Thickness .106″; Base (foot) $2\,^{3}/_{16}$″.

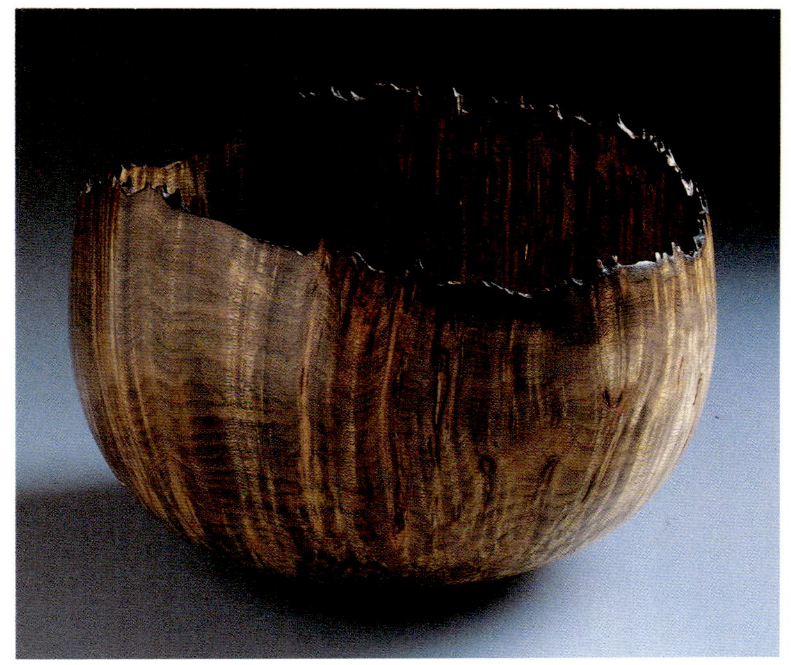

Hap Sakwa: Hemispherical bowl. 1982. Myrtlewood. H. 5¼″–6⅝″; Diam. (rim) $9\,^{7}/_{16}$″–$9\,^{9}/_{16}$″; Thickness .141″.

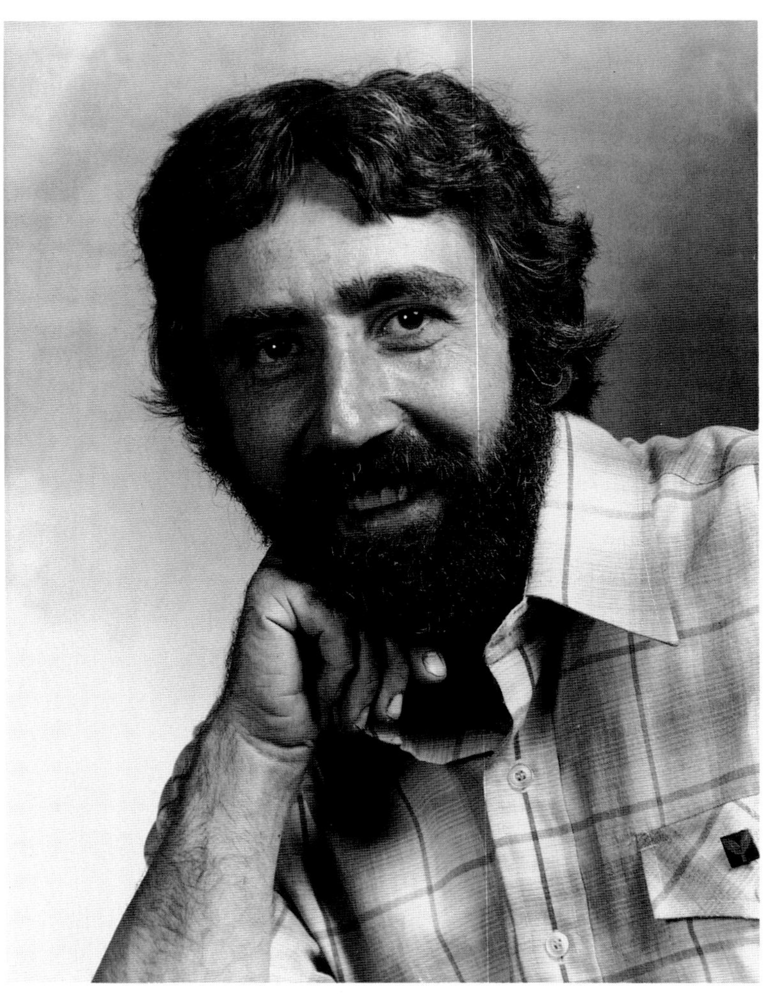

ALAN STIRT

R.D. 4
Enosburg Falls, Vermont 05450

Alan Stirt has a B.A. in psychology from the State University of New York at Binghamton. He started wood turning in 1970 and is completely self-taught in this field.

Mr. Stirt is currently being represented by the following galleries: Appalachian Spring, Washington, D.C.; Jackie Chalkley, Washington, D.C.; The Elements, Greenwich, Connecticut; Frog Hollow Craft Center, Middlebury, Vermont; Gallery Eight, La Jolla, California; The Hand and The Spirit Crafts Gallery, Scottsdale, Arizona; Neiman Marcus, Boston and Dallas; Ten Arrow, Cambridge, Massachusetts; Helen Winnemore Gallery, Columbus, Ohio; The Works, Philadelphia.

STATEMENT FROM THE ARTIST

I became interested in wood turning through a direct emotional response to the beauty of wood. I still remember the excitement I felt on seeing a photograph of one of James Prestini's bowls. That ash bowl opened for me the possibilities of the beauty that could be exposed through the use of simple turned forms. This has remained my primary concern, overshadowing the concerns of technique and personal statement. Over the years I feel that I have developed a rapport with the material so that my best pieces are a collaboration between the wood and myself.

Aside from visual beauty I want my pieces to reveal themselves by being touched. The surface and weight of a bowl should enhance the aspects revealed by the grain and shape. It is important to me that many of my bowls are functional, for I believe that beautiful objects can enhance the lives of those that use them.

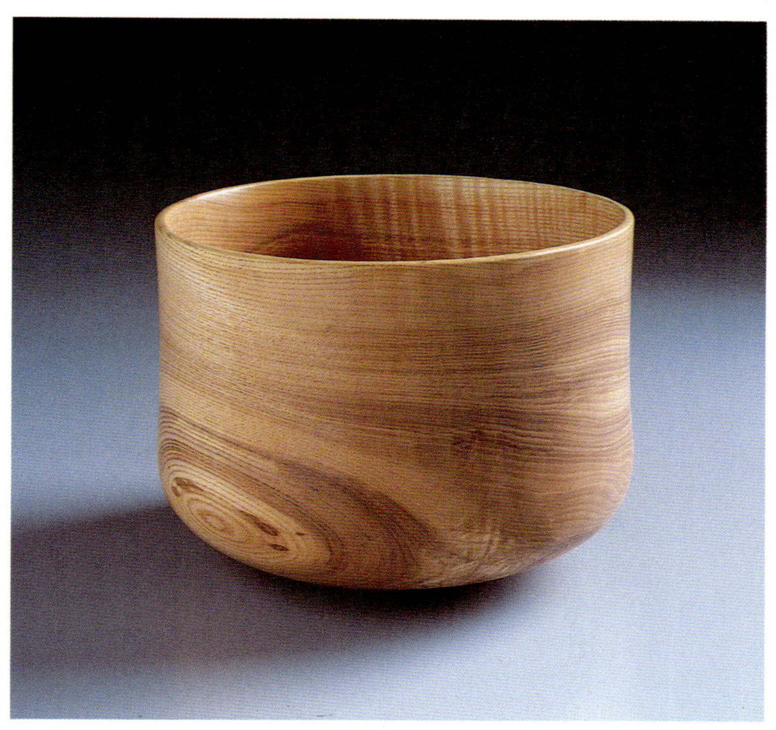

Alan Stirt: Straight-sided bowl. 1982. White ash crotch. H. 5½″; Diam. (rim) 7⁵⁄₁₆″; Thickness .225″; Base (foot) 3⅛″.

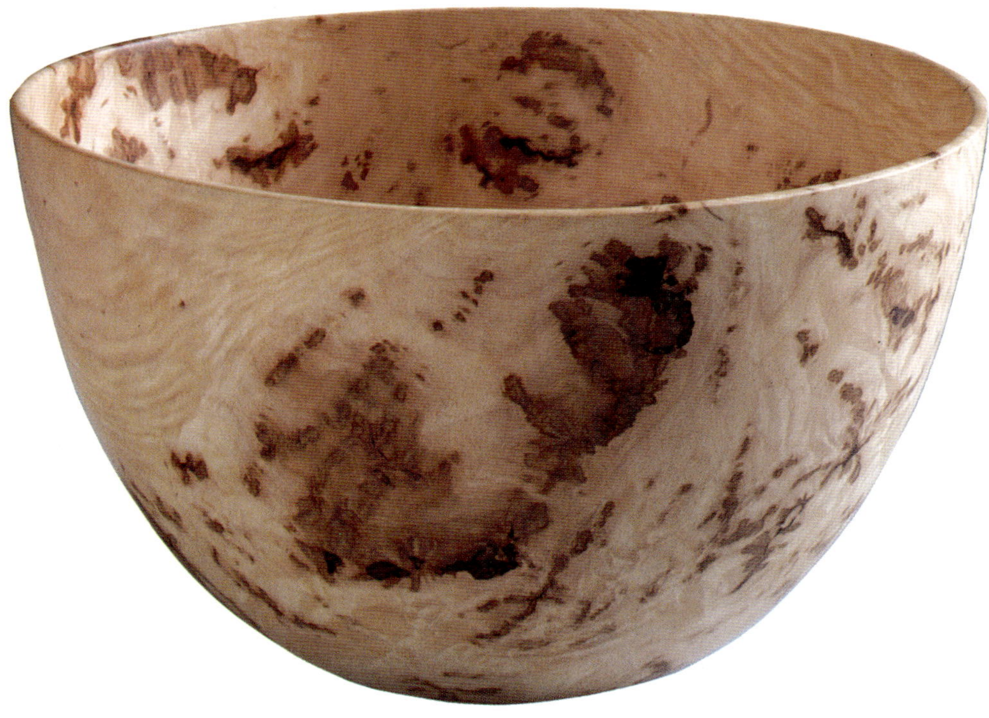

Alan Stirt: Medium-size mottled bowl. 1982. Hop hornbeam burl. H. 4⁵⁄₁₆″; Diam. (rim) 7³⁄₁₆″; Thickness .131″; Base 1¹⁵⁄₁₆″.

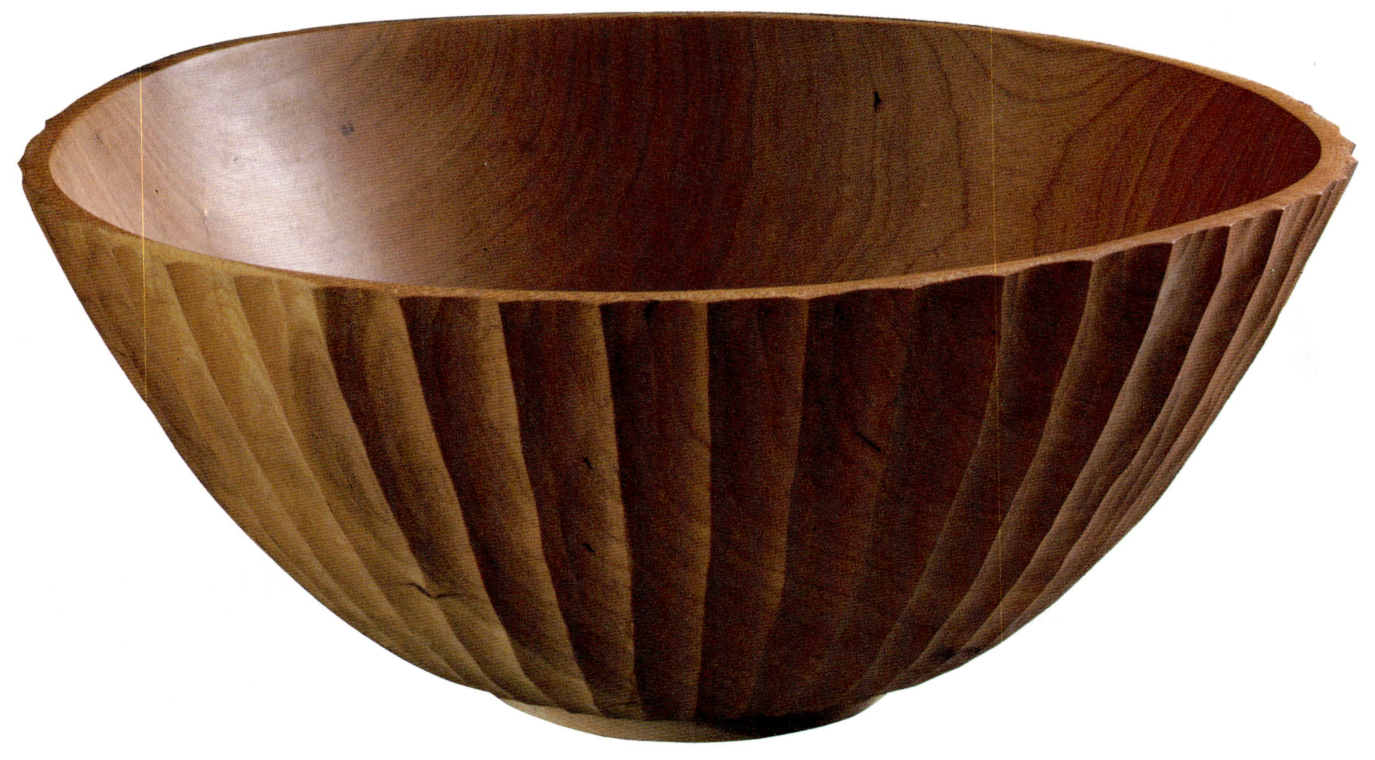

Alan Stirt: Fluted bowl. 1982. Black cherry. H. 4½″; Diam. (rim) 10″; Thickness .225″; Base (foot) 3 5/16″.

Alan Stirt: Medium-size bowl. 1980. Yellow birch burl. H. 3 11/16″; Diam. (rim) 7 1/16″; Thickness .203″; Base (foot) 2 5/16″.

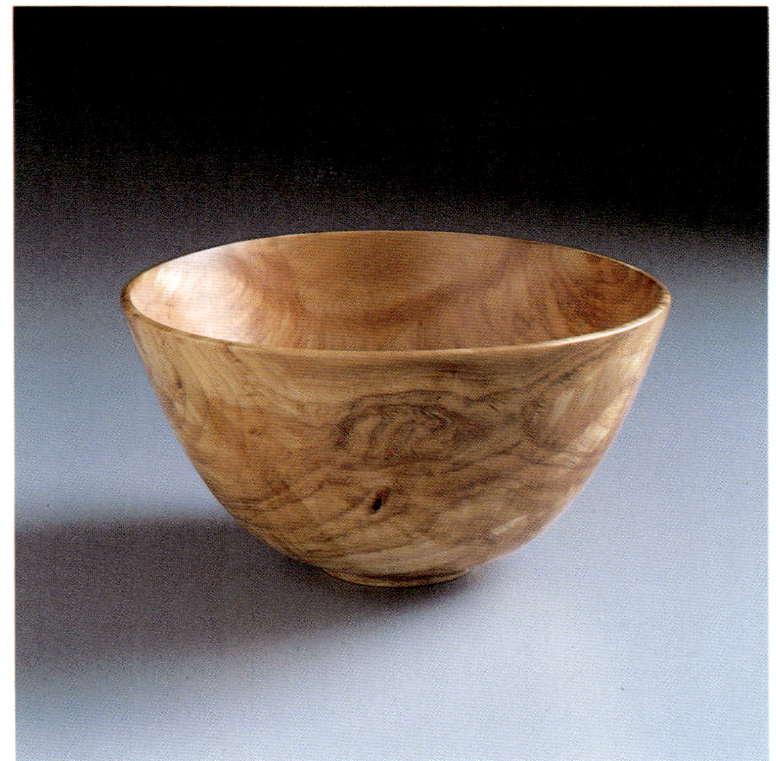

Alan Stirt: Large bowl. 1982. Butternut. H. 6 13/16″; Diam. (rim) 14 15/16″; Thickness .256″; Base (foot) 5⅛″.

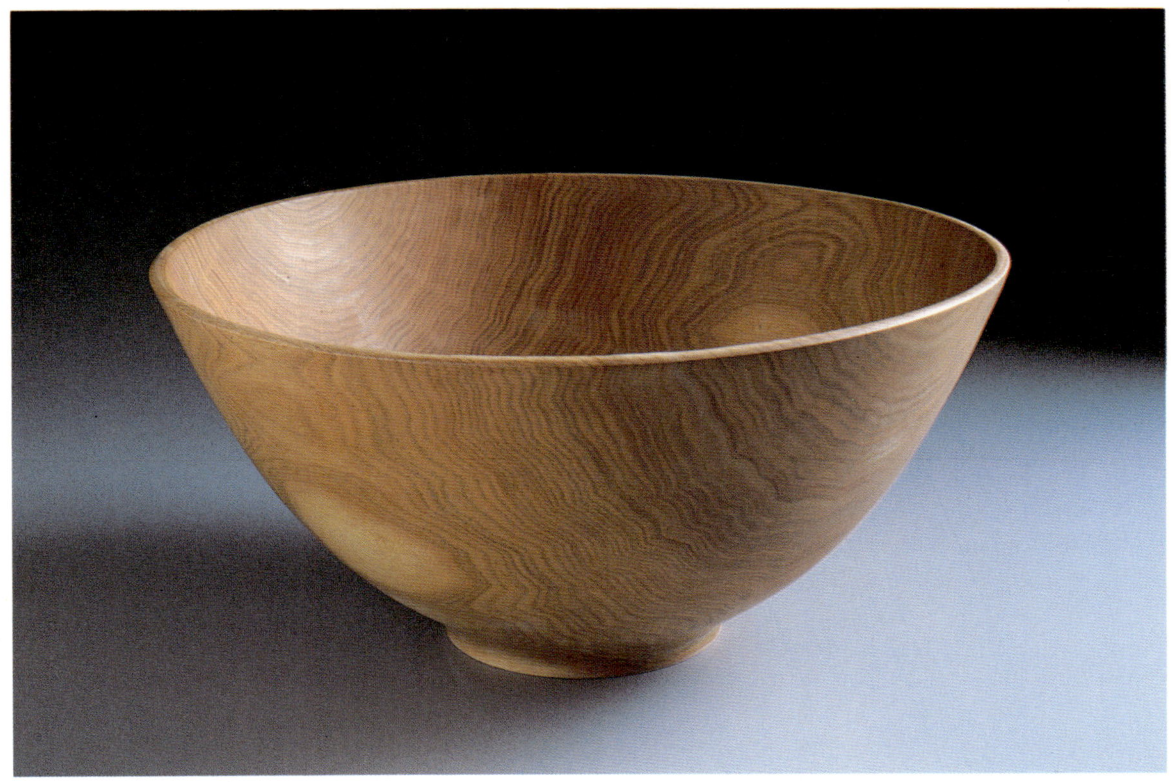

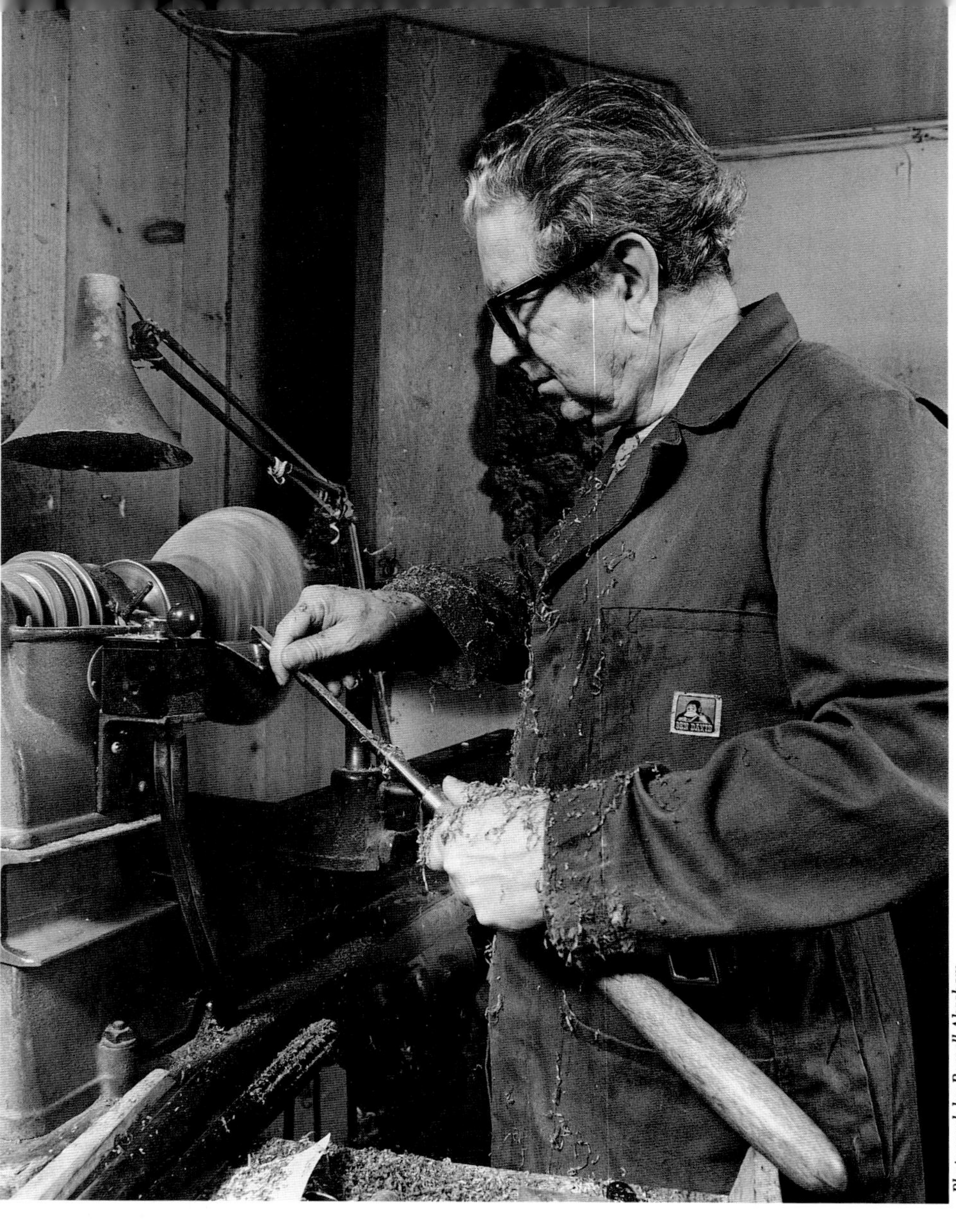

Photograph by Russell Abraham

BOB STOCKSDALE

2145 Oregon
Berkeley, California 94705

A self-taught artist, Bob Stocksdale has participated in the following workshops and seminars in wood turning, among others: Rhode Island School of Design, Providence (1980); Boston University Program in Artisanry (1980); Greenwood Gallery Workshop, Washington, D.C. (1980); International Seminar for Wood Turners, Parnham House, Dorset, England (1980); Mr. Stocksdale's work has been included in the following group and solo exhibitions: Capricorn Asunder Gallery, San Francisco (1980); "American Crafts, 1977," Philadelphia Museum of Art; "The Turned Object," Museum of Contemporary Crafts, New York City (1982–1983); "Living Treasures of California," Crocker Art Gallery, Sacramento, California (1985); Oakland Museum, Oakland, California (1981); Helen Winnemore Gallery, Columbus, Ohio (1981); Contemporary Artisans Gallery, San Francisco, California (1983). Mr. Stocksdale's art is included in the following public collections: Museum of Fine Arts, Boston; Royal Scottish Museum, Edinburgh; Parnham House, Dorset, England; Oakland Museum, Oakland, California; American Craft Museum, New York City; Philadelphia Museum of Art.

STATEMENT FROM THE ARTIST

I work with the rarest woods in the world as well as many common types. My goal is to discover unusual grains and colors in any wood that I work with.

The forms are developed on the lathe, for many times I have to change my initial design to eliminate flaws in the piece of wood. I do not turn bowls as thin as I could, for I try first to give the piece strength and durability and then thinness without being fragile.

Bob Stocksdale: Shallow ellipsoid bowl. 1982. Putumuzu. H. 1½″–2⁹/₁₆″; Diam. (rim) 5⁷/₁₆″–7⁷/₁₆″; Thickness .130″; Base (foot) 1½″.

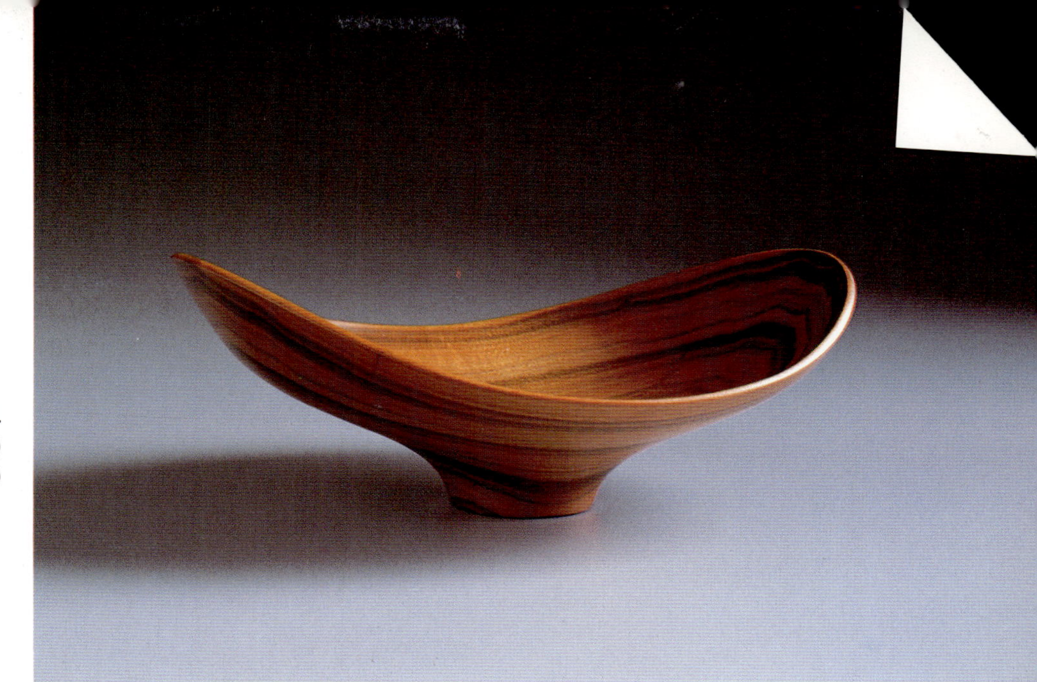

Bob Stocksdale: Medium-size footed bowl. 1980. Ebony. H. 3⁵/₁₆″; Diam. (rim) 8¼″; Thickness .147″; Base (foot) 3″.

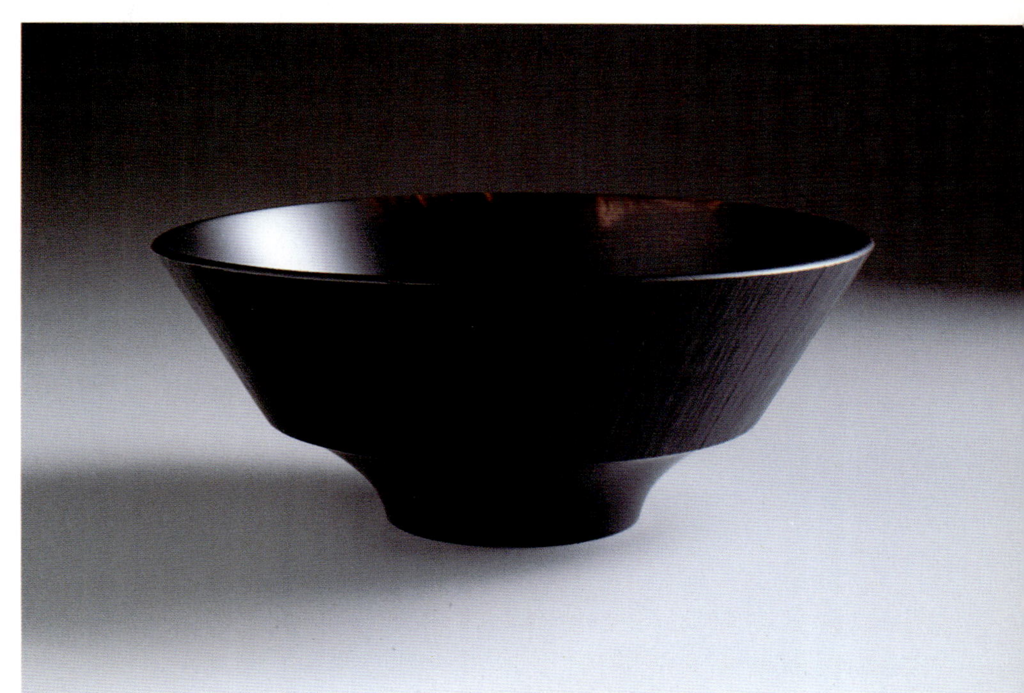

Bob Stocksdale: Ellipsoid footed bowl. 1981. Ebony. H. 2½″–3⁵/₁₆″; Diam. (rim) 5¹/₁₆″–6¹/₁₆″; Thickness .108; Base (foot) 1⁷/₁₆″.

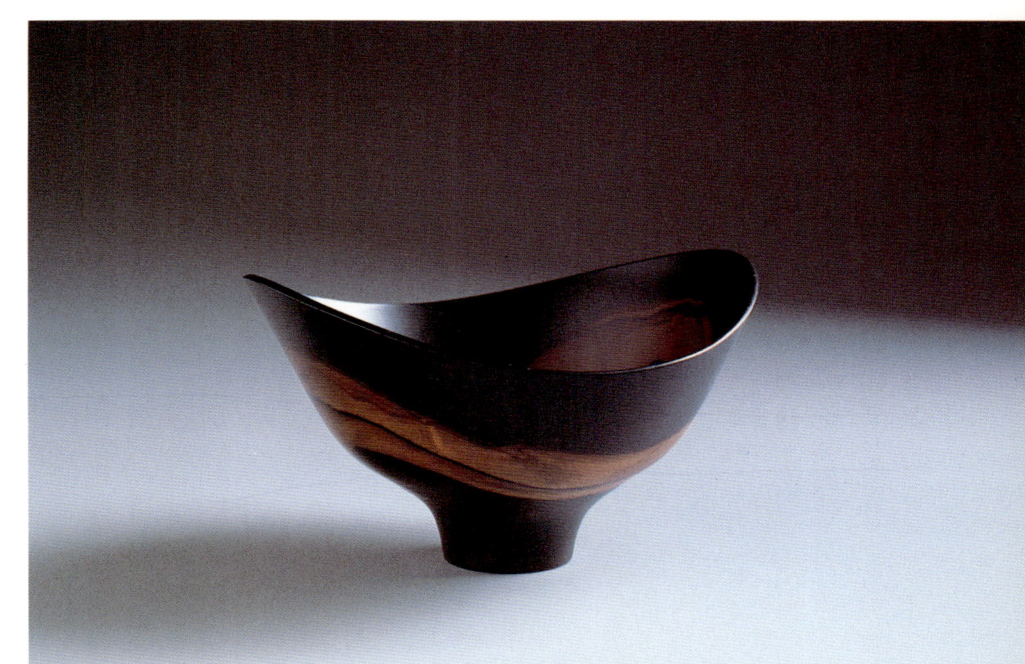

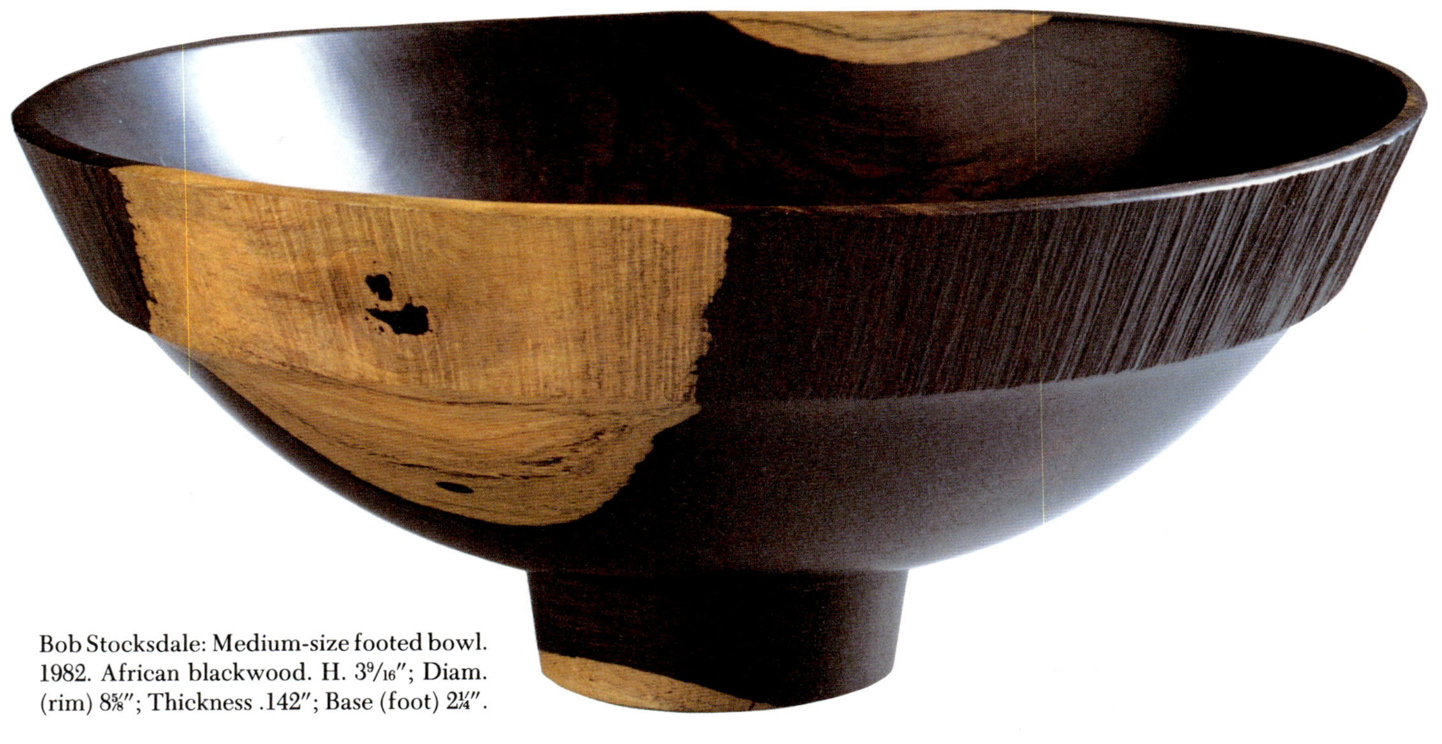

Bob Stocksdale: Medium-size footed bowl. 1982. African blackwood. H. 3 9/16″; Diam. (rim) 8 5/8″; Thickness .142″; Base (foot) 2 1/4″.

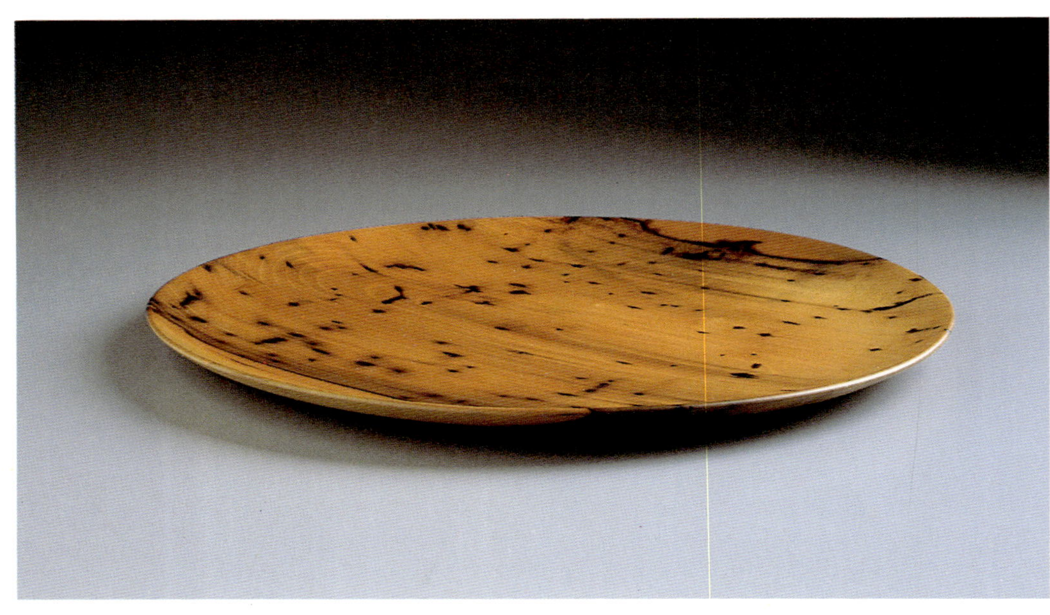

Bob Stocksdale: Flat plate. 1980. Magnolia. H. 11/16″; Diam. (rim) 13″; Thickness .151″; Base (foot) 8 1/16″.

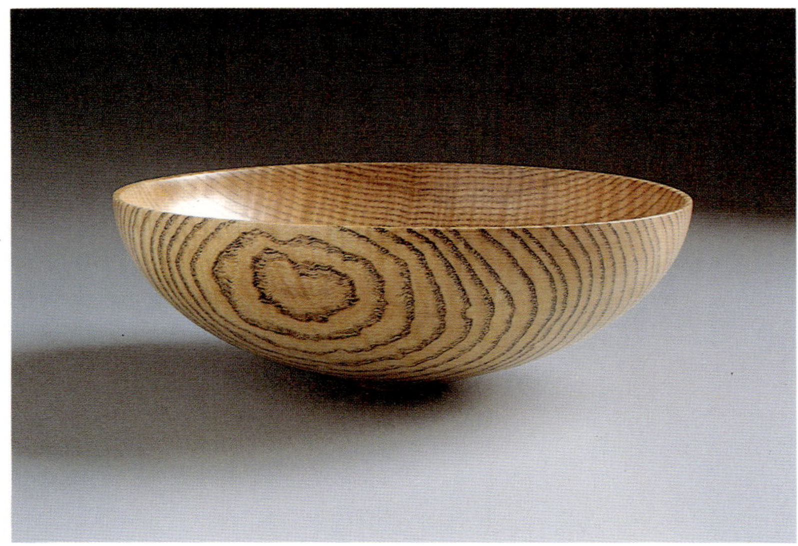

Bob Stocksdale: Medium-size shallow bowl. 1982. Ash. H. $2\frac{9}{16}''$; Diam. (rim) $7\frac{3}{4}''$; Thickness .101″; Base $1\frac{3}{16}''$.

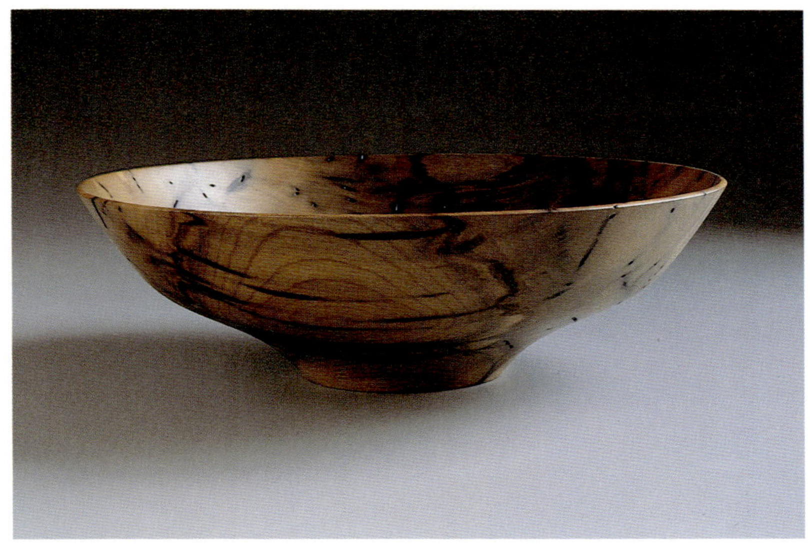

Bob Stocksdale: Medium-size bowl. 1980. Magnolia. H. $3\frac{3}{16}''$; Diam. (rim) $10\frac{1}{2}''$; Thickness .130″; Base (foot) $3\frac{5}{16}''$.

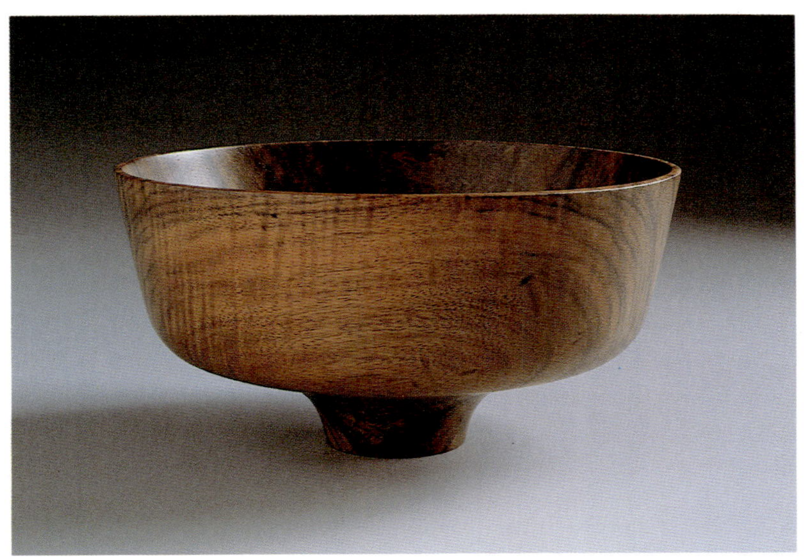

Bob Stocksdale: Medium-size bowl with pedestal foot. 1982. Laurel. H. $3\frac{5}{8}''$; Diam. (rim) $7\frac{1}{8}''$; Thickness .108″; Base (foot) $1\frac{13}{16}''$.

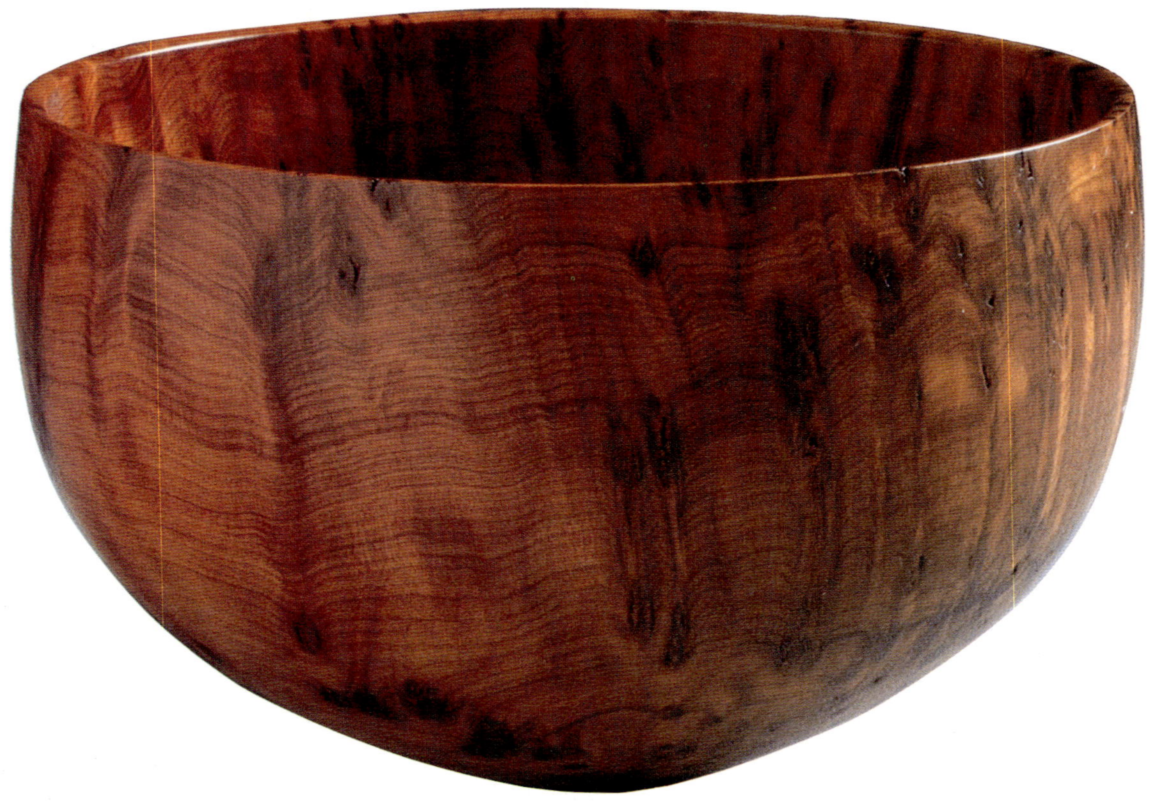

Bob Stocksdale: Medium-size bowl. 1981. Thuya burl. H. 3 7/16″; Diam. (rim) 5 11/16″; Thickness .134″; Base 2¼″.

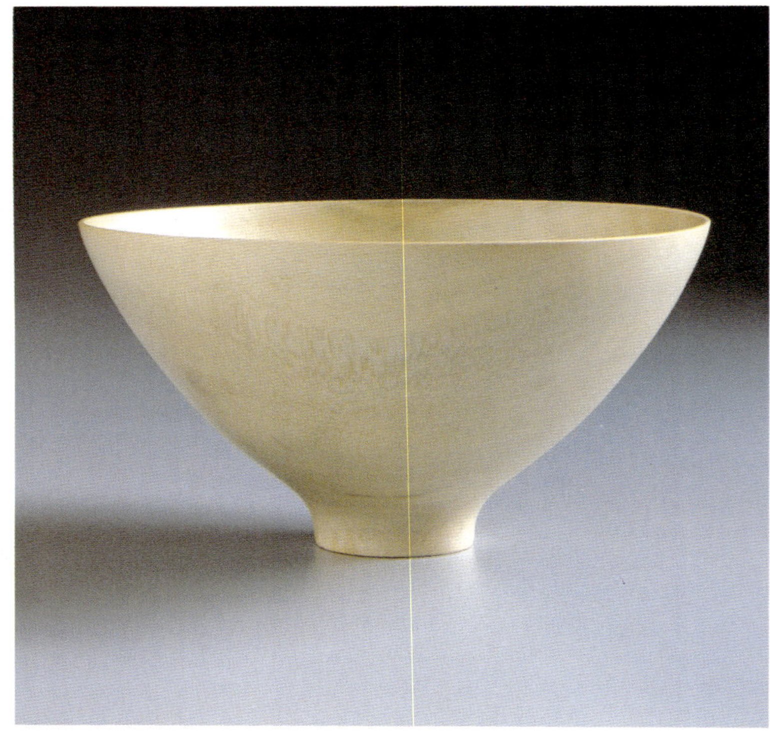

Bob Stocksdale: Small footed bowl. 1982. Holly. H. 3 1/16″; Diam. (rim) 6″; Thickness .074″; Base (foot) 1½″.

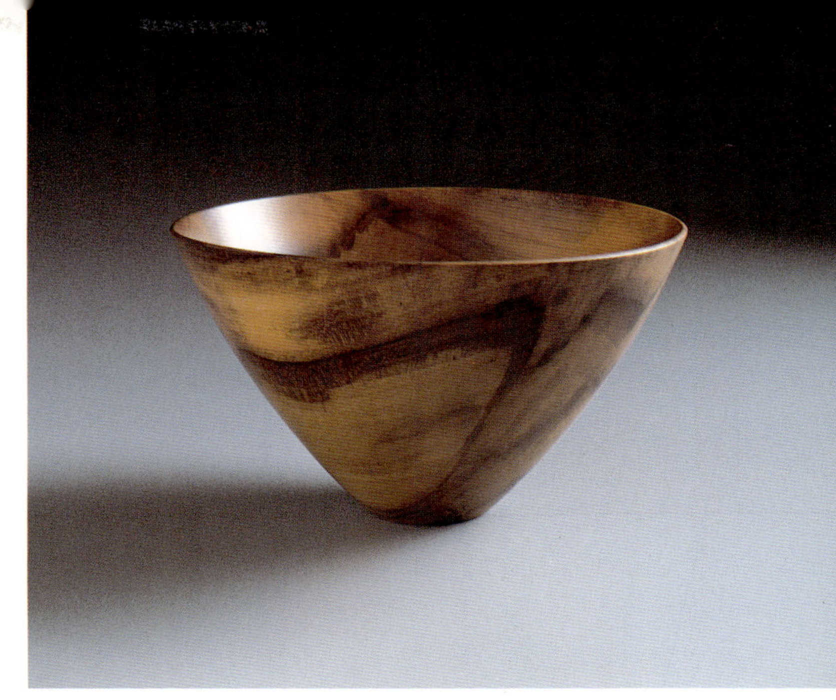

Bob Stocksdale: Medium-size tapering bowl. 1980. Magnolia. H. 3⅞″; Diam. (rim) 6⅞″; Thickness .097″; Base 1¾″.

Bob Stocksdale: Medium-size bowl with tall foot. 1979. Olivewood. H. 3½″; Diam. (rim) 8″; Thickness .097″; Base (foot) 2⅛″; H. of foot 1⅛″.

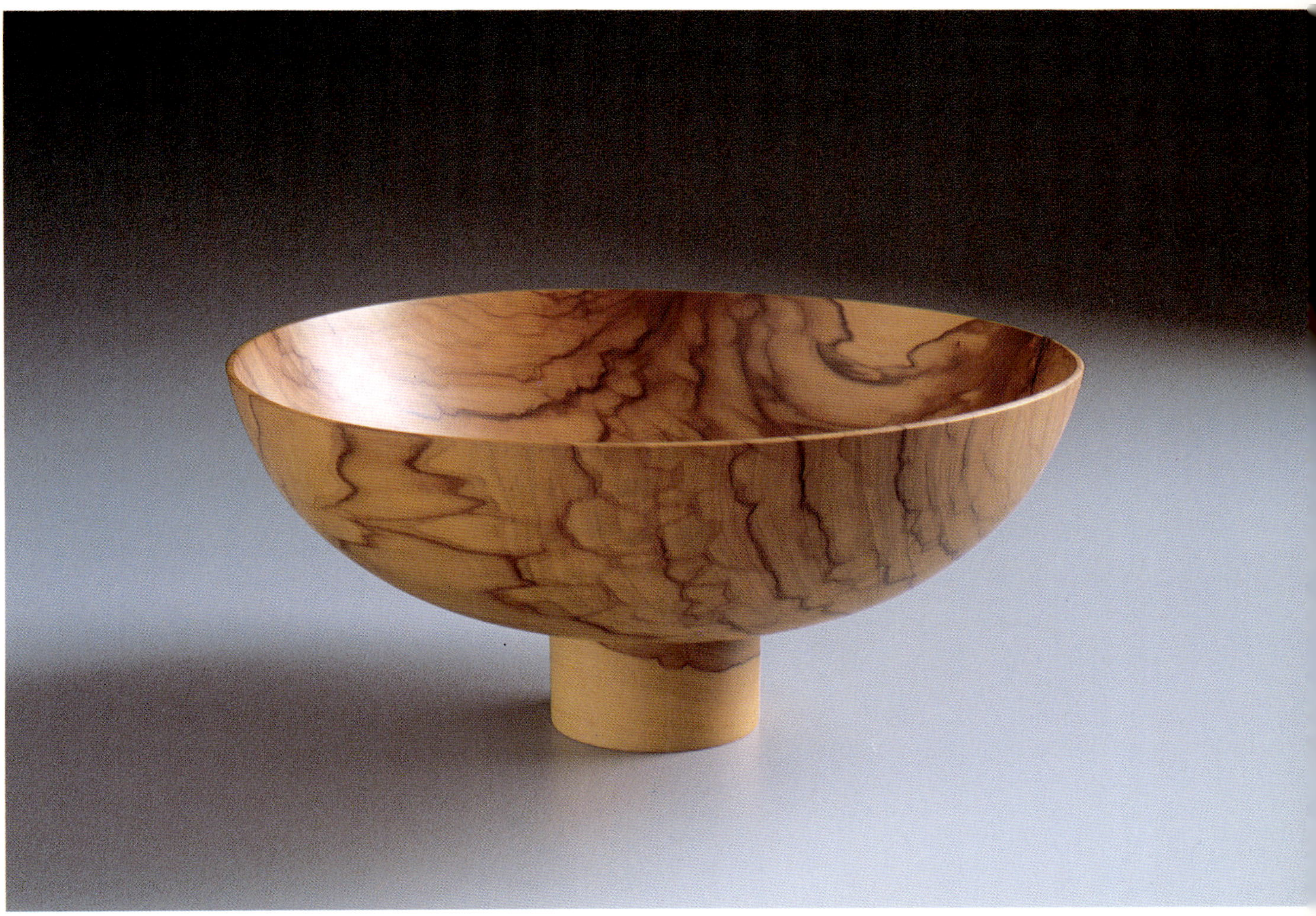

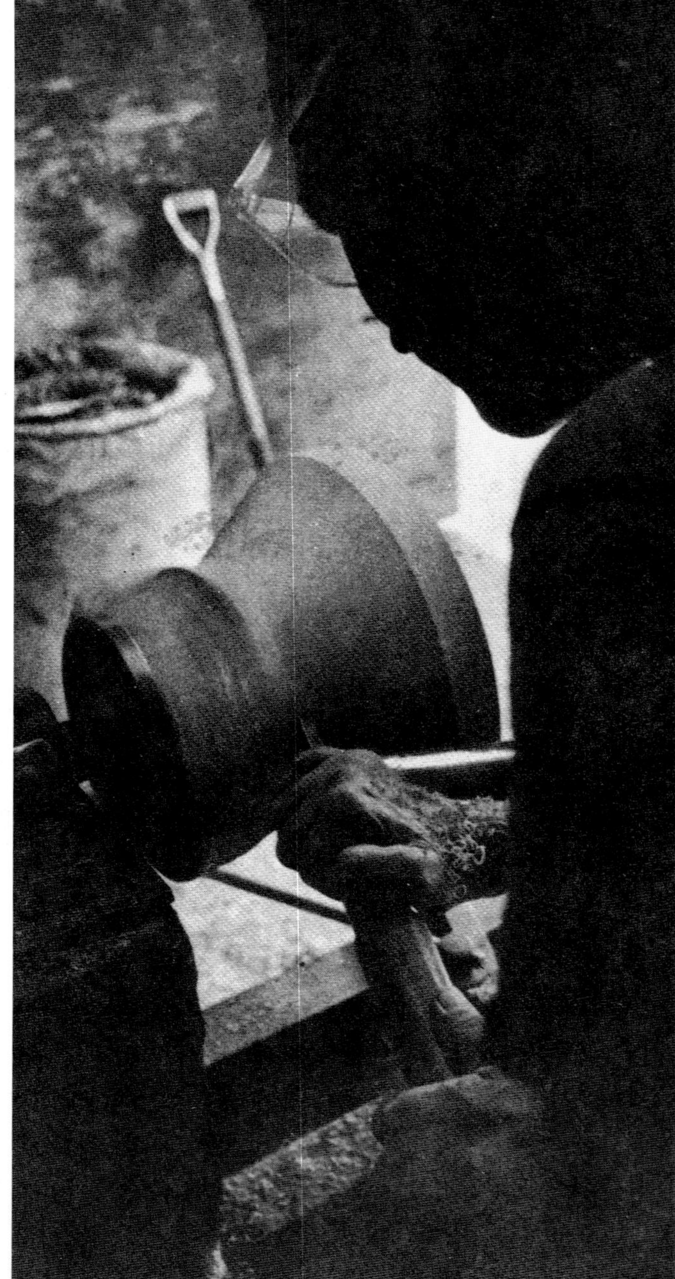

JACK STRAKA
SR 31 QQQ
Keaau, Hawaii 96749

Jack Straka, Big Island craftsman and one of Hawaii's finest woodturners, came to his craft not so long ago. During his eighteen years with the Burroughs Corporation, wood turning was just a hobby. However, feeling the need for a major change in his life, Straka turned toward wood and Hawaii. He studied with internationally known woodturner Peter Child in England. It was in England that Mr. Straka learned the cutting method of turning, rather than the more prevalent scraping method. The cutting method makes it possible to create thinner-walled bowls, a Straka hallmark, and does not chew up the wood, thus permitting a finer finish. Also, the cutting method makes it possible to turn bowls from soft woods. The beautiful satin finishes on Straka bowls are the result of four to six steps of sanding and then finishing with hand-rubbed oil.

Most of Mr. Straka's bowls and other wooden ware are executed in koa, a native Hawaiian wood, because of its beauty and availability. Koa is a dramatically grained wood that varies in tones from deep rosy brown to gold, and it was used by pre-European Hawaiians to fashion their massive canoes. Straka has successfully turned some fifty Hawaiian-grown woods, including lichee, Christmas berry, plumeria, mango, sandalwood, and other native woods like naio, mamani, milo, and hau. Carrying on a native Hawaiian tradition, Mr. Straka will occasionally punctuate the surface of his bowls with patches of fine inlays.

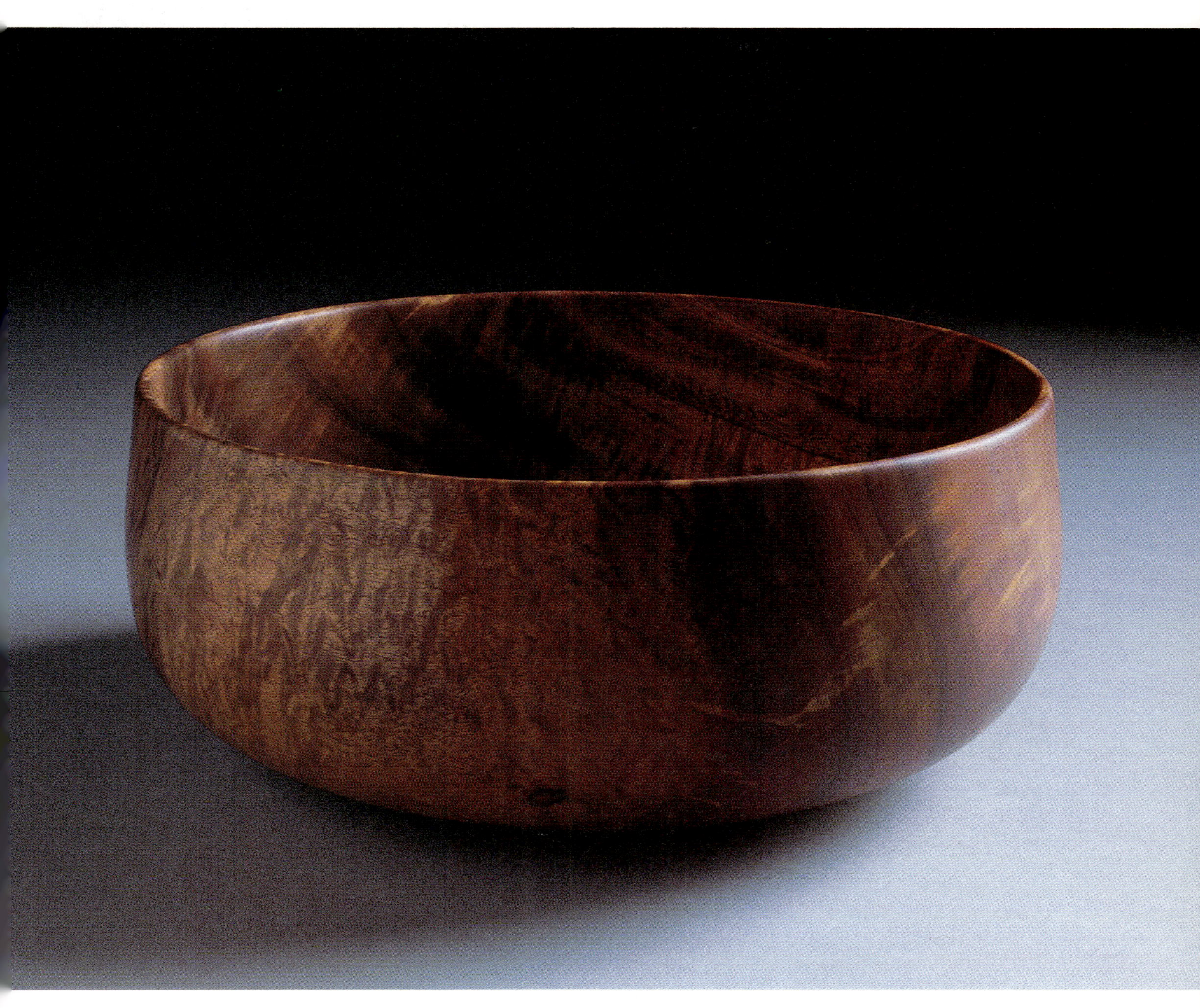

Jack Straka: Large poi bowl. 1984. Koa wood. H. 4 11/16″; Diam. (rim) 11″; Thickness .218″.

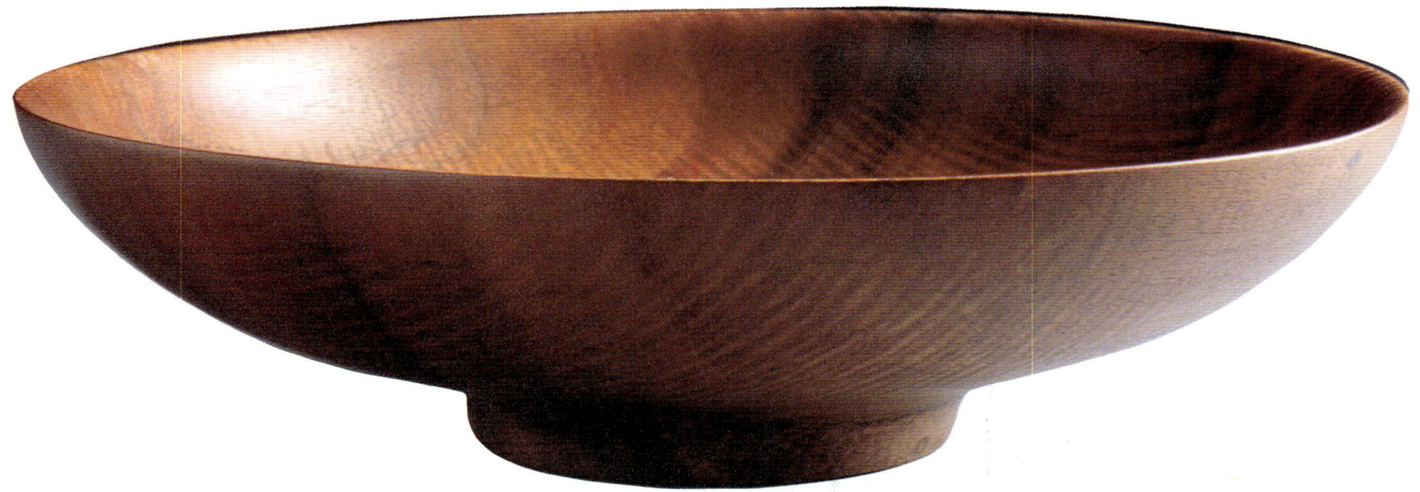

Jack Straka; Shallow footed bowl. 1984. Koa wood. H. 3 5/16″; Diam. (rim) 13″; Thickness .210″; Base (foot) 4⅝″.

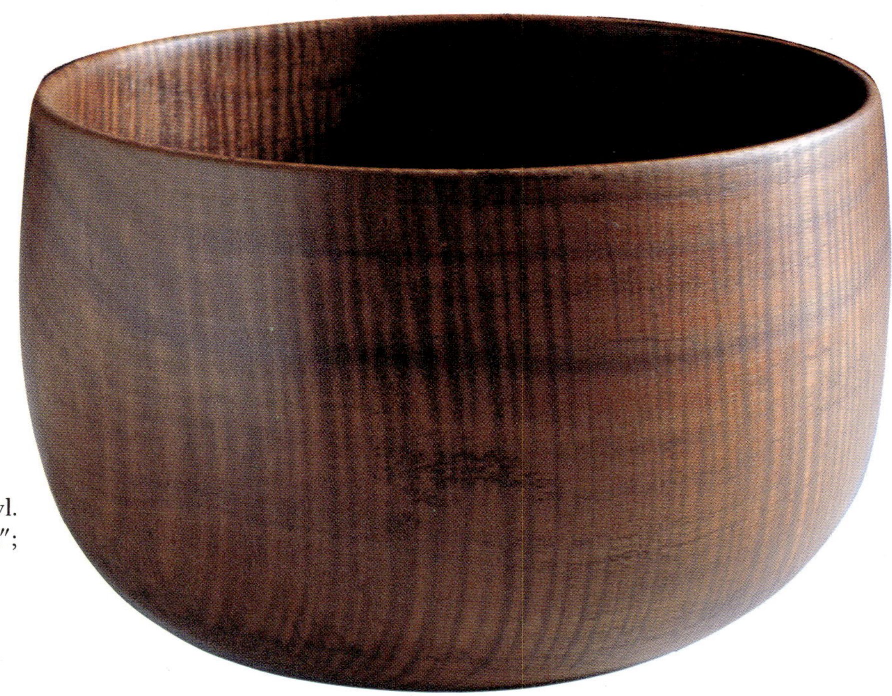

Jack Straka: Deep medium-size poi bowl. 1984. Koa wood. H. 5 15/16″; Diam. (rim) 8½″; Thickness .245″.

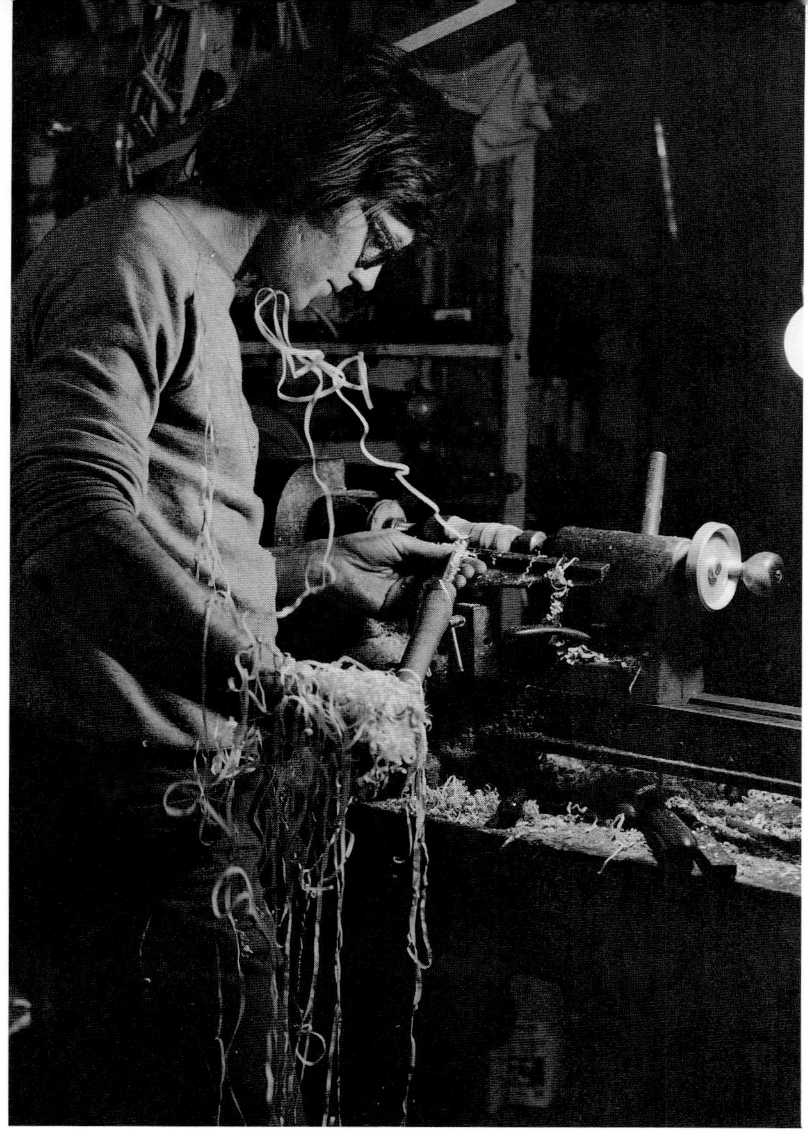

DEL STUBBS

1130 Elmer Street
Chico, California 95926

Raised in a rural environment, Del Stubbs developed a passion for natural beauty and a love of careful handwork. These interests flowered into his becoming a woodturner in 1973 at the age of twenty-one, and soon after he spent a year and a half studying wood turning with Paul English, who had been a turner for forty years. In spite of occasional arguments Mr. Stubbs and his craft live happily together as he continually tries to refine his precision, technique, understanding, and form.

STATEMENT FROM THE ARTIST

Translucent turning came into my work in 1981, beginning with very small pieces. This type of turning has evolved into pieces of up to a foot in diameter, and pieces with walls as little as five-thousandths of an inch thick. Such pieces still represent a considerable challenge to my skill and concentration, and there are only a few days during any month when I can create such bowls successfully.

Contemporary woodworking is taking rapid strides in changing the way that wood is viewed. Translucent turning is my current contribution to this movement. I believe that my efforts have added to the level of skill and technical understanding needed for this particular craft. The most important result, however, is being able to show that when wood has been made thin enough to permit the passage of light, an entirely new form of beauty has been achieved.

The most recent development of my work as a woodturner is the creation of the manzanita "Tulips," which were inspired by the glowing translucent beauty and simple, perfect form of a California poppy. Manzanita is a shrub that grows in the dry foothills of California. It is extremely hard and, while green, very prone to cracking. The technical difficulties in making the "Tulips" still present a considerable challenge, and the loss rate currently hovers around fifty-five percent.

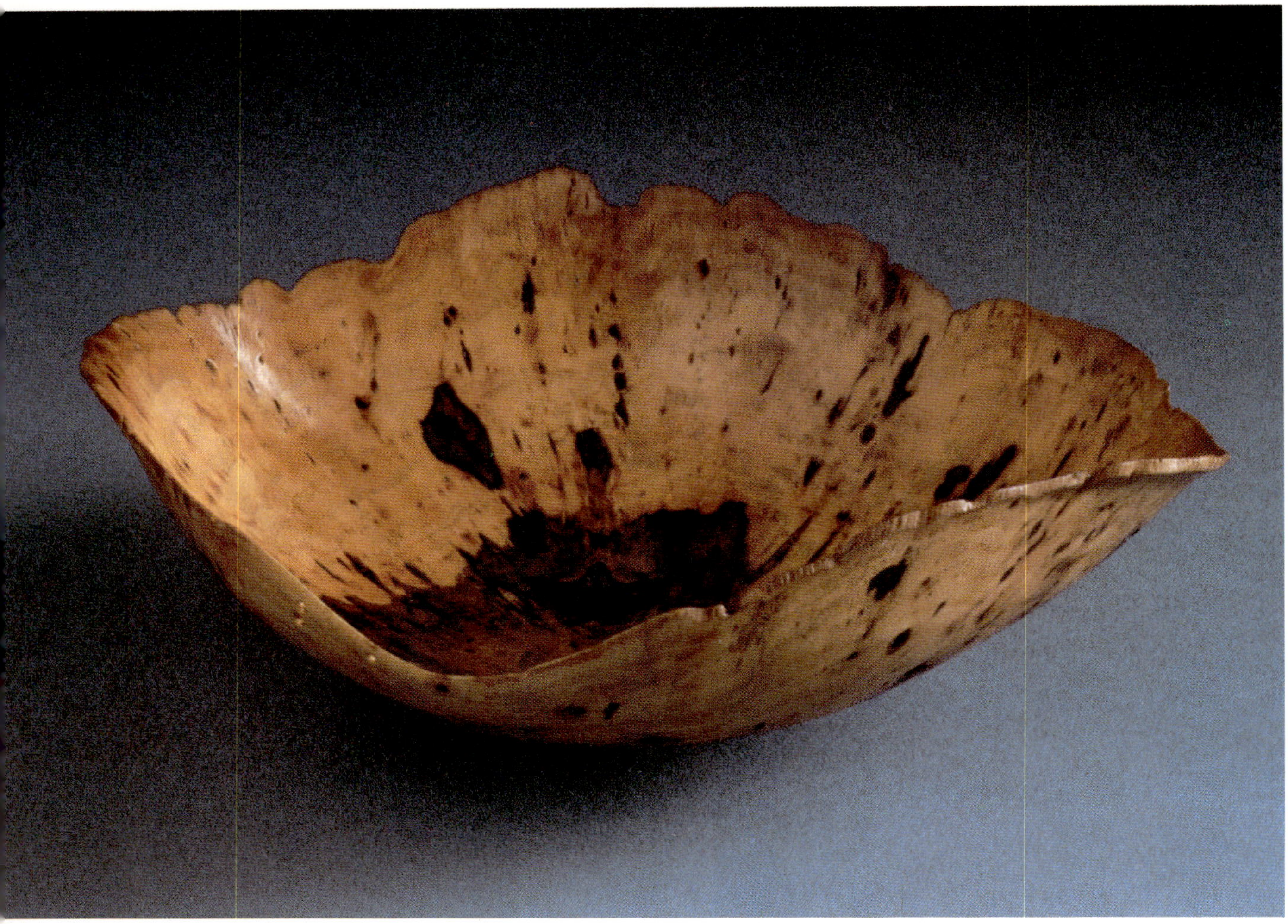

Del Stubbs: Small free-form bowl. 1983. Mistletoe walnut. H. 1⅝″–2¼″; Diam. (rim) 5⅜″–6½″; Thickness .049″; Base (foot) ⅝″.

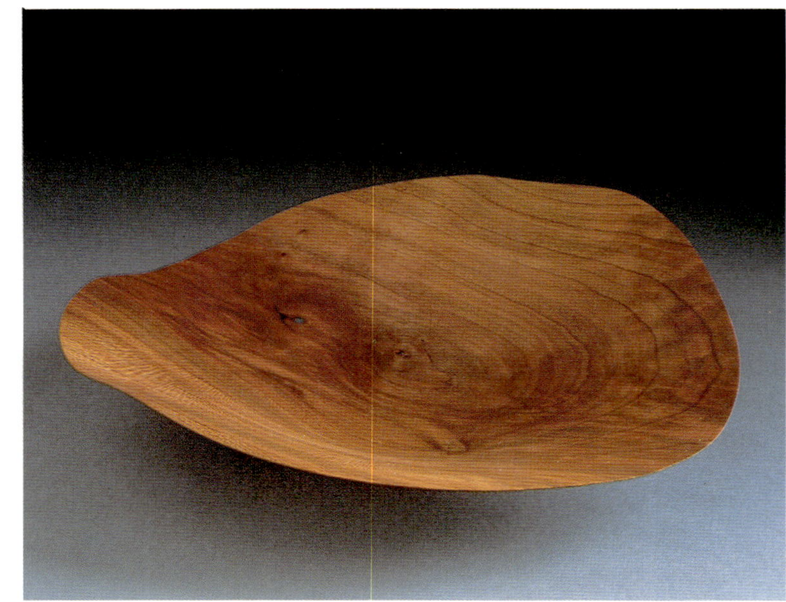

Del Stubbs: Paper-thin, shallow free-form bowl. 1983. Walnut. H. 1 5/16″–3⅛″; Diam. (rim) 9¼″–10½″; Thickness .01″; Base (foot) 1 3/16″.

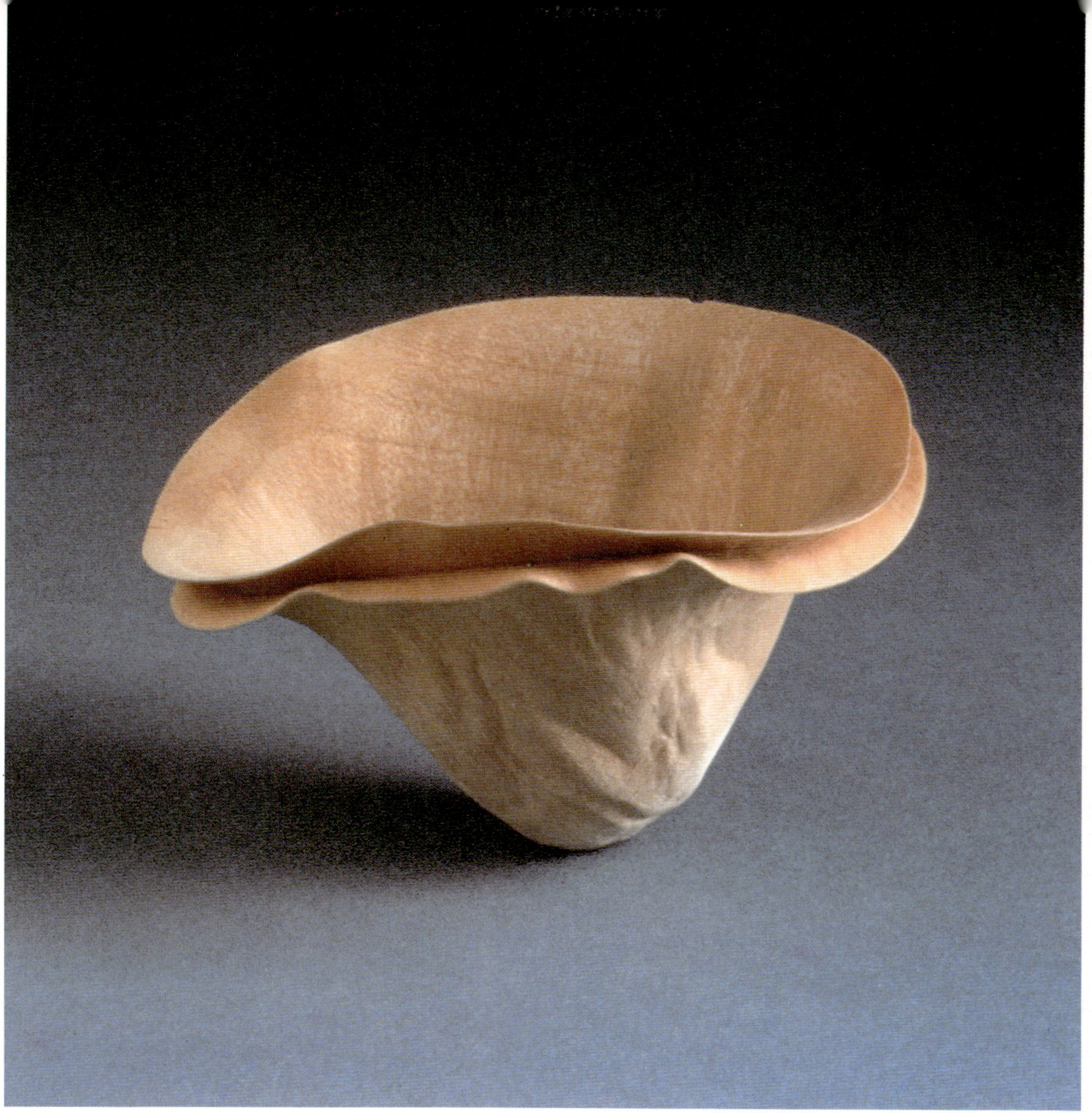

Del Stubbs: Small double-rimmed bowl. 1983. Madrona. H. 1 7/16″–2 3/16″; Diam. (rim) 2 13/16″–3 3/8″ ; Thickness .019″.

Del Stubbs: Small stemless goblet. 1983. Tulipwood. H. 2 7/8″–3″; Diam. (rim) 1 3/4″; Thickness .111″; Base 9/16″.

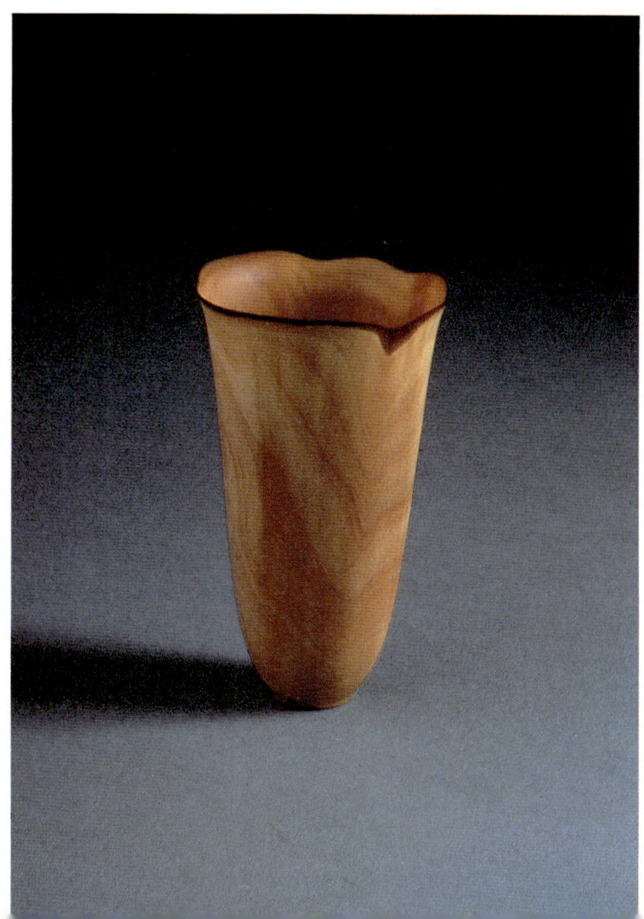

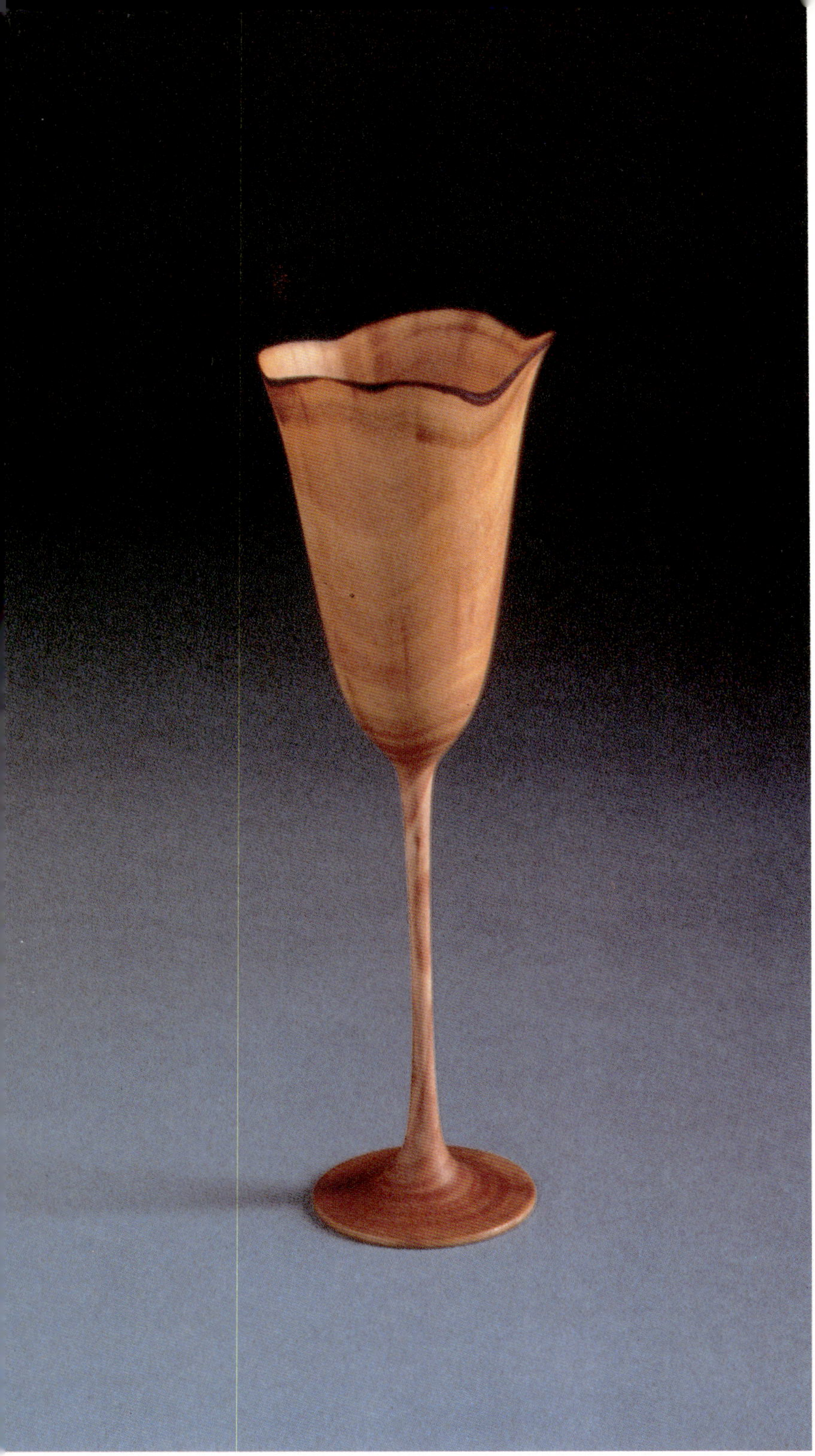

Del Stubbs: Small stemmed goblet. 1983. Tulipwood. H. 5⅛″–5⅜″; Diam. (rim) 1⅝″–1¾″; Thickness .025″; Base (foot) 1⅜″.

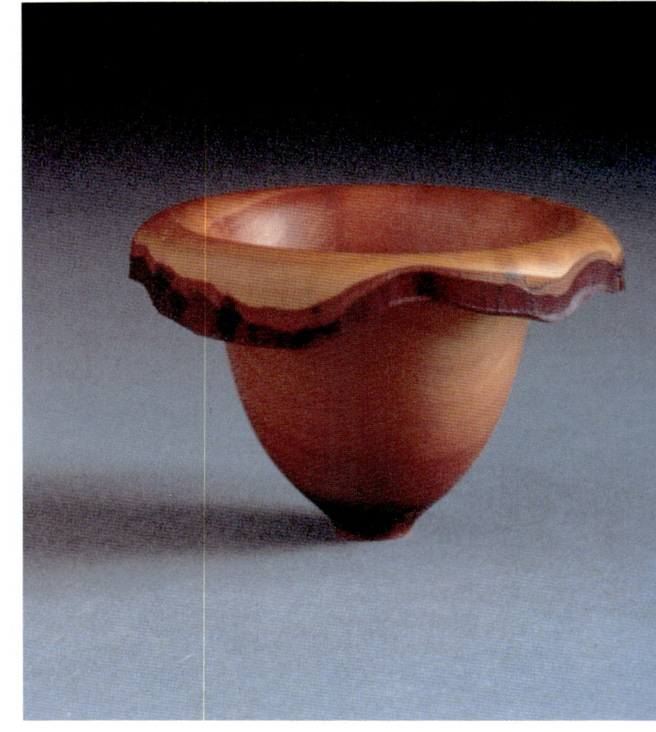

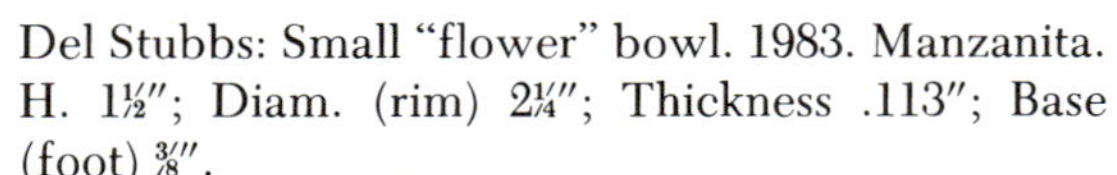

Del Stubbs: Small "flower" bowl. 1983. Manzanita. H. 1½″; Diam. (rim) 2¼″; Thickness .113″; Base (foot) ⅜″.

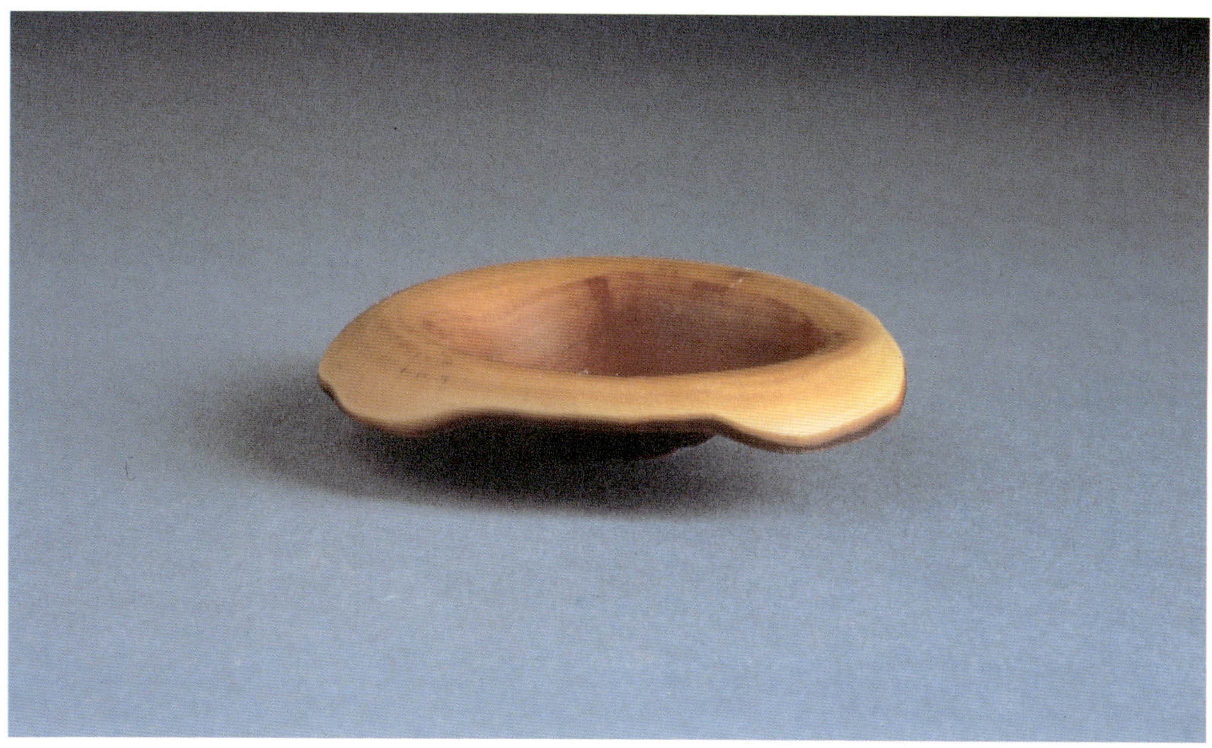

Del Stubbs: Tiny "flower" bowl. 1983. Manzanita. H. ½″; Diam. (rim) 2¼″–2⁵⁄₁₆″; Thickness .121″; Base ⅜″.

Del Stubbs: Small, paper-thin, free-form footed bowl. 1983. Madrona. H. 1″–1½″; Diam. (rim) 4″–4¼″; Thickness .024″; Base (foot) ⁵⁄₁₆″.

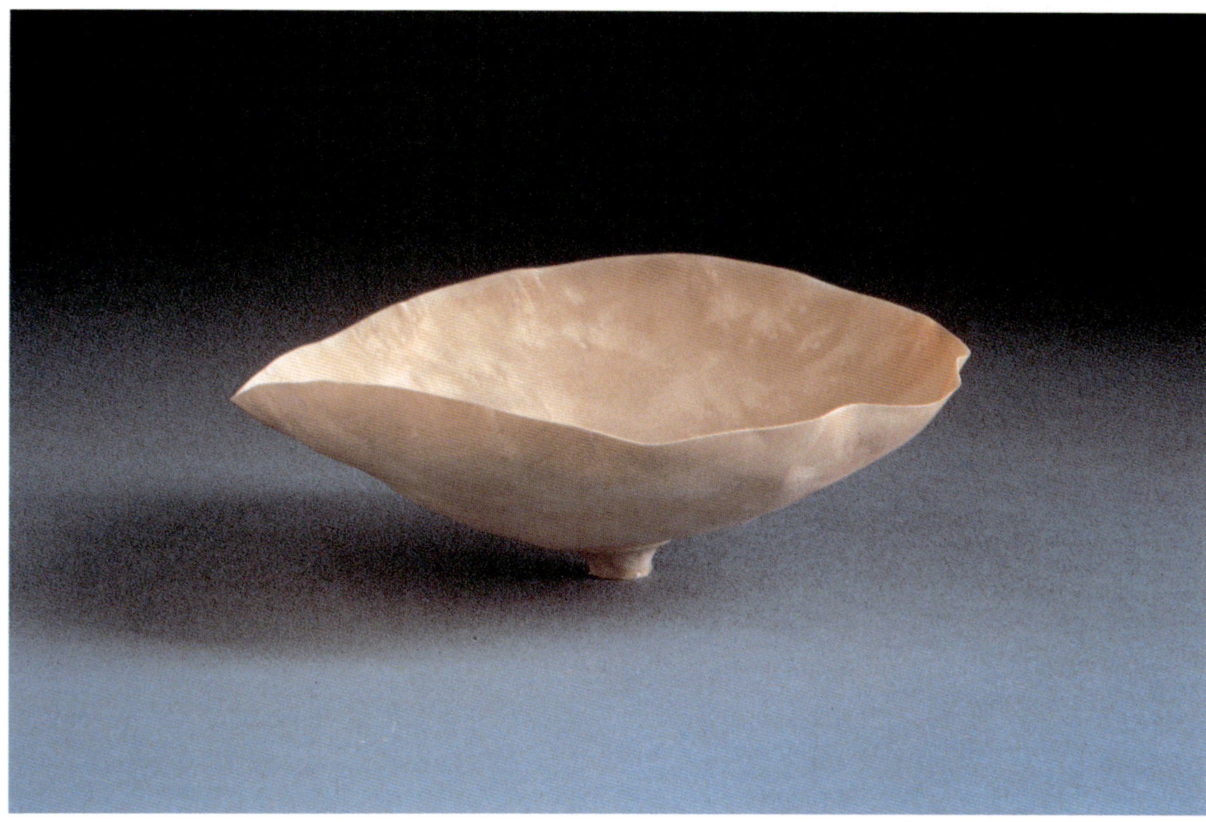

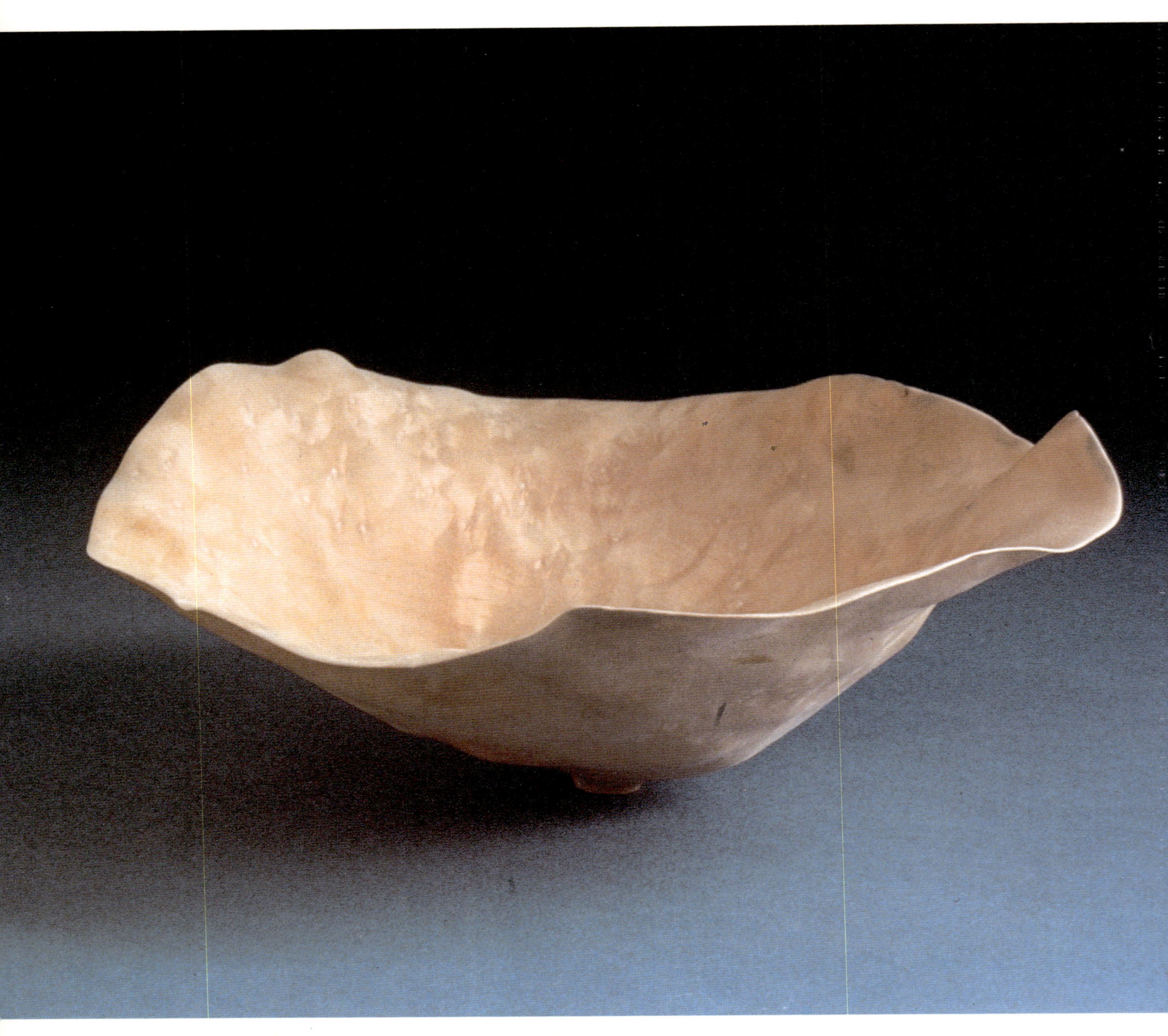

Del Stubbs: Medium-size, paper-thin, free-form footed bowl. 1983. Madrona. H. 1 11/16″–2½″; Diam. (rim) 5 15/16″–6 1/16″; Thickness .025″; Base (foot) ⅜″.